Girl Scout Badges and Signs

REVISED EDITION

Girl Scouts of the U.S.A.
420 Fifth Avenue
New York, N.Y. 10018

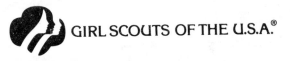
GIRL SCOUTS OF THE U.S.A.®

Betty F. Pilsbury, *President*
Mary Rose Main, *National
Executive Director*

Inquiries related to *Girl Scout
Badges and Signs,* revised edition,
should be addressed to Program,
Girl Scouts of the U.S.A., 420 Fifth
Avenue, New York, N.Y. 10018.

ISBN 0-88441-346-2

15   14

CREDITS

Project Coordinator
Karen Unger Sparks

Authors
Karen Unger Sparks
Chris Bergerson
Candace White Ciraco
Sharon Woods Hussey
Carolyn L. Kennedy
Verna L. Simpkins
Joan W. Fincutter
Martha Jo Dennison

Contributors
Toni Eubanks
Donna L. Nye
Audrey Major
Patricia Connally
Beth Bridgeman
Corinne Murphy
Gayle Davis

Recognition Designs and Art Concepts
Karen Unger Sparks
Chris Bergerson

Illustrators
Susan J. Harrison
Pat Stewart

Text and Cover Design
Keithley Assoc. Inc.

Special acknowledgment is given to the
past authors and consultants who contrib-
uted to the 1980 edition of *Girl Scout
Badges and Signs.*

GSUSA also expresses appreciation to all the
associations and organizations that lent us
their expertise. A special thank-you goes
out to the girls, leaders, and council and
national staff who field-tested and reviewed the badges.

CONTENTS

My Book of Badges and Signs   1

   Be a Badge Explorer!   2

   How Do I Choose the Badges
I Want to Do?   4

   Making a Plan of Action   6

   Other Junior Girl Scout Recognitions   9

   Badge Presentations   9

   Helps and Resources Section   9

Health and Fitness   12

   Dabbler   14

   Across Generations   17

   Becoming a Teen   19

   Caring for Children   21

   "Collecting" Hobbies   23

   "Doing" Hobbies   24

   Exploring Healthy Eating   25

   Family Living Skills   27

   First Aid   29

   Health and Fitness   31

   Healthy Relationships   33

   Making Decisions   35

   "Making" Hobbies   37

   My Self-Esteem   38

   Pet Care   40

   Safety Sense   42

   Sports   44

   Sports Sampler   46

World Citizens   48

   Dabbler   50

   Active Citizen   52

   Celebrating People   54

   Creative Solutions   57

   Geography Fun   60

   Girl Scouting Around the World   62

   Girl Scouting in the U.S.A.   64

   Junior Citizen   66

   Local Lore   68

   My Community   70

   My Heritage   72

   Now and Then: Stories from Around
the World   74

   On My Way   77

   Traveler   79

   Women Today   82

   The World in My Community   86

   World Neighbors   88

Science and Technology   **90**
    Dabbler   92
    Aerospace   95
    Business-Wise   97
    Car Care   99
    Computer Fun   101
    Do-It-Yourself   103
    Foods, Fibers, and Farming   105
    Geology   107
    Math Whiz   109
    Money Sense   111
    Ms. Fix-It   113
    Plants and Animals   115
    Puzzlers   117
    Ready for Tomorrow   119
    Science in Action   122
    Science Sleuth   124
    Science in Everyday Life   126
    Sky Search   128
    Water Wonders   130
    Weather Watch   132

Arts Around The World   **134**
    Dabbler   136
    Architecture   139
    Art in the Home   143
    Art in the Round   146
    Art to Wear   148
    Books   150
    Ceramics and Clay   153
    Communication Arts   155
    Dance   158
    Drawing and Painting   160
    Folk Arts   162
    Jeweler   165
    Musician   167
    Music Lover   169
    Photography   171
    Popular Arts   173
    Prints and Graphics   175
    Textiles And Fibers

    Theater   180
    Toymaker   182
    Video Production   184
    Visual Arts   186

Exploring The Out-of-Doors   **188**
    Dabbler   190
    Eco-Action   192
    Ecology   195
    Finding Your Way   197
    Frosty Fun   199
    Hiker   201
    Horse Lover   203
    Horseback Rider   205
    Outdoor Cook   207
    Outdoor Creativity   209
    Outdoor Fun   211
    Outdoor Fun in the City   213
    Small Craft   215
    Swimming   218
    Troop Camper   220
    Walking for Fitness   222
    Water Fun   224
    Wildlife   226

The Cookie Connection   **228**

Our Own Troop's Badge   **232**

Our Own Council's Badge   **233**

The Junior Aide Patch   **234**

Junior Girl Scout Signs   **236**
    Sign of the Rainbow   237
    Sign of the Sun   238
    Sign of the Satellite   240

Helps and Resources   **242**
    Health and Fitness   242
    World Citizens   243
    Science and Technology   245
    Arts Around the World   248
    Exploring the Out-Of-Doors   251

Badge Index   **253**

My Book
of
Badges and Signs

This is your book of Girl Scout badges and signs. With this book you will explore new worlds and find out about new subjects. Badges are called *recognitions* because they show that you have accomplished something and completed activities to get them. When someone sees the badge, she "recognizes" your accomplishments. Badges, as Juliette Low said, show that you have done something so often and so well that you can teach it to someone else. Choose the badges that interest you and other girls in your Girl Scout troop or group. You might do activities that involve something completely new to you. You might earn a badge because you have a lot of skill in a special sport or hobby, or you might discover a talent you never knew you had. You will definitely discover challenges and fun. Some badges may be difficult to finish. Sometimes you might feel nervous about trying something completely new. But, you will always feel very proud when you have completed the activities and have earned your badge. When people see the badges on your uniform, they know more about you. They know you can demonstrate your new abilities. They can learn what interests you have. And, you know that you have taught more skills and talents to the most important person of all—yourself!

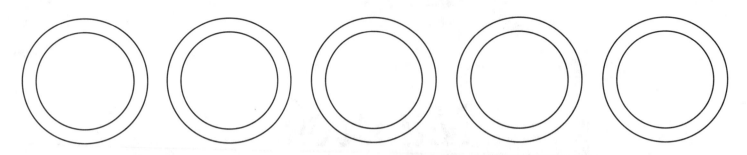

There are 98 badges in this book, including the Our Own Troop's Badge and the Our Own Council's Badge. There are also thirteen badges in the *Junior Girl Scout Handbook*. The badges in this book are grouped by the Girl Scout worlds of interest. The border of a badge indicates the world of interest in which it fits.

BE A BADGE EXPLORER!

Can you find a badge for each world of interest? Which color of the badge borders matches which world of interest? Color in the borders of the five blank badges above so that you have one for each world. Then look through this book and pick one badge from each world that appeals to you. What do you like about the badge designs? Fill in the five blank badges with your copies of the badge designs.

If you explore a little further, you will find a special badge in each world of interest. Can you figure out which badge is special?

What am I?

I keep my name in each world, but I change my color. I have a little bit of everything in one badge. Sometimes Brownie Girl Scouts work on me. If you do me first, you may discover a new world.

____ ____ ____ ____ ____ ____ ____

Answer: Dabbler

What other surprises are waiting to be discovered? Pick one of the worlds of interest. Study the badges carefully. Do you see something that changes when you look at different badges? Look closely at the background colors of the badges.

What are the two colors that badges can have as a background color in this book?

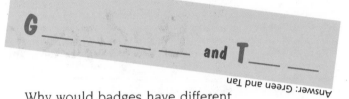

G ____ ____ ____ ____ and T ____ ____

Answer: Green and Tan

Why would badges have different background colors? How can you discover the reason?

If you pick one green badge and one tan badge on the same subject in the same world of interest and compare the two, you will find that the green badge is easier to do and takes less time to finish. The badges with tan backgrounds take more planning and more time to complete. A Cadette Girl Scout may earn a tan badge. A Junior Girl Scout may earn both tan and green badges. Sometimes, you might start with a green badge and find out you like the activities so much that you continue on the same subject with the tan badge. You might begin with a tan badge when you already know a lot about a badge topic and a green badge would be too easy for you. You might pick a tan badge when you want a challenge or when you are really interested in that topic.

What color border do the badges have in the *Junior Girl Scout Handbook*? Why do you think they have that color?

_____

_____

Answer: The badges have a dark blue border. This color is used to indicate that the badges include activities from many worlds.

Look at the picture on the facing page. Is there anything unusual about this picture? If you look carefully, you can discover the designs for 20 badges hiding in the picture. Circle the designs when you find them and try to match them to the badges in the book. How many green badges did you find? How many tan badges did you find?

HOW DO I CHOOSE THE BADGES I WANT TO DO??

Whenever you wear your badges, you are letting people learn a little bit about you. The badges you earn show what you like to do, what new skills you have developed, and what interests you. The badges on your sash or vest are like a map of your interests and talents. Take a look at the different types of badges in this book. Looking over the Dabbler badges can give you an idea of the activities in each world. Also, look at the designs of the badges. The designs will give you an idea of what each badge is like.

Sometimes, you might decide as a troop or group or patrol to earn a particular badge. Sometimes, you might attend a special event, wider opportunity, or camp where you will complete the activities for badges. But, you may also work on your own on a badge that interests you. There are so many badges in this book. How do you choose one? Where do you start?

Why not explore your interests, talents, and skills? Do you know all the things that you do well? Where are you an expert? What do you enjoy? What are your hobbies? What would you like to learn to do?

Meet Julie. Julie is nine years old and thinks of herself as being average—not too short, not too tall, not too fat, but not too skinny. She has two best friends and lots of other girls she knows from school and the neighborhood. She cares about what the other girls think of her. Sometimes she feels close to one group of girls and other times she feels left out and a bit lonely. She is considered to be well-liked by her teachers and her Girl Scout leader. There are times when she feels that no one can really understand her, even her family. But, she loves her family and enjoys doing things with them—when she's not daydreaming or talking on the phone with her friends!

Julie likes to be busy. She is interested in *everything*! After school she is supposed to work on her homework as soon as she comes home. And, usually she finishes it. But, more times than she likes to admit, she'll look out the window or hear a song on the radio and her homework disappears. Instead, she is imagining herself riding a horse as fast as she can across open country with nothing to stop her until she and her horse need a rest. Or, all of a sudden, she is dancing on a bright stage next to the most famous rock star in the world and though she can't see the faces of the crowd, she can hear the audience screaming. Then the lights disappear and everything is quiet. She can't hear anything in her space helmet except the sound of the countdown from mission control—three, two, one, *lift off*—and she feels the spaceship shudder around her. She might remember the camping trip her Girl Scout troop took last year and the scary stories the girls told when they were supposed to be sleeping. Then, she looks down and sees that she still has a lot of homework to do. But, in her imagination, she has explored her interests and has learned a little more about herself and her hopes and dreams.

Her Girl Scout troop has met for the first time. Julie has the chance to choose some badges to work on this year. Because she likes to do so many things, Julie is not sure which badges to pick. She is also curious about some of the badge topics, but she is not confident of her ability to finish all the activities in the badges she is considering.

Julie decides to try the treasure map in her copy of *Girl Scout Badges and Signs*. She gets to CONTEMPLATION POINT and reads the questions. She thinks about her daydreams—maybe there's a clue in those dreams! What are her most common dreams about? Well, she's riding a horse—actually, she loves horses. And, she had a great time on the camping trip. She always has the radio playing (much too loud, her family says) and she and her friends often practice the dances they see on television and videos. She likes math and science—they're her best subjects in school. She has read about the female astronauts and loves to watch when the space shuttle is shown taking off and landing on television. She often imagines herself in a space capsule landing in a place that looks completely different from her community. She has so many interests! She travels on the I'M PROUD OF MYSELF FREEWAY, feeling great that there are so many things she enjoys doing and *can* do! The CHOOSE A WORLD OF INTEREST tollbooth stops her and beyond lies the horrible SWAMP OF INDECISION. How can she choose a world of interest that will have a badge she'd like to do?

HOW ... DID ... YOU ... ANSWER ... THE ... QUESTIONS ... ?

That's it! She can combine her skill in math with her dream of being an astronaut and her interest in adventure in the Aerospace badge. And then try Dance, Horseback Rider, Outdoor Fun, Finding Your Way, Outdoor Creativity, Sky Search, Ready for Tomorrow, My Self-Esteem, Music Lover, Geography, On My Way, World Neighbors. . . . Her list goes on and on. There seems to be a badge for everything she'd like to do—and more!

Why don't you try the map? Which badge will you try first?

Once you have an idea of what you already know and what you are good at doing and an idea of what you would like to try and do that is new, you can begin. Some badges have requirements of activities that you must do. In some badges you may need to do one activity before the others. Usually, though, you can begin with any activity in the badge.

See if other girls would like to do the badge with you. Ask your leader to share her ideas on how you could work on this badge. You could also find an adviser—your troop leader, an older Girl Scout or other adult Girl Scout, a parent, teacher, family friend, or someone in the community, an expert on the badge topic, or a business person or governmental employee. An adviser can assist you in finding resources that will help you with your badge. An adviser can also give you lots of ideas and suggestions. Make sure your adviser is a person who has the time and willingness to help you. It is also important to write a thank-you note to anyone who has spent time helping you.

There are many ways you can do different badge activities. You do not always have to do the first activity first! Read all the activities. Are there any requirements? Some activities are very specific. You do the activity exactly as it is written. Other activities give you lots of room for creativity. You can decide what you want to do. Just remember that each activity you do can only be counted once for one badge. Often, the badge activity might suggest that you "show, describe, create, display, make, or exhibit." What are some ways that you can show someone what you have accomplished?

Here are some suggestions:

_____ Draw a picture.

_____ Take a photograph.

_____ Write a poem or story.

_____ Make a collage.

_____ Draw or design a poster.

_____ Write or record a song.

_____ Write or act out a skit, play, or role-playing exercise.

_____ Keep a journal or diary.

_____ Make a newspaper or scrapbook.

_____ Prepare an exhibit, a diorama, or a shadowbox display.

_____ Give a how-to demonstration.

_____ Prepare a speech or lecture.

_____ Build a model or sculpture.

_____ Make a diagram, a chart, or a list.

_____ Make a video.

_____ Teach what you have learned to someone else.

_____ Put on a pantomime or puppet show.

_____ Invite your local newspaper to record your activities.

_____ Prepare an event that shows others what you have done.

_____ Plan a party or open house when people can come and see your work.

_____ Plan a parade, festival, or carnival.

MAKING A PLAN OF ACTION

Let's make a plan. Before an explorer sets out on a journey, she makes a plan of action. She makes sure that she has everything she needs. Making a plan of action will help you be sure that you will be able to complete the badge you chose.

The first badge I would like to do is:

I can do the activities to this badge myself:

I can get help from the following people and places:

I will need the following supplies:

I will start with Activity Number:

I need to do these things before beginning this badge:

Here is my plan for completing the badge:

You might want to think about how long a badge will take, how easy it will be to find what you need in order to do the badge, and who can help you with different activities. You might not be able to do every badge in the book. You might begin a badge but not finish it. You might lose interest in the subject or the badge might be too hard. Sometimes, you can stop working on the badge for a while and then return to it later. Always keep a record of the activities that you have finished and save what you have created or constructed for a badge activity. Write your initials and the date next to each activity when you have completed it. If someone helped you, you might ask her to initial the activity, too. Your leader or assistant leader should also initial the activities when completed. If you did the activity on your own, explain or show to your leader what you did. When you have finished all the badge activities, you and your leader sign off that the badge has been completed and write in the date of completion. Congratulations!

The important thing to remember is that you should enjoy working on your badges and you should be finding out more about yourself, other people, and the world around you.

Record the badges you have earned on the chart on pages 10–11. Write the name of the badge under the world of interest to which it belongs. When you start to fill the chart, notice in which worlds you have earned the most badges. What does that tell you about your interests?

OTHER JUNIOR GIRL SCOUT RECOGNITIONS

The Sign of the Rainbow, the Sign of the Sun, the Sign of the Satellite, the Sign of the World, the Junior Aide Patch, and the Bridge to Cadette Girl Scouts patch are the other recognitions that you may earn as a Junior Girl Scout. These items are different from badges because they are not on one specific topic. Instead, these recognitions give you greater challenges that use the skills you are gaining in Junior Girl Scouting.

JUNIOR GIRL SCOUT LEADERSHIP PIN

Although there are no strict rules, it is recommended that you earn the Junior Girl Scout Leadership pin during your last year in this age level. To earn this award, you demonstrate your leadership skills through community service and other leadership activities. The requirements are listed in Chapter 8 of your *Junior Girl Scout Handbook*.

BRIDGE TO CADETTE GIRL SCOUTS PATCH

During your last year as a Junior Girl Scout, you may earn this patch. The requirements are described in Chapter 8 of your *Junior Girl Scout Handbook*.

JUNIOR AIDE PATCH The Junior Aide patch is your opportunity to show that Girl Scouting is a sisterhood. To earn this patch, you help Brownie Girl Scouts do activities that prepare them for Junior Girl Scouting. The requirements for this patch are described on pages 230–231.

THE SIGNS There are four signs: the Sign of the Sun, the Sign of the Satellite, the Sign of the World, and the Sign of the Rainbow. The requirements for the Sign of the World are in your *Junior Girl Scout Handbook*. The requirements for the other three signs are on pages 232–237 of this book. Each sign has activities that relate to the worlds of interest and include earning badges and working on projects. Earning a sign truly represents your accomplishments in Junior Girl Scouting.

BADGE PRESENTATIONS

Badges are usually presented at award ceremonies called a Court of Awards. You and your troop may plan to have more than one Court of Awards so that you receive the badges as you earn them, or you may have one big celebration and receive all the badges that you have earned during your troop year. Once you have earned your badges, you may wear them on your sash or vest. Chapter 1 of the *Junior Girl Scout Handbook* contains a diagram that shows the proper placement of Girl Scout recognitions.

HELPS AND RESOURCES SECTION

If you look in the back of this book, you will find a special section called "Helps and Resources." This section contains information, definitions, and extra activities that will help you complete the badges. Throughout the book, you will be referred to this section when needed.

BADGE CHART

Record the badges

you have earned

Health and Fitness

World Citizens

_____
_____
_____
_____
_____
_____
_____
_____
_____
_____
_____
_____
_____
_____
_____
_____
_____
_____
_____
_____

Science and Technology

Arts Around the World

Exploring the Out-of-Doors

Health
and
Fitness

These exercises are good for warming up or cooling down when you are exercising. Never do an exercise that hurts. You should make an effort, but move smoothly so that you do not feel a pain in your muscles or joints.

HEEL RAISES: Stand straight with your hands on your hips and your feet together. Rise up on your toes, then return to the starting position. Try to do this 10-15 times.

Write your personal thoughts, feelings, daydreams, hopes, and stories in a journal! Writing things down can often cheer you up or help you solve a problem. You can also record your accomplishments so that you can compliment yourself on all the great things you have done.

Roller skating and in-line skating are fun ways to exercise. Be careful your first time on skates. Practice in a flat area with no automobile traffic or at a skating rink. You should also wear the proper safety equipment, including a helmet, elbow pads, and knee pads.

ARM CIRCLES: Stand comfortably and hold your arms straight out, palms down. Move your arms in small circles. Change the direction of the circles moving forwards and backwards. Then try making bigger circles. Try to keep your arms straight while you make your circles. Attempt to make 15-20 circles.

BODY BENDS: Stand with your feet slightly apart and your arms raised straight above your head with your hands clasped. Bend smoothly to the right and feel your other side stretch. Then bend smoothly to the left and feel your side stretch. Try five stretches on each side.

In Double Dutch rope jumping, double ropes are used and more than one girl can jump at the same time. Rope turners hold a double dutch rope in each hand. They turn the ropes inward in circles, the left hand turning clockwise, the right hand turning counterclockwise, one after another, in an even rhythm. When one rope hits the floor, the other should be at its fullest height. It is important for the rope turners to let their wrists do all the work.

Jumpers enter the ropes from a position close to the turner's shoulder. The sound of a rope hitting the floor is a signal to move in. The jumpers use an alternating foot step. They should watch the movement of the turners' arms and listen to the rhythm of the ropes, which will help them know when to jump.

Exercise Checklist

- Always begin a physical exercise routine with a warm-up period of exercises and end with a cool-down period of exercises. These exercises ready your muscles for a workout and then relax the muscles after you have exercised them.

- Wear the clothing that is appropriate for the exercise. Layered clothing is always good.

- Do an exercise routine at least three times a week for 20 to 30 minutes for the best aerobic benefits.

- Do different activities so that you don't get bored. Try exercising with friends or exercising alone. Always choose activities that you enjoy.

Many hobbies and activities are relaxing. Playing a musical instrument, singing alone or in a group, listening to music, creating a painting, poem, craft, or something to wear, reading a book, maintaining a collection, or joining a theater group are just some of the ways you can spend your free time.

DABBLER

COMPLETE ONE ACTIVITY IN FIVE OF THE GROUPS.

A.1 Make something that shows the things that are special about your family, the things you enjoy at home, and/or the things you can do with members of a family.

or

A.2 Collect or make pictures of the important events that happen in the life of a family (births, marriages, deaths, etc.). Discuss different ways families celebrate special events. Share ideas about how family members can support each other during difficult times.

B.1 Make a picture alphabet chart or book, a set of cardboard letters, or a safe toy for a younger child. Use what you make with several children. Watch and record their actions.

or

B.2 Spend time with a senior citizen. Plan an activity both of you can enjoy. Determine a way you can stay in contact with each other.

C.1 Pick one food from each of the six food groups.

• Price each item at two stores near your home.

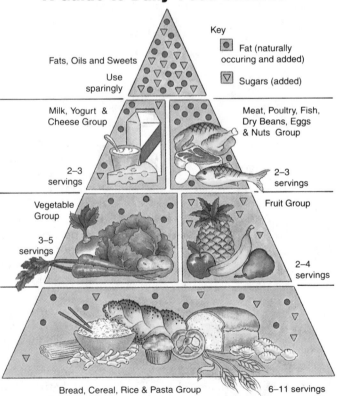

A Guide to Daily Food Choices

Key
- ◉ Fat (naturally occuring and added)
- ▽ Sugars (added)

Fats, Oils and Sweets
Use sparingly

Milk, Yogurt & Cheese Group
2–3 servings

Meat, Poultry, Fish, Dry Beans, Eggs & Nuts Group
2–3 servings

Vegetable Group
3–5 servings

Fruit Group
2–4 servings

Bread, Cereal, Rice & Pasta Group
6–11 servings

• Decide which store offers the best buy in each category.

or

C.2 Visit a place where food is prepared, grown, or processed. Find out how the food gets to consumers.

D.1 Make up a radio, television commercial, or magazine advertisement for a basic home first aid kit. Include all the items to be contained in this kit. Include the reasons why people should buy the kit.

or

D.2 Invite a health educator, police officer, self-defense instructor, or other health and safety professional to your troop or group to talk about the do's and don'ts of personal safety and what you can do if someone tries to harm you. To prepare for the presentation, review the sections, "Safety Do's and Don'ts" "Fire Safety," and "Personal Safety" in Chapter 3 of your *Junior Girl Scout Handbook*.

E.1 Make your own personal health record. Include immunizations, allergies, history of diseases and accidents, family health history, and hospital stays. Keep your health record in a safe and handy place. Keep it up to date.

or

E.2 Find out what a doctor or dentist does at a checkup.

• Learn the name of each piece of equipment and its use.
• Make up a skit or puppet show that will tell other children what will happen at the doctor's or dentist's office when they go for a checkup.

F.1 Make a collage or poster that shows others the things you like about yourself—things you do well, things you are proud of, places you have been, and anything else that makes you special.

or

F.2 Think of some things you might do to improve a relationship with a parent, sibling, friend, or other adult. Try one of your ideas for at least a week.

G.1 With the help of an adult, learn how to take your temperature, pulse, blood pressure, or respiration (breathing) rate.

• Find out what numbers you should expect to have.
• Take readings for yourself at least twice and compare the results.
• Teach one of these skills to another person.

or

G.2 Take care of your own clothes for a week.

• Wash them and iron them if necessary.
• Learn how to sort your clothes. Find out what needs to be washed by hand or what needs special treatment.
• Find out how to make simple repairs, such as sewing on buttons.
• Repair several things of your own or repair items for other family members.

H.1 Discover how you have grown over the years.

- Collect old and recent photographs of yourself or talk to an older family member or relative about your growth.
- List the ways you have changed. What has stayed the same?
- Learn what physical and emotional changes will take place as you become a teenager.

or

H.2 Find out how nicotine, drugs, and alcohol can affect one's health. Share what you have discovered with others.

I.1 Write an imaginary letter to an advice columnist about a problem that girls and teens may have. Share your letter with others. What advice could they give?

or

I.2 Make a list of ten things you love to do. Then, decide which three things you love to do the most. Have some friends do the same thing. Compare your lists and talk about how it felt to limit your choices.

J.1 Help organize and take part in an afternoon of fun for your own troop or group or another troop or group. Include a quiet and an active game or sport, a song, a story, a skit or poem, and a nutritious snack.

or

J.2 Ask several adults or children about their hobbies. Find out about one that interests you. Do or make something related to the hobby.

Date badge completed

My signature

Leader's signature

ACROSS GENERATIONS

COMPLETE FOUR ACTIVITIES.

1 Interview one or more older adults to find out about their lives. Ask about dates, special events, or other important events they remember. Create a painting, time line, or scrapbook showing these important experiences. Give it to or share it with the person.

2 Invite a person over 50 who has a special hobby or skill to your troop or group to demonstrate her talent to you.

3 Read and complete one of the activities in "The Generation at the Top: Senior Citizens" in Chapter 5 of your *Junior Girl Scout Handbook*.

4 Find out how you can participate in the Adopt-A-Grandparent program in your community. If a program is not already organized where you live, contact a nursing home, hospital, or senior citizens' group about starting such a program. Tell your troop or group about the activities you and your adopted grandparent do together.

5 With your troop or group, check with community agencies, schools, churches, or organizations formed to help older people to see if you could volunteer your time and efforts. Try to help where needed.

6 See if you can find women in your community who were Girl Scouts during the 1920s to 1950s. Invite them to share their Girl Scout memories with you. What has stayed the same in Girl Scouting? What is different?

7 With your troop or group, ask for permission to visit a nursing home, retirement home, or senior citizens' center. See if you can participate in an activity there, such as a sing-along, luncheon, game, or craft session.

8 You could write to a family member who lives far away or get a name from a community agency, a retirement home, or a senior citizens' center. Try to discover more about an older person's life by corresponding through letters.

Remember birthdays or holidays that are special to your "pen pal." If you think you might stop writing, be sure to discuss this with your "pen pal" ahead of time.

9 Be an investigator. Look at magazines and newspapers and television shows to see how older people are shown. Are they shown positively or negatively? Discuss your findings with others.

10 In your community or family, or through books and magazines, find out about a person over 65 years old who is still active in a business career or the arts, who has changed careers, or is active in community organizations or government. See if you can discuss what makes this person happy and successful.

_____
Date badge completed

_____
My signature

_____
Leader's signature

BECOMING A TEEN

1 Read the sections, "Changes in Your Body," "Get the Facts," and "Brenda's Advice Column" in Chapter 2 of your *Junior Girl Scout Handbook* and do one of the activities.

2 Make a list of things you have heard about puberty. Compare your list with others. Then find out whether the things on your list are correct or incorrect. You can talk to adults and teens or ask an adult to suggest a book to read.

3 Talk with a health educator, parent, or another adult you trust to find out the following information:

- What are the physical and emotional changes that can take place in girls during the ages of 8–13? The changes in boys during those years?
- What are some of the ways girls can prepare for these changes? Think about nutritional needs, skin care, and personal hygiene.

or

Invite a health care professional (such as a physician, nurse, or health education teacher) to your troop/group meeting to answer questions about puberty. As a troop, you might prepare a few questions in advance.

4 Set up a personal care schedule and follow it. Include combing, brushing, and washing and taking care of your hair; bathing; brushing your teeth; washing your face; and having regular health examinations.

5 Design a poster or T-shirt that will tell others why you feel good about being you.

6 Interview family members about what it was like for them when they reached puberty. You can talk about appearance, school, friends, dating, or any other information that is important to you as a female.

7 Invite two or three older teens to a troop or group meeting. What advice can they give you about becoming a teen?

8 Look through magazines or watch some television programs that show teenagers. Make a list of the characteristics and behavior of teenagers as shown in advertisements, articles, or shows. Ask a teenager if your list is realistic.

9 In a group or on your own, think of as many things as possible that you believe are the positive parts of being a teen. Then, think of what the negative side to being a teenager could be. Discuss the pros and cons with an adult or teen.

Date badge completed

My signature

Leader's signature

CARING
FOR CHILDREN

COMPLETE SIX ACTIVITIES, INCLUDING THE TWO STARRED.

*1 Read "First Aid Guide" in Chapter 3 of your *Junior Girl Scout Handbook*. Make a booklet or display of babysitter safety measures. Include first aid tips and things to do if a child becomes ill, as well as a list of emergency phone numbers. Share your findings with others.

2 Demonstrate that you know how to care for a young child by babysitting or by helping out at home, in a nursery school, with a religious group, or in an informal play group.

3 Make a "rainy day" activities box for younger children. Include supplies for at least six different types of activities. Make sure the activities are safe for younger children to do. Make up one of the activities yourself. Do the activities with a child or a group of children. Which activities were the most fun? Can you figure out why?

4 With adult guidance, prepare and serve several healthy meals or snacks to an infant, toddler, or young child.

DISCOVERY DIARY

What I discovered _____ can do alone:
NAME OF CHILD

_____

_____

What I discovered _____ can do with
NAME OF CHILD

help: _____

_____

_____

What I discovered _____ can do for
NAME OF CHILD

herself/himself: _____

_____

_____

I was surprised to see _____ do:
NAME OF CHILD

_____

The feelings _____ expressed were:
NAME OF CHILD

_____

I never knew that _____

_____

I enjoyed _____

_____

Things that I did to make _____ happy
NAME OF CHILD

were: _____

_____

*5 Spend time with a young child or infant on several occasions. Watch the child carefully. Keep a written or taped discovery diary and record.

6 Demonstrate that you know how to hold, feed, and dress an infant. Do each of these things for an infant several times.

7 Talk to a school nurse or other health care worker about the immunizations children get and why. Find out what health records are necessary for children. Check to see that you have all the immunizations required. Make your own record if one is not available, filling in all the information you can find out.

or

Interview several parents, teachers, and other adults to find out what they think are the most important things to remember when caring for children.

8 Decide what supplies you would need if you were taking a young child on a picnic or other all-day outing. Explain why you would include each item. Check with any adult who supervises young children to see if you were right.

9 Find out what household items can be dangerous for a young child. Make a list of these items and then find out how these are stored in your home. If possible, make a safety check in a home where there is a young child.

or

Go through a toy store or catalog and check for toys that would be safe and those that would be dangerous for children under three years old. Decide on a way to share your findings with adults.

_____
Date badge completed

_____
My signature

_____
Leader's signature

"COLLECTING" HOBBIES

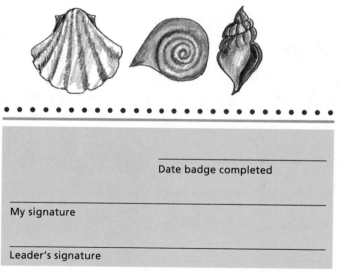

EXAMPLES

Rocks • shells • coins • stamps • autographs • postcards • model cars or airplanes • dolls • baseball cards

COMPLETE ACTIVITY 1, THEN DO FOUR OF THE OTHERS.

1 Before starting a collection, ask yourself these questions. Write down the answers and discuss them with your family or other adult.

- Is the hobby fun?
- Can I afford it?
- Do I have the space for it?
- Is it something that will not harm the environment?

2 Collect enough items so that you will learn something about the subject. Organize your collection, including the name or classification of each object. List when you acquired the object, how much it cost or where you found it, and something special about each item.

3 Arrange, display, or mount your collection so that you are able to show it to others. If possible, display your collection for your troop or other group.

4 Find out something about other people who collect the same things you do. What are the clubs, organizations, or magazines for people with your hobby? If possible, meet and talk with other collectors, or exchange letters to discuss your collection.

5 Read books or magazines about your hobby. Find out your hobby's history. Are there other hobbies that are similar to yours? Have people made careers from this hobby? Present this information in some creative way to your troop or group.

6 Create your own activity related to your special hobby.

_____
Date badge completed

_____
My signature

_____
Leader's signature

"DOING" HOBBIES

Examples

Singing in a choir • games • swimming or other sports • playing a musical instrument • cooking • gardening • hiking • bird-watching • reading

COMPLETE ACTIVITY 1, THEN DO FOUR OF THE OTHERS.

1 Ask yourself these questions and discuss the answers with an adult family member or other adult.

- Is it fun?
- Can I afford it?
- Do I have space for it?
- Where will I do it?
- Can I do it alone or with others?
- Do I have time for it?
- Are there safety or environmental factors to consider?

2 Practice your hobby. Demonstrate or try to teach your hobby to others.

3 Learn something about the history of your hobby and about others who share your hobby.

4 Find out about the kinds of careers that are related to your hobby. Interview someone or collect pictures and stories about people in careers similar to your hobby.

5 Participate in something with other people who also share your hobby, for example, singing with a musical group, hiking with others, playing an instrument in a band, joining a bird-watching club, or going to a garden or flower exhibit.

6 Create your own activity related to your hobby.

_____
Date badge completed

_____
My signature

_____
Leader's signature

EXPLORING
HEALTHY EATING

COMPLETE SIX ACTIVITIES, INCLUDING THE ONES STARRED.

1 Using a large wall chart as a visual aid, teach a younger child or small group of children some beginning steps in cooking.

*2 At two different stores, comparison shop for at least a dozen grocery items your family uses, or compare generic food items with brand name items at one store. Price items that are of the same size. Determine if you are paying more than is needed for the item. Then, get at least two brands or types (fresh, frozen, canned) of each of several products and hold a taste test. Have a family or a group of friends rate the foods without telling them which brand they are tasting. Which were the most popular?

or

Learn how to make several foods. Either grow something to eat in a window box or garden, learn how to bake two or three items without a mix, or make jams or pickles. Compare the cost and taste of what you make to similar products available in stores.

3 Plan a three-day menu for a family of five (three adults, a toddler, and a Junior Girl Scout) who are going on a trip. The family is very concerned about world food shortages and prefers non-meat meals. They don't want to spend too much money. They do want meals that are nutritious and simple to prepare, and they would prefer at least some dishes that require no refrigeration. Make up menus for the meals they will have, including a snack each day.

4 Have a tasting party in your troop. Everyone should bring at least one food item or dish that is a specialty of her family or something that she would like to try. Try to include foods low in cholesterol, sugar, and fat.

5 With others, plan and prepare the food for a large group celebration or gathering. Plan a menu that is nutritious and suited to the special occasion. Plan decorations or a table setting that fits the occasion and the menu selected.

*6 Keep a record of the foods you eat for at least three days. Include any snacks you have. Find out about the food pyramid in Chapter 3 of your *Junior Girl Scout Handbook* and check to see that you are eating the correct proportions of foods from different groups. Do your food habits need improving? What are some good habits?

7 Make up a game to help younger children learn about the four food groups. Play the game with children.

8 Try to discover how much food students at school throw away from their lunch. Meet with the cafeteria manager, parents, your teacher, or your Girl Scout leader and plan ways in which waste could be reduced. Carry out one of your plans.

9 Watch several hours of children's television programming. (Saturday mornings are a good time.) Count the number of food commercials that are shown. How do commercials teach good or poor eating habits? Find out which advertised products are nutritious and which are not. Discuss your findings with others.

Date badge completed

My signature

Leader's signature

FAMILY LIVING SKILLS

1 Read about families in Chapter 2 of your *Junior Girl Scout Handbook*.

- Look for the responsibilities each family member has, the way decisions are made, how problems are solved, what conversations between adults and children are like, and the ways families share and help each other.
- Compare the television and movie families to families you know. How are these families the same? How are they different?

2 Find out about several agencies that help families in your community, county, or state. What help do they give to families? What training and education do people need? Add the information you find to a troop career file, use it to create a community service reference booklet, or create a poster highlighting these agencies.

3 Make up a skit, short story, cartoon, or display showing what family life could be like in the future. What would change the most?

4 Ask several people, including women and men of different ages, girls and boys your own age, and people from different ethnic and religious backgrounds how they would describe a homemaker. You can tape or write down their definitions. Decide on some way to chart or list your results and share them with others.

5 Interview one of the oldest members of your family or members of your community. What household labor-saving techniques and products have been invented since they were young? How have the changes in housekeeping changed family life? Share your discoveries with others.

6 What are the household tasks that need to be done in your home? With your family, talk about each person's responsibilities and activities outside the home (jobs, school, hobbies, volunteer work, etc.). Fill in the chart, "Responsibilities of a Family Member," in Chapter 2 of your *Junior Girl Scout Handbook*. How can you all cooperate and share in the necessary work? Write out a plan for your share of the work and follow your plan for at least three weeks.

or

For at least two weeks, in addition to your regular household activities, do *one* of the following household tasks in your home or in the home of someone you know who could use your help: shopping, meal preparation, laundry, gardening, light cleaning. Ask an adult to keep track of how well you did your household tasks.

7 Keep track of a personal budget for a month. Write down the money you receive, spend, and save. Where does your money go? How much can you save? Try to make a savings plan that you can follow.

8 Discuss with your family a typical household purchase that could cost a lot of money, such as appliances, furniture, or repairs. Do a bit of detective work. Help look for advertisements and compare prices. Show what you've discovered to other members of your family.

9 Make, repair, paint, or refinish an object that will make your home nicer. Use a method you have never tried before. Compare the cost of doing it yourself, having it done by someone else, or buying the object new.

10 What is a parent? What are a parent's responsibilities? Interview several parents. Ask them about how their lives changed when they had children. Try to find out how much having children costs. Create a demonstration about the typical life of a parent.

_____
Date badge completed

My signature

Leader's signature

FIRST AID

1 Read the sections on "First Aid" and "Emergency Telephone Calling" in Chapter 3 of your *Junior Girl Scout Handbook* and complete the activities.

2 Learn and practice first aid for cuts, bruises, sprains, fractures, and fainting.

3 Learn the first aid to be given for a child or for an adult with the following: stopped breathing, severe bleeding, shock, poisoning, and choking. Try to arrange for a professional demonstration. Keep written instructions for these procedures in a safe place where you can review them often.

4 Design and put together a first aid kit. Make a list of all the items included in this kit. Show how each item can be used. (For more help, see Chapter 3 of your *Junior Girl Scout Handbook*.

5 Work with an adult to make your home and troop/group meeting place fire safe. Keep a list of the things you do to make each place fire safe. Leave the safety rules to follow if there is smoke or a fire. Have a practice fire drill, at your home and at your troop/group meeting place.

6 A poison is any substance (solid, liquid, or gas) that causes death or injury when introduced into the body.

- Survey your home for poisonous substances: for example, medicines, cosmetics, cleaning solutions, and plants. Be sure these substances are properly labeled and out of the reach of small children.
- Find out and role-play what to do if a person has inhaled, swallowed, absorbed, or injected a poison.

7 Learn about possible disasters that could affect you, such as snowstorms, electrical storms, earthquakes, fire, flood, or hurricanes. Find out if your community has a disaster plan. Design an evacuation plan in case one of these disasters strikes your home or community. Practice this plan until you can follow it properly.

8 Find out about the kinds of careers and volunteer positions that require first aid training. Choose a career that interests you and learn more about it.

Do Don't Do Don't

9 Learn about what to look for in cases of hypothermia and heat stroke. Describe how treatments differ and what you can do to prevent and/or avoid both.

10 Invite a teacher, park ranger, health professional, or veterinarian to your meeting to talk about Lyme disease or some other disease in your area that can be caught from ticks or insects. Learn what types of precautions should be taken when traveling in an area where it is possible to contract these diseases. Record all information for future reference.

Date badge completed

My signature

Leader's signature

HEALTH
AND FITNESS

COMPLETE FIVE ACTIVITIES.

1 Read about nutrition in Chapter 3 of your *Junior Girl Scout Handbook* and do two of the activities.

2 Try to keep a record of what you drink for a week. Record *everything* you drink. Check to see if you are getting the six to eight glasses of water a day needed by the average person. Remember that all the liquids you drink contain water, including juice, soda, and milk. Try to increase the amount of fresh water you drink and at the same time, try to decrease the number of soft drinks or other sugary drinks you might have. See how long you can stick to this program.

3 Find out what the daily calorie needs are for someone of your height, weight, and age. Plan and prepare a breakfast for yourself that includes one-third of your daily calorie needs. Use nutritious foods. How does eating one-third of your day's calories at breakfast make you feel the rest of the day? Try to plan a week's worth of breakfast menus, all healthy and nutritious.

4 Try three of the exercise activities in Chapter 2 of the *Developing Health and Fitness: Be Your Best!* Contemporary Issues booklet.

5 Read about "Exercise" in Chapter 3 of your *Junior Girl Scout Handbook* and make up your own fitness plan. Be sure to include warming-up and cooling-down exercises. Choose an activity such as walking, jumping rope, jogging, swimming, cycling, hiking, or aerobic dance to do for 20–30 minutes three times a week. Make sure to check for your target heart rate as shown in Chapter 3. You might ask an adult or a professional to check your fitness plan.

6 Find a chart that shows good posture for someone your age. Demonstrate good posture while walking, standing, sitting, and lifting. You can use a full-length mirror to see if your posture is correct. Learn why good posture is important. How does it relate to good health, good appearance, and feeling good about yourself? You could also learn about scoliosis, and other conditions that affect posture and the methods used to correct different kinds of back problems.

doing a number of bent-knee sit-ups. List some of the activities provided. If your community doesn't have one, find out what a fitness trail or circuit exercise course is. With your troop or group, develop a course that could be used by younger children. Invite a group of younger children to the course and demonstrate how it is used.

8 Make a list of games you enjoy that include aerobic activity. Basketball, roller or ice skating, jumping rope, field hockey, tennis, tag, soccer, or softball are all examples. Choose an activity and join a team, club, or group that plays this sport. Participate for at least two months.

9 Make up a card or board game that shows the benefits of healthy eating and exercise. Teach it to members of your troop or group or your family and friends.

10 Learn the healthy ways people use to relieve tension or stress. One way is to tighten all the muscles in your body, hold, then relax. What are some other ways? Practice what you have discovered and demonstrate for others.

7 Visit a fitness trail or circuit exercise course at a school or park. A fitness course usually has a number of stations or "stops", as shown in the illustration. There are usually instructions for an exercise or activity to be performed at each station, such as doing stretching exercises, walking along a low balance beam, or

Date badge completed

My signature

Leader's signature

HEALTHY RELATIONSHIPS

1 Think of as many things as you can that you feel are essential for making and keeping friends. Your list might include being a good listener, respecting others, showing loyalty, and so on. Then survey several people of different ages to find out what they feel makes and keeps a good friend. Compare your list to your survey results.

2 Read the "Decision-Making Story Maze" in Chapter 2 of your *Junior Girl Scout Handbook* and do the activities. Try creating your own story maze or one with your troop or group on decisions you make with friends.

3 Hold a group discussion on friendship. Include these topics:

- The qualities or characteristics that each person likes most about two of her friends.
- The expectations each person has of her friends.
- A difficult choice each person had to make concerning a friend.
- The limits each person might set in a friendship.
- Examples of behaving like a good friend.

(Keep the names of your friends anonymous.)

4 Learn how nonverbal communication can be as effective as verbal communication. Write feelings or emotions, such as fear, shyness, happiness, etc., on pieces of paper. Distribute one to each person in a group. Take turns communicating the feeling on the piece of paper to the rest of the group without talking. Discuss the most commonly used gestures or expressions.

5 Make a list of fun things you can do with friends. Try to think of things that are inexpensive or free. A few examples are putting on a play, going on an outing, or running relay races. What others can you list?

6 Interview the adult members of your family. Ask them to talk about encouraging words they received from family members and friends while growing up and how those words affected them. In what ways can you give encouragement to each other? Practice in a group.

7 With your troop or group, start a monthly "friendship" project. Have members of the troop communicate words of encouragement, congratulations, or advice to someone else who needs or deserves it within or outside the troop or group.

8 Watch a movie or television program or read a book that includes a teenage dating situation. Discuss how the characters handled the relationship. Were there feelings of conflict or peer pressure? Talk about what you would do in similar situations.

9 Talk with an older family member, parent, or guardian to find out how she or he related to adults when still a child. How were this person's experiences different from your own experiences with adults today? Find out what topics could not be discussed when she or he grew up. Are there topics that can be discussed more freely today? Think of some ways by which communication can be increased in families.

Date badge completed

My signature

Leader's signature

MAKING DECISIONS

COMPLETE SIX ACTIVITIES.

1 Read the section on "Making Good Decisions" in Chapter 2 of your *Junior Girl Scout Handbook*. Think of a decision you need to make and try the decision-making steps.

2 In a small group, share your experiences in making a difficult decision. What influenced your decision? What helped you decide? What was the result of your decision? What might you have done differently if you could have had a second chance?

3 Make a list of the important decisions you will have to make within the next ten years. Some might be whether to go to college or whether to get a job, what kind of career to have, whether to buy a car, when to get your own apartment, or whether or not to get married. Talk with at least three friends to find out about their plans for the future. Compare their plans to your own. Are there any decisions that are the same or different? What are some decisions that girls and women make today that they didn't have to make in the past?

4 Create a poster of ways that people pressure or force others to do something they may not want to do. Some statements might be "Everybody's doing it" or "Try it; you'll like it." Share your poster with others and role-play some positive responses to such lines.

5 With your troop or group, decide on a service project. Make a list of everyone's ideas. Discuss each idea. Come to an agreement about what you will do and put your plan into action. How will you evaluate the project? What changes might you make the next time? Chapter 6 "Leadership in Action," in your *Junior Girl Scout Handbook* has some helpful guidelines.

6 Discuss with family members and other adults the ways they make decisions. Can you think of some other ways? Decide which ways are helpful and which are not. Make a list of helpful reminders for when you make decisions.

7 Create a story about a girl who has trouble making an important decision because two of her values are in conflict. One idea might be that her two closest friends want her to help play a prank on a classmate, but she doesn't like hurting anyone.

8 Think of the things and people that influence your decisions, for example, friends, school, family, or the media. Star (*) the people on this list whom you can approach when you need help in making a personal decision. What makes these people special?

9 Discuss the following situations and role-play what you would do if:

- A classmate offered you a cigarette on the way home from school.
- A group of friends stopped by to visit when no adults were home.
- You noticed your sister taking money from your father's wallet.
- Your cousin told you that she was being abused by a relative and wanted you to promise to keep it a secret.
- Your family planned an outing on the same day of your best friend's birthday party.
- A bigger kid tried to bully you in the park.
- A stranger offered you money to sell some drugs.
- Some of your friends started teasing a classmate.

Make up your own situations.

10 Set a positive goal for something you want to do in the next three months. Some examples are completing a badge, getting an "A" in math, making a gift for someone special, or learning to roller skate. Determine how you will reach this goal. Ask an adult to help you decide if this goal is possible to do in three months. Carry out your plan to reach your goal.

Role-playing

Role-playing is acting out a situation that could really happen. When you role-play, you try to say and do what the person you are pretending to be would do and say in that situation. When you role-play, you can experience how someone else might feel and act. You should always have a discussion after role-playing so that you can talk about what happened and how people felt. When you watch a role-playing exercise, think about what you would do in that situation and be supportive of the people doing the acting.

_____
Date badge completed

_____
My signature

_____
Leader's signature

"MAKING" HOBBIES

EXAMPLES

Any of the arts— woodworking · knitting · sculpture · sketching · photography · weaving

COMPLETE ACTIVITY 1, THEN DO FOUR OF THE OTHERS.

1 Ask yourself these questions and discuss the answers with an adult family member or other adult.

 • Is this hobby fun?
 • Can I afford it?
 • Do I have the space for it?
 • Do I have time for it?
 • Are there any environmental concerns?

2 Make some examples of your hobby. Explain to others what is involved in your hobby and what skills you have learned.

3 Find out about other people who share your hobby, for example, carpenters, potters, or photographers. Attend an exhibit, read a book, or interview the people involved.

4 Find out something about the history of your hobby. Share this information with others in some creative way.

5 Display, use, or organize your finished products and show others the work you have made. Describe what you have done.

6 Interview someone or collect several clippings, stories, or pictures of people in a career related to your hobby. Do you think that you would like to turn your hobby into a career or would you like to keep it as a hobby?

7 Create your own activity related to your hobby.

_____
Date badge completed

_____
My signature

_____
Leader's signature

MY
SELF-ESTEEM

1 Start your own journal. A journal is a special book, similar to a diary, in which you can write your thoughts and feelings. You can be creative and write stories, poems, cartoons, or draw pictures. You can be very honest and serious or happy and silly in your journal. You can share your journal or keep it private. It's your book. Try writing about these topics in your journal.

What do you like the best about yourself? How are you special and different from everybody else?

Write two words that each of these people would use to describe you:

Yourself   A neighbor
Your best friend   A teacher

Each time you write in your journal, think about what it tells you about yourself.

2 Create a "brag bag." Write down as many things as you can think of that make you special. You can do this alone or in a group, and you can write positive statements about each other. Look at your list. Write the statements on separate index cards. Toss the cards in a bag; pull out one card each day for a week or when you're feeling "down." Repeat that positive statement out loud or to yourself several times throughout the day.

3 Collect some pictures of people in different poses and with different facial expressions. Select at least a dozen and decide what you think the pictures reveal about each person's self-esteem (what she feels about herself). Do this in a group and discuss your reactions.

4 Create three situations to role-play. They should involve characters who have important decisions to make, and who are tempted to follow the crowd rather than to think independently. Create two endings for each situation: one in which the main character has high self-esteem, and one in which she has low self-esteem.

5 Read the section on "Body Image" in Chapter 2 of your *Junior Girl Scout Handbook* and do one of the activities.

6 Select a real or "pretend" person who you feel shows a lot of self-esteem. Make a list of the characteristics that make this person feel good about herself. What can you copy or learn from this person?

THINGS THAT WORRY ME

Things I Believe Will Definitely Occur:	Things I Believe Might Occur:	Things I Guess Won't Happen:
_____	_____	_____
_____	_____	_____
_____	_____	_____
_____	_____	_____
_____	_____	_____
_____	_____	_____
_____	_____	_____
_____	_____	_____
_____	_____	_____

7 List these twelve items in the order of importance to you:

  Home
  Money
  Career
  Respect
  Car
  Job
  Peace with myself
  Wardrobe
  Family
  Religion
  Fame
  Friends

Ask at least three other friends to do this activity and then compare your lists. Discuss what you think your list means. What do the things that are important to you tell you about yourself?

8 What is a goal? Make a list of three goals you would like to reach in a month. Decide on a plan for reaching at least one goal and then follow it.

9 Think about things that worry you. Do all the things that you worry about happen? In your journal or on a piece of paper, make a chart. Write down all your worries for one week in one of three categories: "Things I believe will definitely occur," "Things I believe might occur," and "Things I guess probably won't happen." At the end of a week, put an X next to the worries that came true. Was worrying worth the time you spent? With a group, come up with ways to think constructively about things that you can really change or improve.

• •

_____
Date badge completed

_____
My signature

_____
Leader's signature

PET CARE

. . . .

COMPLETE FIVE ACTIVITIES, INCLUDING THE ONE STARRED.

(For activities 3–7, if you do not have a pet, think of one you would like to have, and do the activities for your imaginary pet.)

1 Identify four animals that would make good pets. Make a chart or poster showing a picture of each pet and describing the reasons why it is a good pet. Include things like their life expectancy and their daily needs. Make a list of four animals that would not make good pets. Be able to explain your reasons.

*2 Take responsibility for a pet (your own or someone else's) by providing it with the care it needs—shelter, food, exercise, and grooming. Keep a record for two months of how you cared for this pet. What other things must be done regularly to care for a pet? Include the cost of care and the time it takes. What laws does your community have about pets?

3 Find out about the kinds of illnesses most common to your pet, what signs to watch for, and how to protect against illness. Learn how to administer medicine (if possible) or show how to seek emergency treatment for your pet.

or

Read about animal bites in the "First Aid Guide" of Chapter 3 of your *Junior Girl Scout Handbook.* Learn the correct and safe way to approach an animal if it is injured. Show how to restrain it when giving treatment without risk to you or the animal. Learn how to give first aid for the injuries most common to a pet.

4 Learn how to tell whether your pet is a male or female. Find out how often the female of your pet could have babies and how many she could have at one time. Compare her to another kind of pet. In each case, how many young would be produced in five years? Would you be able to find homes for that many animals?

5 Identify two diseases that pets can get and spread, such as Lyme disease. Find out what is being done to control these diseases and what you can do to prevent your pet from getting these diseases. Do something that will help educate people and help prevent a common pet disease.

6 Find out how many people in your community have careers dealing with pets. Visit one of these people on the job or invite her/him to tell you about the work she/he does.

or

Visit an animal veterinary hospital or humane society and find out how these places help pets. Find out if there is something you can do to assist and do it.

7 Do something special for your pet: Make it a special toy, give it some extra exercise and attention, or learn more about your pet and the care it needs.

or

Start a scrapbook of animals. Collect pictures of animals, articles or funny stories about animals, animal laws, animal problems, advertisements for animal movies, or animal cartoons. Share your scrapbook with others.

8 Pretend your pet is lost. Write a newspaper advertisement or notice to display, describing what your pet looks like, where it was lost, and how you can be reached. (For ideas, look at the "lost pet" notices in newspapers.)

9 What is a good diet for your pet? Collect advertisements for pet food. What information do they give you about the nutritional needs of an animal? Read labels on pet food containers and compare them for food values. How would nutritional needs change as your pet grows older?

10 How do you communicate with your pet? Is it possible for your pet to communicate with you? How do you show a pet what you want it to do? How does your pet communicate to you what it wants? Describe some specific behaviors that your pet uses to communicate anger, fear, hunger, and loyalty.

· ·

_____
Date badge completed

_____
My signature

_____
Leader's signature

SAFETY SENSE

1 Find out about four health and safety services your community, county, or state provides to protect you and others. Visit or write to one of these agencies and learn what it does and how to contact it if you need its services.

2 Survey your troop/group or class at school to find out the number and types of accidents they or people close to them have had in the last year.

• Discover how and where these accidents have occurred most frequently.

• Discuss ways to prevent such accidents from happening again.

3 Make a booklet or audiocassette tape explaining the safety rules for four of the following situations:

• Talking to strangers.
• Riding in a car, bus, train, or plane.
• Being at home alone.
• Riding a bike.
• Babysitting.
• Being in public places (elevators, playgrounds, shopping areas, restrooms).
• Swimming, fishing, or boating in a lake.
• Swimming, fishing, or boating on the ocean.
• Ice skating on a lake or at a rink.

Share your booklet or tape with others.

4 Bicycle falls are a major cause of children's head injuries. It has been proven that helmets reduce the number of head injuries nationwide. From your local bicycle or safety organization, learn what you can about bicycle helmets: their ability to protect, their cost, the different types. Then do one of the following:

• Hold an educational event for children and parents or speak to them at one of their community meetings. Your local bike shop or police department can help you plan a fun presentation.

or

• Run a poster contest for the best posters promoting helmet use. Display the posters.

5 Plan, talk about, and practice fire escape routes for your home, troop meeting place, or school. Use the information on Fire Safety in Chapter 3 of your *Junior Girl Scout Handbook.*

6 Plan an activity, a video or musical presentation, skit, or puppet show on safety for younger children. Present it to Daisy Girl Scouts or other younger children.

How many safety hazards can you find in this picture?

_____

_____

_____

_____

_____

_____

_____

_____

_____

_____

_____

(For answers, see page 239.)

7 Conduct a safety check of your home. Spot and correct hazards with the help of family members. Be alert for problem areas that might endanger a family member who has a disability or who is ill, an infant or toddler, or an elderly person who has problems with eyesight or walking. List the following information and post it in a handy spot: phone numbers of police, fire department, poison control center, doctor, and ambulance.

8 Write and act out a safety public service announcement or commercial that could be aired on radio or cable television.

9 Take a hazard identification hike along a bike path, foot trail, horse trail, skateboard course, or other similar place.

• Identify places where you could get hurt or unsafe practices that could cause you trouble.

• Set up some way to warn others of the hazards or work to remove them.

. . . .

_____

Date badge completed

_____

My signature

_____

Leader's signature

SPORTS

*1 Choose a sport, such as basketball, bowling, cycling, frisbee, field hockey, ice skating or roller skating, soccer, softball, volleyball, or another of your choice.

- Learn the rules of the game.
- Practice the skills and strategies needed to participate in your sport.
- Review the "Tips for Playing Sports" in Chapter 7 of your *Junior Girl Scout Handbook*.

2 Show how to select, use, care for, and store the equipment and clothing needed to participate in your sport.

- Visit a sports equipment store or look in a sports catalog to learn more about these items.
- Find out about the facilities in your community that are available for your use.

3 Trace the history and development of your sport. Find out what makes this sport special, the countries in which it is popular, the past and present star athletes, or the outstanding teams.

4 Find out what injuries occur most often from participating in this sport.

- Learn and be able to demonstrate first aid for at least two of these injuries.
- Discuss or list the safety tips you would give to help prevent these injuries.

5 Observe, in person or on television, two events involving this sport.

- Note three of the following: How the game is played, how it is scored, what are the number of players, how the team works together, what are the uniforms worn, what equipment and playing area are used.
- Record your feelings about this event and the new things you discovered.

6 Participate in this sport with others by taking part in a tournament, club, play day, intramural program, or team.
- Follow the rules of safety and fair play.
- Demonstrate your ability to cooperate with others.
- Find out how climate affects your ability to play.
- Discover ways that you can improve your play.

7 Learn to play two games that are similar to your sport, and teach them to a younger group of children. You might want to select a game that is played in another country or one that is traditional in an ethnic or cultural group in the United States.

8 Find out what the life of an athlete is really like.
- Collect information (from books, magazine articles, newspaper clippings, athletes, coaches, etc.) on the type of diet, exercise, commitment, and training required for an athlete in this sport.
- Learn about the types of tournaments and amateur and professional opportunities available for athletes in this sport.

9 Learn how to keep score for or officiate at a sports event.

Find out the duties of a scorekeeper or official and the training needed to do this job.

or

Volunteer as a scorekeeper or official for a local sports event.

_____
Date badge completed

_____
My signature

_____
Leader's signature

SPORTS SAMPLER

1 Discover which sports are available for you and others in your community.

- Search for sports that you can participate in alone and those that involve a team or a group.
- Find a way to tell others about the sports.
- Find out what skills are necessary to participate in these sports.

2 Read a book or watch a video or movie on one of these topics and prepare a talk on it:

- A sports story or collection of sports stories.
- A biography of an athlete or coach.
- The history of a sport or of the Olympic Games.

3 Find out the proper clothing and/or equipment for four different sports activities.

- Visit a sports equipment store or look in a sports catalog or magazine.
- Be able to tell why this clothing/equipment is needed and how it is used.

or

Read the Section on "Playing Sports and Games" in Chapter 7 of your *Junior Girl Scout Handbook*. Choose one sport and organize a tournament with other Girl Scout troops or groups or other groups of friends.

4 Show that you are prepared to help an injured person. Be able to treat three of the following injuries:

- Cut lip.
- Skinned knee.
- Nosebleed.
- Broken tooth.
- Blister.
- Sprained ankle.
- Loss of consciousness.

5 Discuss the rules of fair play and safety when playing in or watching sports.
- Make a list of these rules and post it on the wall.
- Decide what action should be taken if the rules are broken.

6 Take a survey of at least ten people. Ask them what kind of sport they play, how often they play it, why they play this sport, and what advice they would give others who are interested in this activity.

7 Develop a sports presentation for a group of Daisy or Brownie Girl Scouts. As part of the presentation, explain why exercise and sports participation are important to good health.

8 Make a list of sports that one can participate in at any age. For each sport you list, determine how much money is needed for equipment and ongoing participation, what the benefits are to the participants, and whether participation is indoors, outdoors, or seasonal.

9 Attend a sporting event or watch a sport on television, such as a basketball or baseball game, a soccer match, a swimming meet, a tennis match, or a figure skating show. Learn something about the participants or the rules or history of the sport.

10 Help plan a fun-filled play day, games festival, or tournament. Include activities for different ages and skill levels. Participate in a variety of the activities or be a games leader or referee.

11 Learn about the careers available in the sports field. Talk to a person involved in sports, such as an athlete, coach, athletic trainer, sports official, sportswriter, scorekeeper, or equipment manager. Find out about her/his work and the training needed for that job.

_____
Date badge completed

_____
My signature

_____
Leader's signature

World Citizens

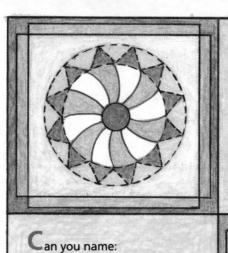

Look at a globe or a map of the world. Find: a country bigger than the United States, a country surrounded by water, a country on the Equator. Invent a game to play with others.

Can you name:
• two women scientists?
• two female politicians?
• two women artists?
• two women athletes?

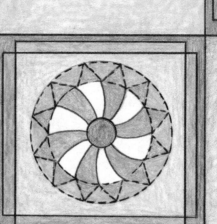

See if you can find something in your neighborhood or area that is more than ten years old? 50 years old? 100 years old? 500 years old? What things will still exist in 10 years? 50 years? 100 years? 500 years?

Imagine that you are one of the first Earthpeople to visit the inhabitants of a distant planet. Because your spaceship is small, you could only bring ten things that would be typical of and represent the people of Earth. What ten things would you bring?

Find out more about a member of your family, an ancestor, or a famous person who shares your cultural, ethnic, or racial heritage. What positive qualities or characteristics does this person have? Write a poem or short story about this person.

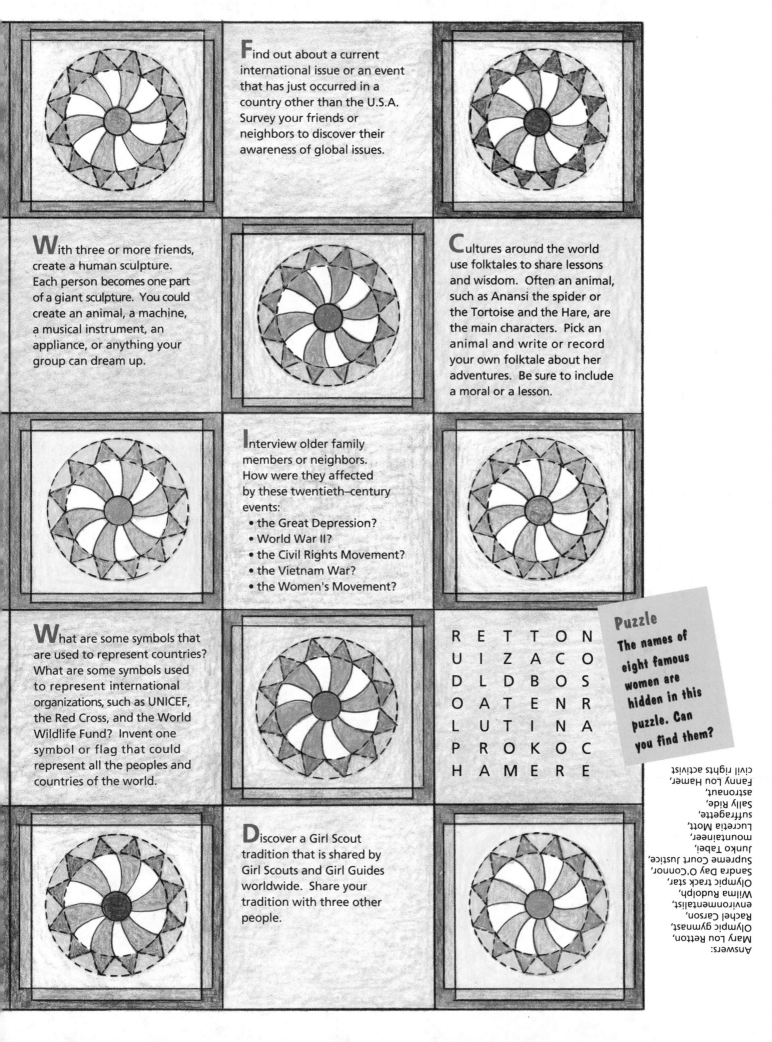

Find out about a current international issue or an event that has just occurred in a country other than the U.S.A. Survey your friends or neighbors to discover their awareness of global issues.

With three or more friends, create a human sculpture. Each person becomes one part of a giant sculpture. You could create an animal, a machine, a musical instrument, an appliance, or anything your group can dream up.

Cultures around the world use folktales to share lessons and wisdom. Often an animal, such as Anansi the spider or the Tortoise and the Hare, are the main characters. Pick an animal and write or record your own folktale about her adventures. Be sure to include a moral or a lesson.

Interview older family members or neighbors. How were they affected by these twentieth-century events:
- the Great Depression?
- World War II?
- the Civil Rights Movement?
- the Vietnam War?
- the Women's Movement?

What are some symbols that are used to represent countries? What are some symbols used to represent international organizations, such as UNICEF, the Red Cross, and the World Wildlife Fund? Invent one symbol or flag that could represent all the peoples and countries of the world.

Discover a Girl Scout tradition that is shared by Girl Scouts and Girl Guides worldwide. Share your tradition with three other people.

```
R E T T O N
U I Z A C O
D L D B O S
O A T E N R
L U T I N A
P R O K O C
H A M E R E
```

Puzzle

The names of eight famous women are hidden in this puzzle. Can you find them?

Answers:
Mary Lou Retton,
Olympic gymnast,
Rachel Carson,
environmentalist,
Wilma Rudolph,
Olympic track star,
Sandra Day O'Connor,
Supreme Court Justice,
Junko Tabei,
mountaineer,
Lucretia Mott,
suffragette,
Sally Ride,
astronaut,
Fanny Lou Hamer,
civil rights activist

DABBLER

COMPLETE ONE ACTIVITY IN FIVE OF THE GROUPS.

A.1 Find out about community workers or city, town, or county employees whose main jobs are to help others. Think of a way to show others what these workers do. You might make puppets and put on a skit for younger girls.

A.2 Discover why the colors and symbols were chosen for the American flag. Design a flag for your neighborhood or community. Think about the colors and symbols that you will use. Show your flag to others and explain your design.

A.3 Draw or make a simple map of your neighborhood. Include important landmarks, buildings, recreational areas, businesses, and other information. Test your map by showing it to others. Do they know what it represents?

B.1 What are the responsibilities of being a good citizen? What rules do citizens follow? Think about being a citizen, a member of your family.

What "rules" does your family have and what rules do you follow to be a good citizen of your family? Create a family document listing these rules.

B.2 Make a list of all the groups to which you belong. What set of rules does each group have that you follow in order to be a member or citizen of that group? Which groups are the most important to you? Which groups have the most influence on you?

C.1 Learn to play cooperative musical chairs and teach the game to others. In this game, one chair is removed each time the music stops, but all the players try to balance on the chairs that are left. The game ends when there is only one chair left and everyone is somehow sitting on it!

• 50 •

I'm so misunderstood!

C.2 Think of a favorite fairy or folk tale. Try to rethink the story from the villain's point of view. For example, what would "Cinderella" be like if one of the stepsisters told the story? Share your new story with others by having a story session, writing it, making a comic strip or picture book, or using some other way to tell your new story.

D.1 Find a way to show where three generations of one family have lived. It could be your family, a relative, or a family in your neighborhood. Add dates and go back further into the past if you can.

D.2 Discover one thing that is special to your family. It could be a celebration, a way of cooking, a saying or story, or other custom or tradition. Find ways to continue this tradition.

E.1 Next time you are in a bus or a car, or taking a long walk, be a geography observer. Try to notice the following: the type of plants you see, how much land is empty and how much is being used, and what is on the land that is being used—plants for farming, parks for recreation, buildings for housing, businesses, schools and churches, or other uses. Think about what you observed. Would you keep the land the way it is or would you make changes? Write a letter about your ideas to someone in your town or county who works in a zoning or land-use department.

E.2 Think about a place that you have never been but that you would like to visit. Why do you want to visit that place? What do you know about it? Is it a real or an imaginary place? How could you get to this place? Draw a travel poster, write a short travel advertisement, or pretend to be a travel agent and try to convince someone else to visit this place.

F.1 Learn the Girl Scout Promise. Think of a way that you could show others that you are following the Promise. Make it a part of your daily actions.

F.2 Learn about three Girl Scout ceremonies. Select a ceremony that you can plan with others and then hold your ceremony.

F.3 Learn the words and music to a Girl Scout song. Perform this with others or teach it to two other people.

G.1 Interview a woman whom you admire. What do you admire about her? What characteristics and skills does she have? How did she develop those characteristics and skills? What can you learn from her and use in your life?

G.2 Read an article or book about a famous woman. Why is she famous? What are her accomplishments? Was her life easier or harder because she was female? What can you learn from this woman's accomplishments?

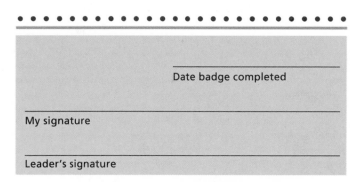

Date badge completed

My signature

Leader's signature

ACTIVE CITIZEN

COMPLETE SIX ACTIVITIES.

1 What are the procedures for registering to vote for an election? Make a poster that encourages people in your community to vote.

2 Interview someone in your family or community who chose or had to leave his home or country in order to exercise freedom.

or

Read a book or see a movie or television program about a fight or flight for freedom. Share what you have learned with others.

3 Choose an issue that is important to your community, such as pollution, homeless families, crime, latchkey kids, drug or alcohol abuse, or not enough child care. Collect and read information on this issue. Try to get some information by listening to someone talk about the issue on the radio, on television, or at a public meeting. You may also want to talk to a friend, neighbor, teacher, or public official to obtain several points of view. Decide how you feel about this issue and be able to explain why you feel this way. Share this knowledge with others.

4 Find out how to do four or more of these:
- Obtain a passport.
- Report a water or gas leak.
- Report an abandoned car.
- Register a bicycle.
- Get working papers or a Social Security number.
- Get a pet license.
- Report a dangerous road condition.
- Handle a parking violation.

5 Find out the name of your state legislative representative and your U.S. congressional representative. Find out when they come up for election again and how they voted on at least one issue that concerns you. Write a letter expressing your opinion on that issue. In your letter explain why you were concerned enough to write to them.

6 Through our Bill of Rights, United States citizens have been given the opportunity to follow any religion they choose. Discover more about what religious freedom really means. Find out about the different religious recognitions that are available in Girl Scouting and share this information with your troop or group. (See pages 239–241 for information.)

7 Find out how the United States justice system works. Learn the difference between a civil and a criminal court. What are the rights and responsibilities of the judge, jury, prosecutor (or plaintiff), defendant, court stenographers, and court officer? Try to visit your local courthouse or plan a mock trial in your troop/group.

8 Besides being a citizen of your community and country, you are also a citizen of the world. Read "Differences in Values" and "Values That Conflict" in Chapter 2 of your *Junior Girl Scout Handbook* and do one of the activities.

_____
Date badge completed

_____
My signature

_____
Leader's signature

CELEBRATING PEOPLE

COMPLETE SIX OF THE FOLLOWING ACTIVITIES.

1 Read about the National Forum on Kids and Prejudice in Chapter 5 of your *Junior Girl Scout Handbook*. What do the Girl Scout Promise and Law state about the ways you should treat other people? Develop your own code of conduct for relating to other people. Share your code with your troop/group, family, or friends. See how long you can live by your code.

2 Create a pretend invitation that could be sent to girls from another country to invite them to a party in your town. When writing this invitation use the language spoken in the country that you have chosen. Plan a meal using recipes that are common to your chosen country. Make decorations for your party in the color of that country's flag or one that represents the culture and arts of the country. Host your party by inviting another Girl Scout group or troop and share with them all that you have learned about the country that you have chosen.

"What a Clique Does"

3 What is a clique? How do cliques develop? How does it feel to be part of a clique? How does it feel to be outside a clique? With your troop/group or a group of friends, think of ways that cliques are different from groups of friends. Make a list of ways that people can be included, not excluded. Try to practice the ways that include people. Report back to your discussion group on your success.

4 What is discrimination? Why do you think it happens? Look in magazines and newspapers for articles on how discrimination is being fought. Read one and share a summary with your troop/group or family and friends.

5 Imagine that you are from another part of the universe and you are circling Planet Earth in your spaceship. You have never visited Planet Earth before and you must make a report to your superiors about this planet. How would you answer these questions in your report?

   a What are the common characteristics of the inhabitants of this planet?

   b What activities do they enjoy?

   c What are their beliefs and what things are important to them?

   d What do they need in order to survive?

   e How do the inhabitants of this planet treat each other and how do they treat their planet?

Share your answers with others. Prepare a skit, role-playing exercise, story, fable, comic strip, or song about your discoveries concerning the inhabitants of Planet Earth.

6 The United Nations has a "Declaration of Human Rights." One of the rights is that all people are born free and equal. Is this the case all over the world? What could be done to make it true? Check if there are any community or local agencies that make sure people have equal opportunity and have all their legal rights. Arrange to visit one of these agencies and speak to the employees there, or write and ask them for information about their work.

or

Write your own declaration of young people's rights. Share it with your friends and family.

7 Find out about people who are "peacemakers." Discover at least three people who are known in your community, in the United States, or internationally for their work in human rights, their work for world peace, or their work to stop prejudice against people of other races and ethnic and cultural groups, against people of the opposite sex, against people of different religions, against people with disabilities, or against people of different ages. What qualities and characteristics do these people have in common? Create a poster or playlet showing an incident from the life of one of these "peacemakers."

8 What is a culture? Explore a culture different from your own. What values does that culture share with yours? What can you learn about this culture, such as its typical foods, folk tales, folk art, music, celebrations, and holidays? Think about your own heritage. What similarities do you share with the culture you investigated? What are the differences? Choose one example of this culture's art, holiday celebration, or food; make it and share it with others.

9 Make a "Human Family" collage, poster, display, or booklet. Include representations from as many different cultures as you can. Make sure the pictures or representations that you use are realistic and accurate rather than stereotypes or made-up characters.

10 Think of problems that might occur when people who are different live or work together. Write some of the problems on slips of paper. In a group, pull out a slip and think of solutions or act out solutions to these problems.

11 Plan a way that you can work with younger girls on a project that would help them understand and appreciate people who are different from themselves. What could you do? How would you know if the girls had learned anything new?

Date badge completed

My signature

Leader's signature

CREATIVE SOLUTIONS

· ·

COMPLETE FIVE OF THE ACTIVITIES.

1 Read the sections on "Conflict Resolution" in Chapter 2 of your *Junior Girl Scout Handbook*. Think of a recent conflict between friends or family members and act out the situation with your troop/group or write, audio tape or videotape an imaginary dialogue for the situation.

2 Investigate some cooperative games. These are games in which everyone is challenged and in which everyone participates and "wins." Many of the games that are played in Girl Scouting are cooperative games, such as "Human Knots" or "Capture the Flag." Teach three cooperative games to others.

Form two teams facing each other. Stand in two lines, two to three feet apart. The players from each team from opposite ends of the line go first. They walk between the two lines towards each other, looking at each other the entire time. When they meet in the middle, they bow to each other and say, "How do you do?" and then keep walking. Neither of these players is allowed to smile, laugh or giggle. Meanwhile, the two teams try everything they can, except touching, to make the player from the opposite team laugh or smile. If the player smiles or laughs, he must join the opposite team.

3 Imagine the following situation. "You are an Ardavanian ruler from the Planet Ardavania. Your planet gets a lot of sun and is very warm, but has very little water. This makes it difficult to grow enough food for everyone. Nearby, the Planet Frazar has only a little sun, but lots of water. Most of the water is ice, which covers three-fourths of the planet. This also makes it difficult to grow enough food for everyone on Frazar. The Frazarians have sent you a message. They want to take over Ardavania. Their spaceships will enter your atmosphere in one hour. With a group or on your own, think of as many solutions as you can to the problem. Would your solution be different if Frazar had no water? How can you reach a solution in which your planet and the Frazarians both win?

4 With a group, try the following:
 a Create a giant machine. Each member of the group acts as a part of the machine—a wheel, a gear, a knob, etc. See how well the group can work together.

Help them find their way out of their group structure.

START

FINISH

b Using drinking straws or toothpicks, try to make a group structure or creation. Each member of the group should help build the structure and should help decide what it will be.

c Sit in a circle. Start with a wound ball of yarn. Toss it to one of the members of the circle. That person begins a story. She tosses the yarn to another member of the circle, who continues the story. The group members keep tossing the yarn, adding to the story until the yarn is unwound.

5 By yourself or in a group, think about conflict. A conflict happens when two people (between friends, family, or neighbors) or two groups (between countries) want the same thing.

Conflicts can also happen inside yourself when you can't decide or are not sure what you want. Think of examples of each of these kinds of conflict. Write the examples on slips of paper. Take turns drawing the examples. For each conflict identify the problem, think of as many solutions as you can, and then try to choose the best one.

6 If you are involved in a conflict, "I-statements" are a useful way to tell someone what "I want, I think, or I feel" without accusing the other person or hurting her feelings. When you start the sentence with "I," you are speaking for yourself. This often makes the situation calmer and it becomes easier to find a solution. Here is an example: Instead of saying, "You make me so mad when you borrow my stuff without asking!" you would use an "I-statement" and say, "I like to know where my things are. I feel upset when I want to use something and it is gone. What can we work out?" "I-statements" can usually avoid an argument in which no one wins. These statements may also make it possible to solve the problem faster. Practice some "I-statements" for the following situations.

- Your teacher accuses you of talking, but it was the person behind you.
- You share a room with your younger sister. She is very messy and you are neat.
- A girl you think is popular asks if you would like to smoke a cigarette. You know smoking is very bad for you.

- You have made some new friends this year. A girl with whom you were friendly last year invites you over to spend the night, but you are not sure yet what your new friends want to do this weekend.
- An older girl dares you in front of a group to steal a lipstick from the drugstore. She calls you a baby and asks if you are afraid.

7 Sometimes a conflict can be caused because people do not listen well. People can become so busy thinking about what they want to say next, that they don't really hear what the other person is saying. Here are some ways to listen:

- Look at the person who is talking.
- Try not to think about other things. Concentrate on what the other person is saying.
- Try not to interrupt or think about your answer.

When the person is finished, try repeating or restating what you heard. You can start by saying, "Did you say that . . .?" or "In other words, . . ." or "It sounds like you said . . ." or whatever feels comfortable to you.

Create conversations for the following situations using the ways to listen described above.

- Your classmate tells you that she heard your best friend say something bad about you. Just then you see your best friend walking toward you.
- Your friend invites you to go shopping on Saturday. Your mother has asked you to watch your younger brother. You really want to go shopping.
- You are responsible for getting your sister ready for school in the morning. This has made you late to class every day this week. Finally the teacher takes you aside and asks you why you've been late.
- You promise to help your friend with her homework tonight. You are having a quiz tomorrow. Your father comes home and suggests that the family go out to a movie.

8 Make a contract with yourself. Try for one week to avoid saying things that hurt or make people angry. What are your results at the end of the week? Share your discoveries with friends. Try making a contract with a friend in which you will both try to avoid saying hurtful things.

Date badge completed

My signature

Leader's signature

GEOGRAPHY FUN

1 Find out about one animal or plant species from each of the seven continents that is in danger of becoming extinct. Find out why. Talk about what you and your troop/group might do to help the situation. How might the people in the United States or other parts of the world influence this animal or plant species?

2 Find out about the seasons in the northern and southern hemispheres. Find a way to demonstrate what causes seasons to occur. When is summer in Australia? What clothes would you bring if you were visiting Chile or Peru in July?

3 Discover new facts about various countries. Select one country to be an expert on. What are the major rivers, capital cities, mountain ranges, animal life, famous geographical features, and so forth? Invent a quiz or game to play with your friends.

or

Make a crossword puzzle or word search puzzle using words from some of the above categories (for example, major rivers, capital cities).

4 Choose a continent and find out about a serious environmental problem that is happening there now. Why is it happening? What influ-

ence do other countries have on this problem? With your troop/group, create a mock television or radio show, panel discussion, or debate about the problem.

5 If you lived in one of the many desert or dry areas of the world, would you be able to carry water for long distances? In many places, women and girls must carry most or all of the water needed in their homes each day.

Try carrying a large pail nearly full of water around a block, a playing field, or a one-acre lot without spilling a drop. Then see if you can carry the container with a small amount of water in it on your head or shoulders for a short distance. Practice until you can walk with the container ten feet without dropping it. Then, try filling two one-gallon milk jugs with water at the start of the day.

Using only this water, see if you can last an entire day using two gallons for drinking, cooking, food preparation, washing, bathing, and flushing the toilet. Think of how you save water during the day. What steps could you continue?

or

Where does your community get its water? Does your community restrict water use? Find out some ways to conserve water and practice two of them in your home.

6 Do the "Reading a Map" activity in Chapter 7 of your *Junior Girl Scout Handbook*.

7 Make a model, a diorama, shadowbox, or other three-dimensional display of one of the following:
  a A city in the Gobi desert.
  b A village on a South Pacific island.
  c A town in the Russian steppes.
  d A village in the African savannah.
  e A large city in Europe.
  f A village above the Arctic Circle.
  g A community along the Amazon River.

8 Find out about world weather patterns. Where do storms and wind come from? How are storms different in winter and summer? How are they different in various parts of the world? Find out about other areas of the world that are affected by natural phenomena: earthquakes, floods, tidal waves, and so on. Which places seem the safest to live? The most dangerous?

9 How is the culture of a people affected by where they live? Make a mural or write a story that shows five different examples of people's adaptations to their environments.

10 Geology shows that once the continents were attached and part of one huge continent. Can you see how they might have fit together? Trace the outlines of the continents on a world map. Then cut the continents apart and try to piece them together. Find out what one continent was like hundreds of millions of years ago.

Date badge completed

My signature

Leader's signature

GIRL SCOUTING
AROUND THE WORLD

Note: For some of these activities, you will need to use the book *Trefoil Round the World*. Some activities will require other resources, such as *World Games and Recipes*, *The Wide World of Girl Guiding and Girl Scouting*, and its *Leaders' Guide*, WAGGGS Girl Guide/Girl Scout Uniform Posters, or WAGGGS Badges Posters. These should be available in your Girl Scout council office or may be purchased through the Girl Scout National Equipment Service. Your local library could also supply you with biographies or reference books about Girl Scouting and the famous people in the Girl Scout Movement.

1 Learn about the lives of Lord Robert Baden-Powell and Olave Baden-Powell and the founding of the Girl Guide Movement. Share your information with members of your troop/group or with a Brownie Girl Scout troop.

2 Learn what the World Association of Girl Guides and Girl Scouts is, and be able to explain why it was formed and what it does.

3 Find out about the world centers operated by the World Association of Girl Guides and Girl Scouts. Which center would you most like to visit? What would you like to do while you are there? How could you prepare for your visit?

Look through the Girl Scout song books. Find a song that you would sing at a world center and learn the words and music.

4 Make a display that shows all the countries around the world that have Girl Guides or Girl Scouts. You may include the different uniforms through photographs, drawings, or cloth costumes. Emphasize in your display the things that Girl Guides and Girl Scouts have in common.

or

Make up a game to help Brownie Girl Scouts learn about Girl Guides/Girl Scouts around the world. Use your game at a neighborhood event, as a wide game at camp, or in helping girls bridge to Junior Girl Scouting.

5 With your troop or group, plan and take part in a special ceremony for Thinking Day that celebrates Girl Scouting and Girl Guiding everywhere.

Do you know?

1 Where Lord and Lady Baden-Powell are buried? _____

2 What Ticalli is? _____

3 What Twinklers are? _____

4 What Sonaeyo tsune ni means? _____

5 Where Pax Lodge is? _____

Answers: 1-Kenya   2-the headquarters for the Girl Guides (Guías) of Mexico.   3-Girl Scouts in the Philippines ages 4 to 6.   4-"Be prepared," in Japanese.   5-London, England.

6 Become an expert about Girl Guiding/Girl Scouting in another country. Learn how Girl Guiding/Girl Scouting started in that country, the age groupings, the uniforms, the Promise, the motto, and the typical activities Girl Guides/Girl Scouts do there. Learn a game, song, craft, recipe, or activity that girls in that country enjoy, and find a way to share what you have learned with others.

7 Find out about the Juliette Low World Friendship Fund. Interview a Cadette or Senior Girl Scout who has participated in a GSUSA-sponsored international wider opportunity.

8 Prepare a skit, role-playing game, or other playlet or musical presentation about Girl Guiding/Girl Scouting, and other countries that are members of WAGGGS. Perform your presentation for younger Girl Scouts.

9 Think about a global problem. How could Girl Scouts/Girl Guides work together to help solve that problem? Plan an outline of a project that could be done worldwide.

• •

_____
Date badge completed

_____
My signature

_____
Leader's signature

GIRL SCOUTING
IN THE U.S.A.

• •

COMPLETE FIVE ACTIVITIES, INCLUDING ONE OF THE THREE STARRED.

*1 Read about Juliette Low in your *Junior Girl Scout Handbook*. Find out what Juliette was like and why she founded Girl Scouting in the United States. Then put on some skits, prepare a booklet, or make a mural illustrating some of her experiences.

2 View "The Golden Eaglet," available from your council office. Discuss in your troop/group ways that Girl Scouting has changed since 1918 and ways it has remained the same.

or

Read *75 Years of Girl Scouting* or interview someone who has been active in Girl Scouting for more than 20 years. What is the same? What is different?

3 Think of something special you can do to celebrate the Girl Scout birthday on March 12 or Juliette Low's birthday on October 31. Invite others to participate in your celebration.

or

Plan and carry out a program that will explain the origin, purpose, and use of the Juliette Low World Friendship Fund.

4 Talk to your leader, another volunteer, or a staff member of your Girl Scout council or visit your Girl Scout council office to discover what adults do in Girl Scouting. Make a chart, diagram, or list showing five different Girl Scout volunteer and/or staff jobs. Which job do you think is the most interesting? Why?

5 Find out the name of your Girl Scout council and write it on the pyramid in Chapter 1 of your *Junior Girl Scout Handbook*. Find out how many councils there are in the United States and which ones are near you.

or

Make a map of your council area. Show the cities and towns within it, the council office and/or program or service centers, and places important to Girl Scouting.

6 Get involved in a local, council, or intercouncil event. Participate in the planning and organizing of the event.

*7 Interview your leader, a Girl Scout volunteer, or a staff member about the services provided by GSUSA, the national Girl Scout organization. How could you easily show what GSUSA does? What Girl Scout councils do? What troops and groups do?

8 Find out about the books that Girl Scouts used in the past. You could borrow some old Girl Scout handbooks, *75 Years of Girl Scouting*, or the *Girl Scout Collector's Guide*. Or you might interview women who were Girl Scouts in the past to see the changes in Girl Scout uniforms over the years. Your council office may have materials to help you. Show the changes that have happened over the years by drawing pictures, making a poster, or making a paper doll with different uniforms.

9 Borrow a copy of *Wider Ops: Girl Scout Wider Opportunities* from your leader, a Cadette or Senior Girl Scout, or your council office. Read the section on the Juliette Gordon Low Girl Scout National Center to learn about the kinds of opportunities that are offered there. Tell others in your troop or group about the opportunities you liked the most.

*10 Memorize the Girl Scout Promise and the Girl Scout Law. Complete the activities about the Girl Scout Promise and Law in Chapter 1 of your *Junior Girl Scout Handbook*.

11 What are the different age levels of Girl Scouting? What are the differences and similarities among them? Invent a simple game, quiz, or puzzle that you could play with other girls relating to the age levels in Girl Scouting.

12 What is the Girl Scout motto? Think of some ways you could follow the Girl Scout motto in your daily routine. Then follow through on this.

• •

Date badge completed

My signature

Leader's signature

JUNIOR CITIZEN

COMPLETE FOUR ACTIVITIES.

1 Citizenship begins at home and in your community. What is a good neighbor? Make a list of ten things you think make a good neighbor. How are these things related to good citizenship?

2 Rights as well as responsibilities are associated with being a citizen of a country. Make a list of some of the rights and responsibilities that you think come with being a citizen of the United States. What rights are guaranteed by the Bill of Rights and the U.S. Constitution? Ask different members of your community what they would include on their list and then compare and discuss your answers.

3 Talk with someone who has been a citizen of another country or who has lived or worked in another country. Have the person describe what it was like to live in that country as compared to living in the United States.

4 Design rules, regulations, or laws that might be needed for two of these situations:
   - Pets in the first town on the moon.
   - An amusement park next to a school.
   - A toxic waste dump next to a farm.
   - A town where everyone owns boats and no one has a car.

- A five-story building with no elevators and only one inside and one outside staircase.
- A bicycle path near a truck highway.
- A busy highway near an elementary school.

5 The American flag is one of the symbols that is used to represent our nation. Learn about your flag. Read about ceremonies in Chapter 1 of the *Junior Girl Scout Handbook* and participate in a flag ceremony in your Girl Scout troop or group.

6 Visit a branch of the city, town, or county government that makes policy or laws for your community, or visit a branch of the government that enforces the laws of your community.

7 Interview someone who works for your local government. What kind of job is it? Is it an elected, appointed, or Civil Service position? What services does the job provide?

8 Design and carry out a small project to show you are a good citizen of your community. You may do your project on your own or with the help of others. Spend at least two hours carrying out the project.

Date badge completed

My signature

Leader's signature

LOCAL LORE

1 Prepare a "time capsule" using a box or other container in which you put objects or pictures of objects that represent your life and the life in your community at the present time. Store your time capsule in a special place. Who will open your time capsule? When?

*2 Contact your local newspaper or library and ask to see photostats or microfilm of newspapers from the past. What was happening in your community ten, 20, 30, 50, 100 years ago? How has your community changed? Share your information with your troop/group, family, or friends.

3 Which ethnic groups have lived in your community or area? Discover a game, a song, a dance, a kind of folk art, or a special dish that is part of the heritage of two of these groups. Share your discoveries with others in your community.

4 Select a section of your community in which you can easily get around. Explore this area for signs of history. You might want to do this with others or with an adult. Look for older buildings, trees, memorials, building foundations, and names of streets that tell you something about the past in this area.

Write down all the signs of history you can find or take photographs of the different signs of history you see. Make a display or create a quiz game to share with your family, friends, troop, or group.

5 Read about the "Leadership Hall of Fame" in Chapter 6 of the *Junior Girl Scout Handbook*. Find out who the leaders of your community have been in the past and who the leaders of your community are today. What leadership qualities do they share?

*6 Visit your community's Chamber of Commerce, historical society, historical museum, a local library, or other agency and request a copy of an old map of your community. Compare this map with your community today. What has changed? What has remained the same? What do you think will happen to your community in the future? Draw a map or make a diorama of how you think your community will look in the future.

7 Communities can change quickly. Preserve a building that you find particularly attractive or appealing by photographing or drawing it. Make a display for others.

8 Visit an old graveyard. What unusual names can you find on old tombstones? Do any people with these names still live in the community? Make a list of epitaphs that you can display.

or

Help weed and clean up a neglected graveyard or other historical site.

9 Find out if your community has any projects or events that will help preserve the community's history. Ask if you can help out.

- -

_____
Date badge completed

_____
My signature

_____
Leader's signature

MY COMMUNITY

COMPLETE SIX ACTIVITIES, INCLUDING ONE OF THE TWO STARRED.

*1 Plan a walking tour or bicycle tour of your neighborhood. What are the most interesting, beautiful, or unusual things that people should see? Make a cassette tape of the tour that gives the directions to follow and the descriptions of neighborhood features.

or

Design a pamphlet that includes a map of your tour, directions, and descriptions. Share your cassette tape or pamphlet with friends, relatives, or newcomers to your area.

*2 Read in Chapter 1 of the *Junior Girl Scout Handbook* about the different types of troop or group government that Junior Girl Scouts can choose. What type of government does your community, town, or city have? Who makes the decisions for your community? Find out what were the most recent decisions or laws made by your community government. Share your information with your neighbors.

3 a Design one or more of these communities:

• A city in a dry area with very little water.
• A city underneath the ocean.

- A town on a river that often floods the area.
- A farming community on the Planet Mars.
- A city with many people but not very much usable or fertile land.

b After designing your new community, pretend you live there. Draw a picture, write a short story, create a short play, or write a song about a typical day in your life. Share your creation with your family, friends, or troop/group.

4 Help solve a community problem. Look at your community. What would you change or improve to make life better for young people? Write a letter about your ideas to government officials in your community or neighborhood, or write to a local newspaper. Or, survey (ask questions and record the answers) at least 20 people to see if they agree with your ideas. Send the results to your community government or discuss with your troop or group.

5 What are the best things about living in your community? Write an advertisement, draw a poster, or make up a song that could be used in a commercial that promotes your community.

6 Look in your telephone book at the page or pages that have the telephone numbers for your local government and community services or agencies. Call or write to someone at the community services listed and find out what they do to help the community.

or

With your troop or group, see if you may visit one of the community service agencies. What can you find out about the work it does in the community?

7 What are some of the businesses in your neighborhood or community? What do they manufacture or what services do they provide? Choose one that interests you and find out more about it. Arrange to visit the business or to speak to some of the employees and managers.

8 What do people in your community like to do in their free time? What recreational opportunities does your community offer? Are there cultural activities available? Are there sports facilities? How could you let others know about all that is available in your community?

or

Work with others to improve, restore, or beautify a recreational or cultural center for children or adults in your community.

9 Are there people in your community who are hungry? Homeless? In need of clothes or other necessities? Who is helping? Find out what you can do to help your neighbors.

Date badge completed

My signature

Leader's signature

MY HERITAGE

1 Find out more about your heritage. Do you know your family history or the history of people who share your racial/cultural/ethnic heritage? Display what you find out, perhaps through a chart, a timeline, a family tree, journal entries, a story, or a collection of photographs or mementos.

2 Look around your room or your home and choose one object that you believe you would want to keep with you as you grow up. Why did you choose this object? Why is it important to you? Next, ask older friends or relatives to show you and tell you about an object that they have had for a long time. Why have they kept it? Why is it important to them?

3 See if you can discover the meaning of your first name, your middle name, or your family name. Find out about others with the same name.

4 Find out about famous people from the past who shared your heritage. What did they accomplish? Why are they still famous today? Think about something you would like to do that could make you famous. Think of a way you could accomplish this dream and write out a simple plan or timeline with your dream as the goal.

Can you guess the meanings of these names?

Draw a line connecting each name with its meaning.

1 Aisha	A Flower
2 Layla	B Born at night
3 Yuki	C Fair lady
4 Flora	D Thanksgiving
5 Susan	E Light
6 Sarah	F Lily
7 Helen	G Snow
8 Jennifer	H Life
9 Carmen	I Song
10 Kelake	J Princess

Answers: 1-H 2-B 3-G 4-A 5-F 6-J 7-E 8-C 9-I 10-D

5 Make a toy, learn a game, a song, or dance, or cook a special dish that one of your ancestors might have enjoyed. Share what you discovered with others.

6 Begin a "wisdom list" of quotations, sayings, and advice your parents, grandparents, and other older people have shared with you and prepare a booklet that includes your favorite ones.

7 Ask older people to tell you about their lives, interesting events, or special stories they could share. Can you discover something about your heritage?

8 Start a diary or scrapbook of your own memories. Write about some important events from your past childhood and include important recent happenings. Try to continue your diary at least once a week.

9 Find a way to celebrate your heritage. What have you inherited that makes you the person you are? How can you show that you are proud of your heritage? Share your ideas with others.

Date badge completed

My signature

Leader's signature

NOW AND THEN:
STORIES FROM AROUND THE WORLD

1 Rich oral traditions are often part of many cultures worldwide. Storytelling was a way to pass on information before a written language was invented. Stories developed that explained many natural phenomena, such as the sound of thunder in a storm, or the phases of the moon, or the passing of seasons. Find a legend that explains a natural phenomenon, such as a type of weather, a constellation, or a geographical feature. Learn this legend and share it with a group.

2 Many cultures have legends that include a "trickster" character, such as the Coyote in some southwestern American Indian cultures, Ananse the Spider in some West African cultures, or the Fox in some Southern European cultures. Read some "Trickster" legends and perform one for your troop or group or make up a contemporary legend with a "trickster" character and share it with others.

3 Many fairy tales share common elements:
  • There is a quest or a journey.
  • Things appear in sets of three.
  • Characters get magical "tools" such as magic swords or shoes or carpets.
  • The main character must overcome some sort of obstacle or become a better person before reaching her goal.

Try creating a modern fairy tale that includes these traditional elements. How could you share your creation with others?

4 Many stories from around the world end with a "moral"—a lesson about right and wrong behavior. Storytelling is a way that cultures can share what is considered acceptable and good behavior by members of that culture. Read a story from the past with a moral. In your troop or group, share your stories with "morals" and discuss the lessons that are being taught.

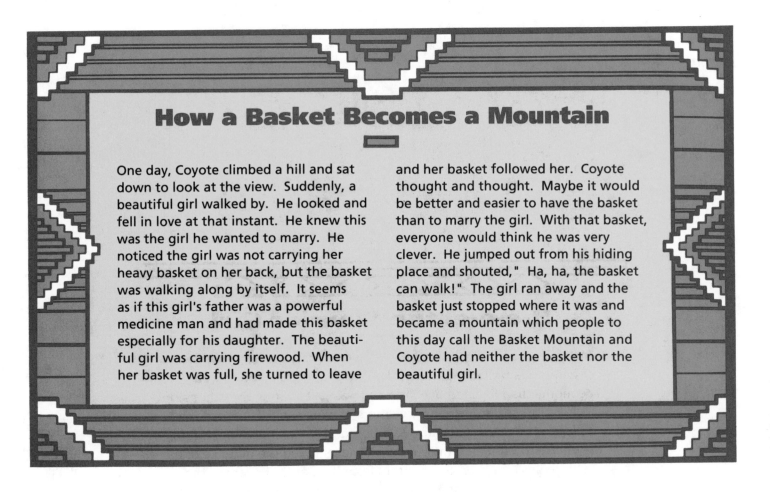

How a Basket Becomes a Mountain

One day, Coyote climbed a hill and sat down to look at the view. Suddenly, a beautiful girl walked by. He looked and fell in love at that instant. He knew this was the girl he wanted to marry. He noticed the girl was not carrying her heavy basket on her back, but the basket was walking along by itself. It seems as if this girl's father was a powerful medicine man and had made this basket especially for his daughter. The beautiful girl was carrying firewood. When her basket was full, she turned to leave and her basket followed her. Coyote thought and thought. Maybe it would be better and easier to have the basket than to marry the girl. With that basket, everyone would think he was very clever. He jumped out from his hiding place and shouted," Ha, ha, the basket can walk!" The girl ran away and the basket just stopped where it was and became a mountain which people to this day call the Basket Mountain and Coyote had neither the basket nor the beautiful girl.

5 Some of the modern "myths" and stories that are told at sleep-over parties and at camp show how storytelling continues to be a popular way to pass on cultural "rules" of behavior. Share some modern myths or stories. What are the morals of the stories?

6 Some older fables and fairy tales have stereotypes. (Read more about stereotypes in Chapter 5 of your *Junior Girl Scout Handbook*.) Some common stereotypes are that women are weak and must be rescued by men or the evil characters have a physical disability like a curved back or a limp. Find a fairy tale or fable which you can modernize by taking out the stereotypes and making it a more contemporary, realistic story.

7 Professional storytelling can be a career or a hobby. Professional storytellers can perform in schools, at libraries, at community events and fairs, at storytelling competitions, and on television. Check with your school system, university or college Literature or Folklore department or library, your local community library, or historical association to find out if a professional storyteller will be performing in your community. If you cannot attend a performance, watch a video of a storytelling performance. Look for ways the storyteller makes the story exciting through her voice and her gestures.

8 Many cultures share a tradition of stories whose morals concern protecting the environment. Find and read some of these stories and do one of the following activities:

• Perform one of the stories for Daisy or Brownie Girl Scouts.
• Create a modern fable on the same theme and perform it for Daisy or Brownie Girl Scouts.

H-e-e-e, the Warrior Girl

Many years ago, a Hopi mother was carefully styling her daughter's hair in the butterfly patterns that the young girl loved to wear. The mother had finished one side and was just starting the other side when they saw some enemy warriors moving sneakily toward the village. The young girl grabbed a bow and some arrows and ran to the village to warn the other people. Then she led the defense of the village until the men could return from the fields. Together, they beat the enemy. In honor of her efforts, a kachina doll was made to look like her with the hair on one side of her head completely styled and the hair on the other side of her head hanging loose.

_____

Date badge completed

_____

My signature

_____

Leader's signature

ON MY
WAY

COMPLETE FOUR ACTIVITIES.

1 Choose a spot away from your hometown that you would like to visit for a weekend.

Decide how you will get there, the people and places you will want to visit, what you will wear, and what you will take with you.

Then, if possible, go to the place you have chosen or write to its Chamber of Commerce for tourist information.

2 Choose three countries in different parts of the world you would like to visit.

• Find out if you will need a passport or a visa to visit these countries.

• Find out how you would travel to these countries: plane, train, boat, car, etc.

• Find out about two or three famous attractions that you would like to see.

3 Pretend you are visiting a place you have never been before, either inside or outside the United States.

Write an imaginary letter from this place describing the people you might meet there and what you could do and see while you were there.

or

Design two or more postcards from this place to send to a friend. Add messages to tell your friend about the postcard pictures.

4 Imagine your troop or group is traveling to a place where none of you can speak the language. Also, no one there can speak your language.

Make up a skit. Some girls are from your troop. Some girls are from the other country. In your skit show ways the two groups would communicate in order to find a place to stay, to order a meal, to get directions to see famous tourist sights, to take a train or a bus, etc.

5 Choose a food specialty from a region of the United States or from a country you would like to visit:

* Find a recipe for this food specialty in a cookbook or magazine.
* Prepare this food specialty and have a tasting party.

6 Imagine spending a week's vacation in at least three of the settings below. You may take only ten articles of clothing for each trip. Which items of clothing will you take? You may compare your lists with the lists of other girls in your troop or group.

* Your grandmother's house in the summer.
* A cabin in snowy mountains in winter.
* An alligator farm in a swamp in the spring.
* A wooded campground on a lake in the summer.
* A city hotel in the fall.
* A raft or a barge trip on a river in the summer.
* A cattle ranch in the early spring.
* A cruise to a sunny island in the winter.

7 Read about the "TAP" steps in Chapter 1 of the *Junior Girl Scout Handbook* and do one of the activities from those pages.

8 Find out about the Chamber of Commerce, traveler's services, or visitor's services in your community. Be a guide for someone who is visiting your community, or create or organize a packet describing your community for a visitor.

9 Visit a travel agent or ask one to come to a troop/group meeting. Find out:

* How a travel agent helps plan trips.
* What an itinerary looks like.
* How a computer is used to make reservations and to plan trips.
* Ways to meet the residents of the areas you'd be visiting.
* What types of transportation are used in traveling.
* What training is needed for a job in a travel agency.
* How trips are "packaged" to be more affordable.

Date badge completed

My signature

Leader's signature

TRAVELER

COMPLETE SIX ACTIVITIES.

1 Pretend you are a travel agent or a tour director. The groups listed below have asked you for advice planning their trips. For each group, plan a trip that will meet the groups' needs. Include the transportation used, the place or places they will stay and visit, what activities they can do once they reach their destination, and how much you estimate the trip would cost.

- A sixth-grade class with four accompanying adults who want to visit two historic sites.
- A couple who enjoy the out-of-doors and do not want to damage the environment or waste fuel.
- A Junior Girl Scout troop that includes some girls in wheelchairs who want to have a fun weekend nearby.
- A group of college-age students who would like to visit a city and a national or state park in one week-long trip.
- A family with three children, one of whom is deaf, who enjoy cultural activities.
- Two retired women with limited funds who love to travel.

2 Draw up an itinerary for a week's visit to a country you would like to visit someday. Find out the important sights to see. Share with a friend what you have found out about the culture of this country—such things as houses, any special kind of clothing, a special cuisine, folk arts or crafts, typical music or dance, folktales or literature. What languages are spoken? What holidays are celebrated? Are there any historical events that had an impact on world history? What can you find out about the natural environment and the geography of this country? Did finding out about the country make you want to visit it more?

or

Create something that will help a friend understand the country you would like to visit someday using two or more senses—sight, touch, hearing, taste, or smell.

3 Design travel brochures or posters for three different places of interest to you. Your brochures or posters should make others want to visit these three places.

or

Design three different travel brochures or posters for the same place that would be of interest to three different types of tourists or travelers. Make sure to describe the audience for each brochure or poster.

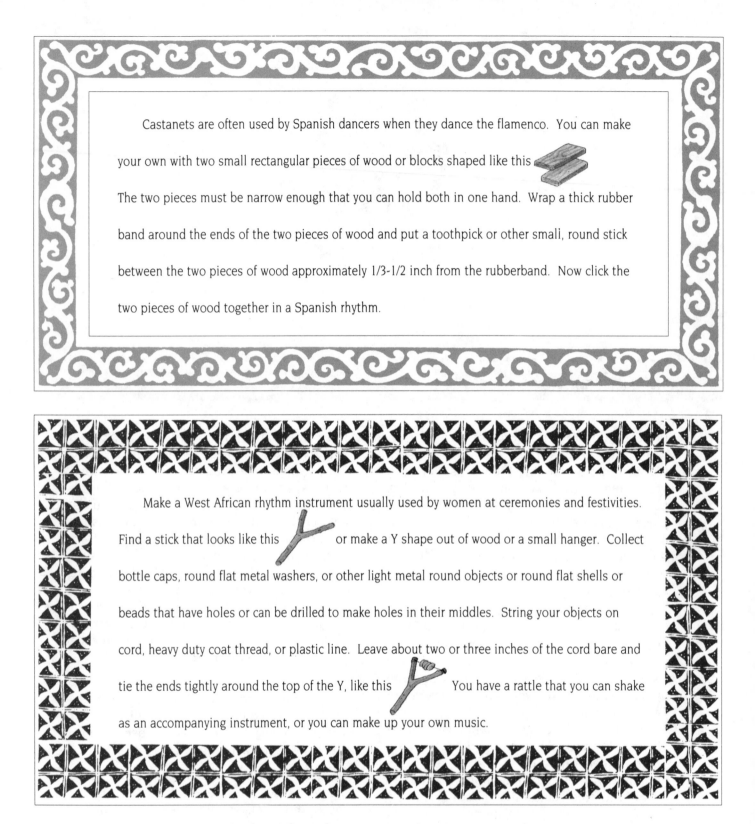

Castanets are often used by Spanish dancers when they dance the flamenco. You can make your own with two small rectangular pieces of wood or blocks shaped like this. The two pieces must be narrow enough that you can hold both in one hand. Wrap a thick rubber band around the ends of the two pieces of wood and put a toothpick or other small, round stick between the two pieces of wood approximately 1/3-1/2 inch from the rubberband. Now click the two pieces of wood together in a Spanish rhythm.

Make a West African rhythm instrument usually used by women at ceremonies and festivities. Find a stick that looks like this or make a Y shape out of wood or a small hanger. Collect bottle caps, round flat metal washers, or other light metal round objects or round flat shells or beads that have holes or can be drilled to make holes in their middles. String your objects on cord, heavy duty coat thread, or plastic line. Leave about two or three inches of the cord bare and tie the ends tightly around the top of the Y, like this. You have a rattle that you can shake as an accompanying instrument, or you can make up your own music.

4 Make or learn at least one of the following from a country or culture of your choosing:

- A poem or story in the style of that country.
- An article of traditional clothing.
- A folktale puppet or toy.
- An example of a traditional craft or folk art.
- A musical instrument from that country.
- A typical song from that country or a typical dance.

Share what you've accomplished with a group of younger children, telling them about the country or culture and showing them how to make or do something similar.

5 A representative from a friendly distant planet is visiting the Earth for the first time. You have been chosen to be her host and you will choose what she will see during her two-week visit. How will you plan her stay? What will she see? What are your reasons for the sights and activities on your itinerary?

6 Participate in a trip that lasts three days or more. Help in the planning. Read about planning trips in Chapter 1 of your *Junior Girl Scout Handbook*. Ask your leader about the guidelines in *Safety-Wise* for planning trips. On your trip, keep a diary or log, collect postcards, take photographs, make a video or slide show, or make drawings of your travels and share them with others when you return.

7 Interview an older Girl Scout who has participated in a national or international wider opportunity. Find out how she applied and prepared for it, and what her experiences were.

8 Find out about four of the following careers: travel agent, conference planner, tour guide, hotel manager, pilot, airline flight attendant, train conductor, cruise director, or cruise ship captain. What education or training do you need? What are the average salaries? What other requirements or skills are needed? If possible, interview someone who has worked or is working in these careers. Share your information with others who could be interested in these career areas.

9 Find out about safety and travel. Ask your leader or council staff person about the guidelines for trips and travel in *Safety-Wise*. What are some safety rules to follow in these situations:

• Visiting a major city for the first time.
• Taking an airplane trip.
• Backpacking in a national wilderness area.
• Taking a group of younger girls on an excursion.
• Taking a cruise or sailing a small yacht.
• Planning a two-day trip by car.
• Taking a train across country.
• Planning a bus trip.
• Visiting an amusement park.

• •

_____
Date badge completed

_____
My signature

_____
Leader's signature

WOMEN
TODAY

....

COMPLETE FIVE ACTIVITIES.

Growing up female is a unique and sometimes challenging experience. If you enjoy the activities in this badge, you may also want to explore some of the booklets in the Contemporary Issues series: *Girls Are Great: Growing Up Female*; *Decisions for Your Life: Preventing Teenage Pregnancy*; and *Into the World of Today and Tomorrow: Leading Girls to Mathematics, Science, and Technology*.

1 Become an investigative reporter. Find out about the women who live and work in your community. Try to find the women who have made unusual choices or who feel they have made a success out of their lives. See if you can locate and talk to a community activist or find a woman who is famous for her artistic or creative talent. Are there women in nontraditional jobs? Make a list of the diverse careers and interests of the women in your community.

2 Become aware of the different types of self-help and support groups that are available for and organized by women. See if the women in your community have organized groups that help women with their problems or with the stresses they might face. Visit or get information from these groups and find out what services they provide. How does Girl Scouting support women and girls in the community? How does Girl Scouting make women and girls feel positive about being female?

3 Find out whether a group of women meets regularly in your community to work in the creative arts: dance, drama, literature and poetry, quilting, pottery or ceramics, weaving, sculpture, painting, etc. Ask if you may attend one of the meetings or if you may interview one of the members of the group.

4 Interview women in the community who are raising children. Talk with women of various backgrounds, ages, and experiences. If possible, interview women who care for children as a career: day care or nursery school professionals. Find out how they manage their time. Some of the questions you might ask are: Were they trained in child development or parenting skills? What do they like best? What do they find most difficult? What kind of support do they receive or would like to receive? Share their answers with others.

5 Did you ever wonder how Girl Scouting or the local day care center or your neighborhood association began in your community? Are there groups concerned with environmental and social issues? Who are the people organizing and motivating others in your community? Find out who the women are who get things done. Attend a meeting of one of these community groups or speak with the organizers.

6 Sometimes being an older woman in a society that emphasizes young people is not easy. Interview a woman over the age of 65. Ask her to describe the advantages and disadvantages of growing older.

7 Make a list of women leaders—local, national, or international. What characteristics do they share? How do women develop stronger leadership skills? Think of some ways in which women could develop stronger leadership skills.

8 Your city, town, county, or state often provides resources for women who have been hurt domestically, physically, economically, or emotionally. These services may include a safe house for women and children who need a temporary place to stay or agencies that help female victims of crimes. Find out what types of services in your community are provided for women. Prepare a list of their phone numbers. Make that list available for distribution.

or

Find out if your community has a list of women's services. How are people made aware of it?

_____
Date badge completed

_____
My signature

_____
Leader's signature

WOMEN'S STORIES

● ●

DO FOUR ACTIVITIES, INCLUDING THE ONE STARRED.

*1 Read "Girls Can Do It" in Chapter 6 of the *Junior Girl Scout Handbook* and choose one of the following activities:

- Select a magazine article, biography, autobiography or collection of short essays and read about a possible female role model. Make a list of the characèristics that made her successful. Which of these characteristics do you share with your role model and which could be important for your life and your goals?
- Interview a woman whom you feel is a good role model for you. Record the results with your troop/group, family, or friends.
- Collect pictures from magazines or newspapers or draw pictures of contemporary female role models and make a display. Set up your display at a troop/group meeting or at another location where it can be viewed by people in your school or community.

2 Make a chart of all the women in your family as far back as you are able to discover. Next to each name, record some information about each woman: her job, her accomplishments, her talents, or any other information

you can find out. What does this chart demonstrate about your family? Are you similar to any of these women? In what ways? Show your chart to your family and your troop/ group.

or

Imagine one of your female ancestors. What kind of person was she? What were her accomplishments and skills? How are you similar to her? Create a way to describe this woman to others.

3 Interview a grandmother, an older female relative or friend, or a female senior citizen and ask her to describe to you the changes in her life, in her community, and in the world that have occurred since she was the same age as you are now. Ask her how women's lives have changed. Which times did she feel were the best? Why?

4 Create a display, poster, map, drawing, story, or skit about one of the following:

- The first female President of the United States.
- The life of a woman 100 years from now.
- A country in which women own the businesses and control the government.

Have you heard of Babe Didrikson Zaharias?

Many sportswriters consider her to be the greatest athlete who ever lived—and definitely the world's greatest female athlete. She lived from 1914–1956 and at the age of 15 broke national records in the javelin and basketball throw. She was the top athlete in many sports.

Can you unscramble their names?

xignob _____

mimgniws _____

thoingos _____

ginnfec _____

sniten _____

draillibs _____

flog _____

talkblabes _____

Answers: boxing, swimming, shooting, fencing, tennis, billiards, golf, basketball.

5 Create a quiz, puzzle, word search, card game, or other kind of activity on women in history and share it with your friends, family, troop, or group.

6 Present a skit, puppet show, musical play, dance, or shadow box/diorama on one of the following situations:
   • Laura Ingalls Wilder moving to a new part of the American West.
   • Sojourner Truth meeting Abraham Lincoln.
   • Dr. Dian Fossey first making contact with gorillas.
   • Amelia Earhart flying solo across the Atlantic.
   • Wilma Rudolph winning her three Olympic gold medals.

   See page 241 for more ideas.

7 Watch the news on television, listen to the news on the radio, or read newspapers or newsmagazines every day for one week. Keep a record of the number of times women were mentioned, the reason they were mentioned, and their names and nationalities. What did you discover by keeping this record?

8 Write a letter or plan a visit to an organization in your community or state that is involved in issues concerning women. Share what you have learned with your friends, family, troop, or group.

_____
Date badge completed

_____
My signature

_____
Leader's signature

THE WORLD IN
MY COMMUNITY

. . . .

COMPLETE FOUR ACTIVITIES.

1 Design or use a prepared map of your neighborhood, county, parish, town, or community. On your map, highlight the contributions of people from different ethnic groups, either from the past or the present. These could be restaurants, shops, street names, statues, or memorials, businesses, names of parks, trails, historic houses or buildings, agriculture and plants, specific neighborhoods, etc. See how many different ethnic groups you can find.

2 Open your community telephone book to any page. How many different family names are on the page? Open to another page. How many different family names are there? Find one name that you think is unusual or interesting. Imagine the family history of a person with that name and write a short story, poem, or diary entries. Or, create a song or draw pictures that show the exciting things that have happened in that person's life.

or

Find out the origin of the name. What can you discover about its history?

3 Read the section, "Other Kinds of Prejudice and Discrimination" in Chapter 5 of the *Junior Girl Scout Handbook*. Survey your community or school to find out how easy or hard it is for

people with disabilities to get around. If possible, interview a fellow Girl Scout or someone you know with a disability as a part of your survey.

4 Participate in a cultural event, parade, or a festivity of an ethnic group other than your own. Find out the meaning and background of the event.

5 Visit a restaurant that serves food that is different from the food your family cooks. Ask the waiter or restaurant manager about the different ingredients and styles of cooking. Ask whether it has been necessary to change the recipe because of different tastes or available ingredients. Ask about any special holiday recipes or dishes that are not on the restaurant menu.

6 Find out from your school principal or a school secretary if there are any students in your school who have recently arrived from another country or section of the United States. Ask the students before or after school or during lunch to tell you the similarities and differences between their new community and their old community. Share with them some of your favorite things about your community.

7 Help organize a backyard or neighborhood fair, a fun olympics, a sports day, or other event. Create a special activity or game that shows others all the different types of people who live in your community.

8 Try to learn more about the history, customs, and heritage of an ethnic group different from your own that is represented in your community. Demonstrate what you have learned through a skit, puppet show, series of drawings, a short story, a shadow box display, clay figures, or a speech.

_____
Date badge completed

_____
My signature

_____
Leader's signature

WORLD NEIGHBORS

1 Remember a time when you felt hungry. How did it feel? About one billion people in the world are always hungry. One billion hungry people means one out of every five people in the world never get enough food to eat. Many of these people are children. Try to imagine what it is like to just have one cup of boiled rice and water—or even less—as the only food you would eat all day. Read about some countries where many of the people are hungry in newspapers, newsmagazines, or books from your library. Talk with your troop/group or group of friends about world hunger. Think of some ways you can help the hungry, either at home or abroad, and follow through on one idea.

2 Choose three languages and learn how to count to ten in each of them or how to say hello, good-bye, thank-you, and you're welcome. Share what you've learned with a friend.

3 What games do children play in other countries? Learn three new games from three different countries. Teach these new games to your troop, group, or younger girls.

4 What are your favorite items of clothing? What kind of clothing or style of dress do you think is typical of girls in your community? In the United States? Find out the typical or the traditional type of clothing of women in several different countries. Think of a way to display these different styles.

5 What kind of home is typical of your community? What kinds of materials are used to build homes and buildings in your area? Why do you think those materials are used? Find out about the different kinds of homes people have in other countries. How could you show others what you've discovered?

or

There are many people in the world who do not have a home. A lot of these people are children. Some of these people live in the United States. With your Girl Scout troop/group or a group of friends, think of some ways you could help people who do not have a place to live.

GLOBAL VILLAGE

Some people have called the Planet Earth a "Global Village." People who are in countries that are far apart learn about each other's values, customs, and news events through television and radio. The United States exports food, machinery, manufactured products, and technologies to many countries. It also imports many products and resources. No country can make all the products its people want or grow all the food and materials its people need. Look around your house, school, or supermarket. Read labels to see where products come from. Here is a list of some common items and their origins.

Bananas	Ecuador
Coffee	Brazil, Colombia, Uganda
Sugar	Dominican Republic
Tea	Sri Lanka, Indonesia
Chromium	Turkey
Newsprint	Canada
Natural Gas	Russia
Petroleum	Middle East
Rubber	Liberia, Thailand
Tin	Bolivia
Wool	Australia
Vanilla	Madagascar
Television sets	Japan
Olives	Spain
Shoes	Italy, Taiwan, Brazil
Clothing	South Korea, Philippines, Hong Kong, Taiwan
Cocoa	Ivory Coast

Can you find these countries on a map?

6 Read about Emily Mabaya and Sidshean O'Brien in Chapter 6 of the *Junior Girl Scout Handbook*. Look in newspapers, news magazines, on television, or contact organizations and groups to find out more about projects in other countries that help the environment, promote peace, or work to raise the status of women or children.

7 Find out about organizations that help children around the world. Share with others what you've learned about the needs of children in other countries and how these organizations help.

8 Pick a country that interests you and discover all you can about how children live in that country. What kind of school do they have? How often do they go to school and what subjects do they study? What sports and games do they play? What kinds of foods do they eat? What holidays do they celebrate? Try to imagine what it's like to live in that country. Share your information with others.

Date badge completed

My signature

Leader's signature

Science and Technology

THE 🌎 -f

ASKS QUESTIONS

Which side of the roof will the rooster's egg roll down?

FIGURES SOLUTIONS

Lying there in the yard so neat
was something very good to eat.
It had neither flesh nor bone.
But in 21 days it walked alone.

What is it?

$$\begin{array}{r} 2625 \\ -1388 \\ \hline = ANSWER \\ -1235 \\ \hline = \quad ? \end{array}$$

+ (sun over mountains)

&

$22 \div 11 = ?$ + (lawnmower) + (person rowing boat)

EXPLORES DILEMMAS

Can you fit a penny on a drawing of this table without going over the lines?

Is the slanted line behind the bar continuous?

Which line is longer?

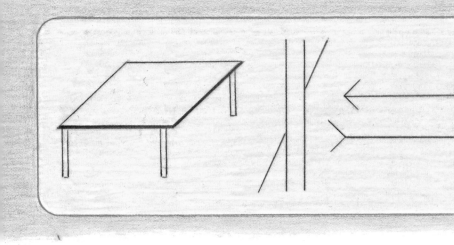

INVESTIGATES MYSTERIES

Stare at the fish at left to the count of 30. Then shift your gaze to the empty fishbowl and count to 20. Now try staring at the flag to a count of 30. Now try staring to the left of the flag. What do you see?

Answers: Rebus—The World of Today and Tomorrow. Asks questions—Neither. Roosters don't lay eggs. Hens do. Figures solutions—An egg. Explores dilemmas—You can fit it if you hold the penny on its side. Yes, it is the same line. Both lines with arrows are the same size. Investigates mysteries—You should see an "after-image" of the fish in the bowl. You should see a flag that has white and red stripes and a white and blue background.

DABBLER

COMPLETE FIVE ACTIVITIES.

A.1 Do at least two things that an astronomer, chemist, geologist, meteorologist, oceanographer, or physicist might do in her work:

- Look at some stars and planets through a telescope and identify five constellations.
- Read about pH in Chapter 7 of the *Junior Girl Scout Handbook* and do one of the activities.
- Collect and identify five rocks and minerals or visit a place of geological interest in your area.
- Make a barometer, wind vane, wind speed indicator, or rain gauge and use it at least three different times.
- Test household products to find out whether they are acids or bases. (Ask an adult to help.)
- Find out what makes things float. Compare how things float in salt water with how things float in fresh water.
- Make a battery.
- Turn a nail into an electromagnet.
- Think up your own project.

B.1 Take care of a plant or garden for two weeks and keep a record of what you did, the changes you observed, and some of the things you learned.

or

B.2 Keep a record of all the times that you use water in a single day. Review your record and determine the times you could have used less water or the times that water was wasted by not being recycled. Develop a personal water conservation plan that you can follow.

C.1 Visit a corporation, bank, real estate office, or other business and find out what kind of work is done there.

D.1 Design the ideal troop meeting place. Plan for a space that will hold 25 people or more. Determine what kinds of furniture and equipment you would want. Check phone directories and newspapers to develop a resource list of people who would be of help if you actually did construct your meeting place.

or

D.2 Make something that is powered by wind or water.

or

Be a paper engineer. Make at least two things out of paper. These could be a drinking straw, a building, a bridge, a statue, etc.

E.1 Find something that needs to be repaired and fix it yourself or help someone else fix it.

or

E.2 Volunteer to do a helpful job for your classmate or science teacher that involves scientific equipment or a science project. Find out why the task needs to be done and the best way to do it.

F.1 Make silver polish by adding a small amount of lemon juice to cream of tartar. Mix together with a plastic or wooden spoon until you have a paste. Then put a little of this paste on a cloth and clean tarnished silver by rubbing it gently. After the tarnish is gone, rinse the piece of silver in water and shine it with a soft towel or cloth. If you can't find any silver, test your polish on a piece of scrap metal.

or

F.2 Visit a science museum, planetarium, observatory, weather station, or laboratory. Ask questions about things you see and the activities that take place.

G.1 Find out about creatures that lived many years ago. Do one of the following:
- Learn about dinosaurs. Pick one that interests you and become an expert on it.
- Find out about ancestors of animals living today, such as the horse.
- Pick a point in time at least one million years ago and write a short story or create a picture or display about what a time traveler might see.
- Predict how you think a modern-day plant or animal might look in a million years.

or

G.2 Fingerprint yourself and the members of your family and notice any similarities or differences.

H.1 Watch the moon once a week for five weeks. Draw the moon's shape, and record the date and time with each of your five drawings.

H.2 Find five ways that science or math can help someone to do her job.

I.1 Asking questions and finding the answers are important parts of a scientist's work. Practice these skills by playing this game. One person thinks up an action or an event and the result or evidence of that action or event. She describes to the other players only the result or evidence. For example, she could say, "There is a small pile of dried twigs next to a tree." The action is, "A bird is building a nest in the branches overhead and during its work some pieces have fallen to the ground." The players try to discover the action or event by asking questions that can only be answered by a yes or a no.

or

I.2 Use a calculator to solve the following problems. After you do each one, turn the calculator upside down to read the word that the numbers "spell." At the end you will have a sentence that tells what one girl does in the summer.

	number	word
a $75 \times 75 - 87 =$	_____	_____
b $1000 \times 60 - 2265 =$	_____	_____
c $810 \times 710 + 2245 =$	_____	_____

Now make up your own math problems to spell at least three different words.

AEROSPACE

COMPLETE SIX ACTIVITIES.

1 Put together a simple model glider or make your own out of balsa wood. See if you can make your glider fly straight, stall, loop, bank right, bank left.

or

Make and test-fly three different designs for paper airplanes.

2 Invite someone who works in or with the aerospace industry to talk to your troop or group about her work experiences. Ask what she thinks about the future of aerospace.

or

Talk to some older people in your community about what it was like to fly before 1950. You might ask about: early aircraft, barnstorming, dirigibles, coast-to-coast travel, Amelia Earhart, a Powder Puff derby, and military flying during the two World Wars. Share what you find out with others.

3 Watch a space launch in person or on television. Keep a record of your observations including:

- Date and place of launch.
- Country and origin of space vehicle or satellite.
- Kind of space vehicle or satellite.
- Purpose of the mission and, if possible, whether it was successful.

- Something new that you have learned from the mission.
- Conditions that could affect the launch.

4 Visit an airport, an airplane cockpit, a control tower, a space center, an aerospace museum, or a planetarium, or see an air show. Make a list of at least four new things you learned as a result of your visit.

5 Make and fly your own kite. Experiment with it to find out which winds are best and how to make the kite fly better. You could also learn about kites from different countries and their uses.

6 Put on an air show and invite other groups to participate.

- Have races for different kinds of model aircraft, such as gliders and airplanes, with awards for different achievements, such as longest flight, best stunt, most accurate flight.
- Have a kite-flying contest.

or

Attend a motorized model airplane show. How much time and money does it take to build a plane? Learn how a plane is controlled.

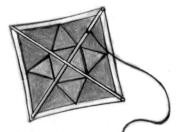

Take a sheet of typing paper or other thin paper and cut a square shape. Decorate the paper with magic markers. Use drinking straws as the supports of your kite like this

and attach your flying string or cord as shown. Find an open place away from poles and power lines and try flying your kite.

7 Make a list of at least ten different jobs that are involved in air transportation. Find out more about two of the jobs.

   or

   What is NASA? Write for materials that will help you learn about the U.S. space program: National Aeronautics and Space Administration Headquarters, Washington, D.C. 20546.

8 Find out about the women who have become astronauts. Do a brief biography on one of them to share with others or develop some informative display about women in the astronaut program.

9 Astronauts or space colonists must do daily tasks and routines very differently when they are in space. With some friends, think of the many things that you would have to consider when designing a space station (a spaceship that orbits around the earth like a satellite and on which a crew can live for long periods of time). How do people live, eat, sleep, bathe, and work? What do they do for entertainment? Make a drawing or a model of a space station that would meet the needs of its residents, or create a short play or skit of a typical day in space.

   or

   An important food supply for an astronaut is dehydrated food (food from which the water has been removed). Explore food markets, health food stores, or catalogues to find out about the different types of dehydrated food that are available. Plan a menu using dehydrated food for different meals. If possible, try out your menu.

• •

_____

Date badge completed

_____

My signature

_____

Leader's signature

BUSINESS-WISE

COMPLETE FIVE ACTIVITIES, INCLUDING THE ONE STARRED.

*1 Think about a business you could start now by yourself or with others, or one that you might be interested in starting in the future. Make a business plan that tells:

- What product you will make or what service you will provide.
- Who your customers will be.
- What the name of your business will be.
- How you will get the money or supplies to start the business.
- How you will make your product or provide your service.
- How much you will charge for your product or service.
- How you will find the right place to locate your business and get your product or service to the customers.
- How you will advertise your product or service.
- How you will keep accurate records of income and expenses.

2 If possible, take part in running the business according to your business plan for at least a month.

or

If you can start your business, carry out the advertising part of your business plan.

or

Create an imaginary advertising campaign.

3 Demonstrate the way you would present yourself and your product or service to your customers. You could do this by demonstrating the correct business manners when you meet customers, when you speak to them on the telephone, or when you write them a business letter.

4 Find out about opening a savings or checking account for a business, about the services offered by the bank for business customers, and about the amount of interest the bank pays for business accounts.

There are not too many things that a penny can buy, but you can use a penny to test the theory of probability. Flip a penny. Can you predict how many times "heads" will show and how many times "tails" will show? The theory of probability states that heads will probably show one out of every two times you flip the penny. Try flipping a penny repeatedly.

What happens?

5 Invite someone who owns their own business to talk to your group. Ask them some of the questions from Activity #1.

or

Visit a business and find out what goes on there.

or

Watch a film or television program on economics or business and share what you find out.

or

Find out about types of savings accounts. Decide what kind would work best for you.

or

Compare the advertising used by two companies that sell the same product. Decide which product you would probably buy and why.

6 Use the profits (if any) from your business to carry out a project that will benefit others.

or

Find out how some businesses use their profits to help others. Find out about things like foundations and grants.

7 Review magazines that are devoted to business. If possible, find some that are written for women and for people who own their own businesses. Develop a list of magazines to which you would subscribe if you had your own business.

8 Write and complete your own activity.

• •

_____
Date badge completed

_____
My signature

_____
Leader's signature

CAR CARE

COMPLETE SIX ACTIVITIES, INCLUDING THE ONE STARRED.

This badge must be done with an adult partner who has experience working with cars.

*1 Look at the owner's manual for the car with which you will be working. What does the owner's manual tell you about this car? What advice does it contain about keeping this car in good condition? Read about the different parts of a car (i.e., cooling system, steering and suspension system, exhaust system) and any special features it has (i.e., options: turbo engine, four-wheel drive, power brakes, air conditioning).

2 Develop a safety check for a car. Find out about things that need to be checked regularly. Include in your safety check the tires, battery, lights, turn signals, emergency flashers, back-up lights, windshield wipers, spare tires, the jack, flares, and seat belts. If you live in an area with hot and cold seasons, find out what you need to check when the weather changes.

3 Many states have automotive safety checks that are required in order for car owners to register their cars. What are the requirements in your state? Work with a car owner to find out if her car would pass the safety checks.

Drive the car from the starting line to the finish line.

4 How do you know if something is wrong or needs repair by looking at a car's instrument panel or steering column? Learn what the lights, buzzers, dials, or gauges tell the driver.

5 Arrange a visit to an auto mechanic's place of business so she can tell you about her work and show you some of the tools used on the job.

or

Ask an auto mechanic to give you and your friends a demonstration of maintenance work. What maintenance work could easily be done by a car owner?

6 Learn how to check the air pressure in a tire and how to fill a tire to the proper pressure or release air from a tire.

7 Learn how to check the windshield cleaning fluid level in a car. Learn what mixture should be added in different seasons or temperatures. Read the label on commercial washer fluid to learn how it should be used.

8 Make arrangements with a tire salesperson to talk with you about the construction of tires, the proper rotation of tires, periodic tire checks, and the causes of tire tread wear.

9 Your troop is going camping. On the way, the car you're in gets a flat tire. Create the following:

A short skit on what safety procedures the passengers should follow.

or

A short presentation, with the help of your adult partner, that demonstrates how to safely change the flat tire.

10 With an adult, show that you know how to do three or more of the following things to a car or truck:

• In a cold engine, check the fluid level in the radiator and add water or antifreeze, if needed.
• Check the oil level and add the right kind and amount of oil, if needed.
• Check the liquid level in the battery and add the right kind and amount of water or, if your battery is maintenance-free, find out how long it should last.
• Check the liquid in the brake fluid reservoir and add the right amount of fluid, if needed.
• Check the power steering fluid if the car has power steering.
• Check the automatic transmission fluid if the car has automatic transmission.

11 Wash or wax a car or truck after receiving permission from the owner. Clean the inside as well as the outside of the car. Check the owner's manual to see what type of cleaner to use. To conserve water, find out how to wash the car without letting a hose run continuously.

Date badge completed

My signature

Leader's signature

COMPUTER FUN

1 Find computers being used for at least ten different purposes. To do this, look through books, newspapers, or magazines, watch television, or go in person. Share what you have found with your troop members.

```
Computers help people perform calculations
much faster and more easily than was possible
with only pencil and paper.  One million is
an easy number to calculate with a computer.
Can you show one million without a computer?
Count how many words are on the opposite page.
If every page had the same number of words,
how many pages would you need to have a
million words?  If you had a piece of paper
the same size as this page, and if you filled
the page with as many X's as you could, how
many pages would you need to have one million
X's?  Think of three other ways you could show
one million of something.
```

2 Spend at least two hours learning something new from a computer, either by taking computer assisted instruction at a school or learning center or by using a computer educational toy.

3 Help put on a demonstration of computer toys and games for your troop.

4 Visit a business, bank, or other place that uses a computer to solve problems.

- See the computer in action and find out some of the things for which it is used.
- Find out what language the computer uses, how information is put into the computer, and how information comes out.
- Learn how to use an automatic banking machine.

5 Invite someone who works with computers to talk to your troop or group. Find out what she/he does with the computer, what training was necessary, and what other people are involved in keeping the computer working properly.

or

Interview four different people and find out how computers affect their lives.

6 Visit a computer store. Compare different kinds of personal computers. Ask someone to explain the basic options available to the average buyer. Decide which one you would buy.

7 Read a computer magazine. Make a list of the types of information that can be found in the magazine and how this would help you use computers.

8 Learn how to do some basic computer operations. Demonstrate your ability to do the following:

- Format a disc.
- Insert a software program.
- Create a file.
- Print stored information.
- Save something you have created.

9 Play an electronic computer game at least five different times. Keep a record of how you do. What skills are needed? How can you improve?

or

Be a computer games reviewer. Play at least three different video games and write a brief review of your opinions of each. Include in your review: comments on the objective of the game, the skills required, the eye appeal and quality of the graphics, the interest level, and the educational value.

10 Design your own computer fun activity.

Date badge completed

My signature

Leader's signature

DO-IT-YOURSELF

1 Visit a hardware store or someone's workshop and find out:

- The name and proper use of tools that could be used to: cut glass, spread putty, mend a crack in plaster, paint a room, square a corner, level a table, cut wood, or pull out a nail. Review the list of tools in the "Simple Home Repairs" section of Chapter 4 in the *Junior Girl Scout Handbook* before making your visit.
- The proper care and safe storage of tools.

2 Visit a lumberyard or home supply store or talk to a building contractor or mason to find out about some of the following:

- The best kinds of building materials to use in your area.
- The kinds of exterior care needed for homes and buildings in your area.
- Different types of paint and how they are used.
- Different materials that are used for the interiors and exteriors of homes.
- Materials that can be used to save energy.

Share what you have found out.

3 Learn about the drawings, blueprints, or plans that are used to guide work on building projects. Have a professional engineer or other adult explain how blueprints are used to make repairs or to build a new project.

Make your own building plan to redesign a room in your home.

1 FOOT = ¼ INCH

4 Create something out of wood that involves boring one or more holes, using nails or other types of material fasteners, and measuring and cutting the wood.

5 Watch a building or repair project going on in your town or neighborhood. Observe the work on several different days. Find out as much as you can about what is being built and keep a record of what you see.

6 Create a model of your dream house. Be able to explain to others what materials you would use to build the house and why you chose those materials.

or

With a model construction set, build at least one of the models suggested in the directions that come with the set and build two other models of your own design.

7 Discover ways in which you can make your home more energy-efficient. Local utility and power companies often have special exhibits, booklets, or consultants who can help you. With the help of your family, practice one of the energy-saving methods you have learned about.

8 Talk with a home economics teacher, someone at a local hardware or home center store, or another adult to learn how to remove common household stains. Choose from the following list, to discover how to remove stains from three different materials: aluminum, brass, bronze, copper, brick, stone, cement, synthetic carpeting, wool carpeting, formica, lacquer furniture, leather, linoleum, vinyl flooring, marble, porcelain, silver, ceramic tile, and wood.

9 Take on a project of reupholstering, recaning, or retaping the seat of a chair. Find out what materials and tools are needed for the project. Share your completed project and how you accomplished it with your troop/group.

10 Read the owner's manual and find out about the repair and maintenance for a piece of equipment or large appliance in your home.

11 Write to the Consumer Information Center, Pueblo, Colorado 81009, to find out what materials and resources are available to help you with this badge. Look for information that will compare different products, identify faulty equipment, and describe repair techniques.

_____
Date badge completed

_____
My signature

_____
Leader's signature

FOODS, FIBERS, AND FARMING

COMPLETE SIX ACTIVITIES.

1 Plant and care for a garden that contains at least three vegetables your family or friends can eat. Keep a record of how you prepared the soil; when you planted and harvested each crop, how often you watered, weeded, and added fertilizer; how you kept out pests; and how you could improve your garden in another year. Harvest each crop at the proper time and share your vegetables with others. (This activity counts as *two* activities.)

or

Plant a window box, container, or indoor garden with at least three different miniature vegetables or herbs. Keep a record of the type of container you used and the preparation of the container, the vegetables and herbs you planted, the date you planted them, the care you gave your garden, and the harvesting of your crops. Share your vegetables and herbs with others.

2 For at least two weeks take care of an animal, such as a chicken, rabbit, or lamb, that is usually raised for food or fiber. Keep a daily record of what you did.

or

If you cannot take care of an animal that is usually raised for food or fiber, choose one you would like to raise. Interview someone who raises this type of animal or find out more about it. Record how you would take care of this animal for two weeks.

Include the kind and amount of food, feeding schedules, where your animal would live, how it would get its exercise, and special health problems of this animal.

3 Talk to the county cooperative extension agent and/or some farmers, ranchers, or people in the fishing business in your county or a county nearby to learn about agriculture or fishing. Find out about food products that are raised in your area. Make a display that can show others about what you have learned.

or

Invite someone to talk to you about the farming methods used in a developing country.

4 Spend several days living and working on a farm or ranch, either on your own or with your family or troop. Learn about life there by helping with the work and by asking questions about what you see. Keep a daily journal of your experience.

or

If you live on a farm or ranch, invite some girls who do not live on one to visit you. Help them experience life on a farm or ranch.

What is a food chain?

Farmers grow corn and other plants that are fed to cows and other animals, which are then eaten by people. It takes 15–17 pounds of grain and plants to make one pound of meat suitable for people to eat. Figure out how many pounds of meat you eat each week. (If you are a vegetarian, try this for a friend who eats meat.) Now figure out how many pounds of grain it took to produce the meat you ate. Could eating less meat provide more food for people who are hungry? What do you think?

5 Try your hand at food processing. Make butter, cheese, yogurt, raisins, applesauce, or a processed food of your own choice.

or

Grow sprouts from mung bean, alfalfa, or other seeds. Make sure you choose seeds that have not been treated with chemicals. Use your crop in salads or sandwiches or as a side dish.

or

Make something from natural fibers. You could spin wool into yarn, weave cotton cloth, knit or crochet.

6 Go to a county fair or other exhibit on agriculture. Discover two or more things about foods, fibers, or farming that you didn't know before. Share what you find out.

or

Enter something you have grown, raised, or made from an animal or plant product in a county fair or other similar exhibit.

7 Visit a food or fiber processing plant. Learn all you can about the steps involved in getting the finished product from the field to you. You might visit a:

- Cannery.
- Flour mill.
- Cereal plant.
- Feed or meal company.
- Frozen food processing plant.
- Wool or cotton mill.
- Citrus processing plant.
- Meat, fish, or poultry packing company.

8 Find or describe three weeds or three insects that cause problems to gardeners or farmers in your area. Identify the pest, the damage it does, and the way to control or eliminate it. What pest and weed control methods can you discover that do not use chemicals? Share this information with others.

9 Visit a veterinarian or invite one to come to a troop/group meeting. Find out about the work she does. Find out, if possible, the care that farm animals need and the common diseases that they may develop.

_____
Date badge completed

_____
My signature

_____
Leader's signature

GEOLOGY

1 Find out about the different types of training or education geologists need to do their jobs. Learn about other careers that relate to studies of the earth. You might arrange to have a professional in this field come and visit your group or you might visit a geologist to discuss her field of work.

2 Search for clues in your community or in a place you visit which show one or more of the following:
   - Where a glacier had been.
   - Where a volcano had erupted.
   - Where erosion had happened.
   - Where water once covered the area.
   - Where the earth has shifted.
   - Where intense heat has been present.
   - Where strong winds, tides, or currents have affected the area.

   Discuss, describe, or show others what you have found.

3 Locate photographs of the earth taken from a high altitude. Photos that have been taken from a satellite would be best. Use these photos to find:
   - Major oceans and land areas.
   - Mountain ranges, fault lines, and volcanoes.
   - The area where you live.
   - Rivers, lakes, and other inland waterways.
   - Other features of interest.

4 Start a rock collection. Go on an exploration hike to see how many different kinds of rocks or minerals you can find. Bring back a few specimens to examine in greater detail. Learn about the different classifications and groupings of rocks. Organize and label your rocks. Use reference books, museums, or the advice of another rock collector.

5 Find out about one way in which fossils are made. Make a simulated fossil by pressing a leaf, rock, skeleton, bone, or dead insect into some soft plaster of Paris and allowing it to harden. This could also be done with some mud layered in a shallow box. Look carefully to see the details made in the impression when the item is removed.

   or

   Go on a fossil hunt in an area of your choice and see what you can find. Can you find impressions, molds, or casts? Study your specimens to see what you can discover about them. Find out what your state fossil is if your state has one. Share your experience with others.

6 In past or current history, find examples of volcanic eruptions, geysers, earthquakes, and tsunamis (the Japanese word for a fast-moving ocean wave that is caused by an earthquake or a volcanic eruption on the floor of the ocean). Find out what causes each of these to happen. Pick one of these and demonstrate to others what you've learned.

7 To discover firsthand the effects of weathering on the land, do two of the following:

- Go for a walk in your neighborhood and observe the chips, cracks, and rough areas in the sidewalk. Think about all the things that help to make these happen. What *natural* processes are occurring that might have caused the changes in the sidewalk? Tell how the same natural processes that helped to crack the sidewalk will also help to disintegrate rock.
- Discover what happens when water gets into cracks and spaces in rocks and then freezes. Fill a small enclosed plastic container with water and then freeze it. What happens to the container? What does this mean for areas where there is water that freezes?
- Visit a cemetery and look at the effect of water and wind on the different types of headstones. Do some types of stone last longer than others? Can you discover why?
- After a severe windstorm, rainstorm, or snowstorm, take a survey of how the land surface has changed. What do you think might have happened to the land if the storm had been more severe or there had been several storms in one year?

8 Find out what makes up soil. Collect two cups of soil from a site of your choice. Spread the soil out on a light-colored sheet of paper. Using a stick to help separate the contents and a magnifying glass to get a closer look at the particles, separate the various particles into groups. Make a list of the different particles you have found. Discuss with your group what you have found, what might grow in the soil, where the things in the soil might have come from, and how soils in other areas may be different.

9 Observe waves in motion. Find out where waves get their energy and motion. You might make a wave bottle or a model of a beach to help you discover what effect waves have on the shoreline. People have developed ways to interfere with the effects of the waves on the shoreline. Put a jetty (a wall that is built out into a body of water), a groin (a short wall built at a right angle to the shore to trap moving sand), or a breakwater (a structure protecting the near shore area from breaking waves) into your model to learn what effect this has on the power of the waves.

10 Find out how water carries things and when it leaves them behind. Do at least two of the following:

- Shake up a jar of water with some gravel, sand, silt, or clay. Watch which settles first and how layers of sediment form.
- Look for fossils of water life in nature or in things made of stone (for example, in buildings or tables).
- Look closely along a shoreline for debris, such as shells, pebbles, plants, bottles, and decaying matter. Figure out where they came from, how they got there, and what is likely to happen to them.
- Find out what causes cloudiness in water. You may need to use a filter, a plankton net, a magnifying glass, or even a microscope.
- Watch how water drains from various surfaces after a heavy rainfall. How does water change things?
- Find out how humans have had an effect on the surface of the earth. You could survey your own area or learn about what is happening elsewhere in the world. Decide whether the effect you investigated was beneficial to the earth and why.

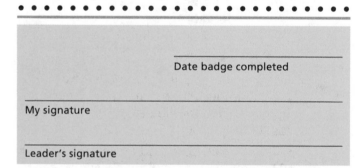

Date badge completed

My signature

Leader's signature

MATH WHIZ

1 Find as many different examples as you can of how math is used every day. These could be balancing a checkbook, using money, cooking, cutting a cake into equal pieces, or other ways. Compare your list with someone else's.

2 Look for geometric shapes around your home, school, playground, or other area. You can check floors, walls, doors, windows, leaves, flowers, or other items. Make a chart or list of your findings.

3 Make up a prediction, such as, "I think that one out of every five people walking down Main Street between two and three o'clock will be wearing jeans."
   • Make up a plan to check your prediction. Then carry it out.
   • Compare your prediction with the results.

4 Plan a party with your troop or group. Decide how much of each food item you will need. If you are going to divide something large into smaller pieces, determine how many times you will have to divide it to have the right number for everyone. Figure out how much you need to spend on the food and drinks.

5 Design new equipment for your school or neighborhood playground, using what you know or learn about geometry, symmetry, and measurement. Make models with clay, soft woods, or other materials.

or

Draw something to scale. It could be a map of your neighborhood, a sketch of your room, or a drawing of yourself. Decide what your scale will be and show it on your drawing.

6 Keep track of your activities for one week. Make a graph showing how much time you spend eating, sleeping, working in school, doing homework, watching television, and enjoying other activities. Share your graph with your troop or group.

7 Make up your own code for sending messages. Show how you could send and receive messages in at least one kind of code or cipher.

8 Have a contest to find out who can calculate most accurately the numbers of objects of a similar size that can fit into a large container.
   • Choose the container and the objects, such as popcorn, beans, or marbles.
   • Let the contestants measure the container and a small number of the objects and then calculate their answers.
   • Give an award to the winner(s).

Draw a square divided into 9 equal spaces (3 x 3). Put a penny on each square (9 pennies). Two players take turns removing one penny at each turn. A player must always leave at least one penny in each row or column. The last person to play wins. If a player takes a penny that makes a column or row empty, she loses. Play at least ten games. Try to discover a strategy for winning the game.

9 Find math or numbers in one of your favorite activities. Ask a teacher or another adult for help if you can't think of how math is involved.

10 Use metric measuring tools to take 12 measurements such as: your height, the length of your arm, the width of your hand, the length of your foot; your weight, the weight of a pet or friend; the dimensions of your room; the average speed of your car in town and on a highway; the temperature indoors and outdoors.

Date badge completed

My signature

Leader's signature

MONEY SENSE

. . . .

COMPLETE FIVE ACTIVITIES, INCLUDING THE ONE STARRED.

1

1 Read about developing a budget in Chapter 4 of the *Junior Girl Scout Handbook*.

or

Develop a troop budget. Include such expenses as equipment, supplies, troop trips, and other activities. Income might include troop dues, cookie sale proceeds, and money earned in special projects. There is a sample troop budget in the Helps and Resources section (see page 241).

2 Think of companies you like or whose products you are familiar with, such as fast-food restaurants, cosmetic companies, sporting goods companies, clothing or toy companies, entertainment companies. Find a copy of a company's annual report in your library or write to the customer relations department of one of these companies asking for an annual report. (Annual reports describe the financial status along with the current and future plans of a company.) Read the report or ask an adult to help explain it to you and find out how a company is doing and what its plans are.

or

Follow the stock of a company for a month as it is reported in the newspaper, or on a financial news program. Explain why you would or wouldn't buy stock in this company. Report your findings to your troop or group.

3 Contact a local bank, money management firm, or brokerage firm and find out:

  a How to open an account.
  b The types of jobs people have in the company.
  c The training necessary for one of those jobs.
  d What a typical workday is like for a person working on the account.

or

Invite someone who works for a bank, money management, or brokerage firm to talk about her job with your troop or group.

4 Visit a bank or other type of financial institution. Find out about the type of work that employees do.

or

Find out what happens at a stock exchange. If possible, visit one in a city near you. Create a role-playing exercise, play, skit, or presentation that would demonstrate for others how a stock exchange operates.

5 With a group of friends, form an "investment club."

   a Choose two different ways that you would like to invest and save money.

   b Invest equal amounts of money in each. You could use "pretend" amounts of money.

   c Follow your investments for three months, and then compare how each of them did.

*6 Find out about different ways to invest and save money. Learn about at least five of the following and determine which would be best for you.

- Mutual funds.
- Money market accounts.
- Tax-deferred annuities.
- Savings accounts.
- U.S. Savings Bonds.
- IRAs (individual retirement accounts).
- Government bonds.
- Interest-earning checking accounts.
- Stocks

7 Interview local businesspeople. Find out how they manage their finances and how they use their earnings. You might learn what stocks they would recommend and what factors influence their decisions to buy and sell stocks.

8 Interview five people (adults and/or children) to find out how their values affect the way they spend money. You might ask: If you were given an extra $20, how would you spend it? Would you spend it differently if you had earned it? Record and share your findings.

9 Find out about career opportunities in the business and financial world. Decide on one job you might like to have and find out more about it.

10 Talk about some good things in life that money can't buy, and make a scrapbook of pictures or drawings. Then have fun for free—take a nature walk, attend free community events, visit a city council meeting, go window shopping with sister troops, have a picnic.

_____
                          Date badge completed

_____
My signature

_____
Leader's signature

MS. FIX-IT

1 Find out what to do and whom to call, in each of the following emergencies. Learn in which ones you can do something to help and when it is best to leave the area until the emergency is over.

- Something goes wrong with the furnace.
- Something goes wrong with the hot water heater.
- Toilets get clogged.
- The thermostat won't shut off or fails to turn on the furnace.
- The smoke alarm or security system won't shut off after an emergency is over or turns on accidentally.
- Gas is leaking in the kitchen or other part of the house.
- A washing machine is overflowing.

2 Do at least three of the following:

- Have someone show you what to do if the lights go out while you are home alone.
- Show that you know three or more safety rules to follow when using electricity.
- Look at the electrical panel box where you live, if possible.
- Find out about fuses and circuit breakers and how to change or reset them.
- Find out how to turn off the electricity in case of flood, storm, or other emergency.
- Know how and whom to call in your community or in your building (landlord, superintendent) in case of an emergency.

3 Learn to replace a washer in a faucet. Find out what other fixtures in and around your home require washers. Keep some spare washers in your repair kit for future use.

4 Review the inner workings of the toilet tank. With the lid off, flush the toilet tank and watch how the apparatus works. Learn the names of the parts, some of the common problems, and how to do the repairs. Demonstrate how to repair a leak. Find out what changes you could make that would save water.

5 A good home repair person always has a flashlight in her repair kit. Learn how to take care of your flashlight and how to make some simple repairs.

6 Windows and screens can cause problems when they won't open or close properly. Demonstrate how to do two or more of the following:

- Open a window that is stuck.
- Replace a broken windowpane safely.
- Repair or renew caulking.
- Repair a hole or rip in a screen.
- Replace a worn-out window screen.

7 Demonstrate your ability to hang an item on a wall. Learn about the different types of walls and what types of fasteners are best used for each. Observe the different ways items such as mirrors and shelves are hung in your own home.

8 To help conserve energy during the cold months of the year, learn how to weatherstrip your windows and doors.
or
Learn about window and house designs that are energy-efficient.

9 Repair something with one or more of the following: nails, tacks, screws, bolts, staples, screw eyes, wire, electrician's tape, putty, caulking material, or glue.

10 Do two or more of the following. Ask an adult for assistance.

- Help paint or refinish a piece of furniture.
- Help fix a crack or hole in a wall, sidewalk, or driveway.
- Help with some painting, papering, or other repair work.
- Help rewire a lamp or replace the cord on an electrical appliance.

11 Pick one small appliance and learn about the simple repairs that can be done without a repair-person. Bring the appliance to a troop meeting and demonstrate one common problem and how to repair it.

Date badge completed

My signature

Leader's signature

PLANTS AND ANIMALS

1 Create a deck of "creature cards." Cut out pictures of at least 25 different creatures that walk, crawl, fly, hop, or slither. Separate the pictures into groups that possess similar characteristics, such as the way they move, the way they look, the way they bear their young, what they eat, and so on. Explain your reasons for the groupings. Try using your cards with younger girls to play a game.

2 Observe an animal, such as a dog or a cat, over a period of time. Note how and when it plays, eats, uses its senses, and hunts. Observe how it behaves when it meets up with another of its species. If possible, view a video or read a book about a creature in the wild that is in the same family as a tame or domestic animal. (If you observe a house cat, you could read about a lion.) Note behaviors that are the same and behaviors that are different.

3 Go on a fossil or dinosaur hunt. Visit a museum, fossil site, or library and learn about animals that lived long ago. Learn about what the world was like when they were alive and talk about why some of these types of creatures no longer live on the earth.

4 Learn about one plant and one animal "pest." Discover why humans consider these plants or animals to be pests. Find out if these pests are important to a food chain. Find out who in your community can help control these pests, learn how diseases from these pests are being treated, and find out what is being done about them in your community. Some species to choose from: deer ticks, rats, cockroaches, fleas, tansy ragweed, poison oak or poison ivy, kudzu.

5 Grow something in one of the following ways:
   • From plant parts, such as from jade plant leaves, or from a spider plant "baby," or from a pineapple head.
   • From a root part, such as a ginger root or sweet potato.
   • From a seed, such as an avocado or dried flower seed.

   Keep a record of observations that you can share with your troop or group. Learn what your plant needs in order to grow healthy and strong.

6 At a zoo or in your favorite animal books, go on a "world wildlife safari." Find the names of animals that:
- Have a thick fur coat for a cold climate.
- Have long fingers for grasping branches.
- Have bright colors for attracting a mate.
- Have a body part that can reach tree branches while the animal is still on the ground.
- Have long legs for wading.
- Have a dark color for living in shadows.
- Have a tongue that reaches in hard-to-get places.
- Can spit when they are upset.
- Have big ears that help to cool their blood in hot climates.
- Use water for cooling.
- Use the earth for cooling.
- Have patterns for camouflage.
- Have voices that communicate.
- Have body movements that communicate.
- Are an endangered species.
- Have behavior that marks territory.
- Have a nose that helps find food.
- Have a footless way of moving.

or

Make up a zoo "safari" for a group of younger girls. Afterwards, discuss what they liked best.

7 In your house or a local shopping center, go on a plant sleuth walk. List as many ways as you can that plants are used by people. Star those ways that might have involved science and technology in developing a product or process from plants. Try to identify those plant products that come from a different country. Share your list with your troop or group.

8 Visit a botanical garden, a plant nursery, or a greenhouse. Learn different ways that plants are grown, and some ways of changing a species of plant to bring out a desired characteristic or to strengthen the species.

9 Talk to someone who works with plants or animals, such as a researcher, wildlife biologist, geneticist, botanist, or marine biologist. Find out what led her into the field of work and what she likes most about the job. Find out what some of the concerns are about the field of work.

10 Teach an animal to behave in a new way or train a plant to grow in a new or different way. Ask an adult to help you. Find ways to do this without causing fear, pain, or harm to the animal.

Date badge completed

My signature

Leader's signature

PUZZLERS

COMPLETE SIX ACTIVITIES.

1 Here is a strategy game, Dara—A Game from Africa, from *Games for Girl Scouts*. It is a fast game with different moves each time you play. Can you develop some winning strategies?

• You need: A smooth patch of earth and a stick, a sidewalk and chalk, or a large piece of paper and pens or pencils and 12 counters such as beans or pebbles for each player.

• How to make: Construct a grid of 30 circles, five across and six down. You can scoop the circles out of the earth, draw chalk circles on a sidewalk, or draw circles on paper.

• How to play: Each player places 12 pieces in the circles on the playing grid. Initially, you can not have more than two pieces in adjacent circles. Players take turns moving pieces one space at a time. You can move in any direction, including diagonally. Jumping is not allowed. The goal is for each player to get three of her pieces in a vertical or horizontal row. Whenever this happens, she can remove one of her opponent's pieces. The game is over when one player can no longer line up three pieces or all of one player's pieces have been removed.

2 Read "Think Like a Computer" in Chapter 7 of your *Junior Girl Scout Handbook*. See what directions you could change and still have the game work out.

3 Perform three card tricks that use mathematical or logical thinking. Have the group try to guess how you performed the tricks.

4 Play the game of Nim several times with another person. Try to figure out how to win every time. To play:

a Put nine pennies in three rows, with four pennies in one row, three in the next, and two in the last row.

b The two players take turns removing pennies, using these rules: A player can take away pennies from only one row during a turn. The player can take as many pennies as she likes from the row, but must take at least one.

c The player who takes the last penny is the winner.

5 Play a game that involves logic and strategic thinking (a method of careful planning). The game could be chess or checkers, or another board game. Play the game at least five times. Each time you play, make notes about what helps to win the game. Are there moves to avoid, or a sequence of steps to take? Play the game again after you have reviewed your notes and see if your skill improves.

6 The quickest path from one point to another is not easily found in a maze. Mazes have been used as puzzles, they have aided animal studies, and garden hedges have been clipped into mazes as outdoor decoration. Find out about mazes and then design your own on paper. Try your maze on others and see how well they can solve it. You might try timing those who solve your maze and then test them after a week or so. Does their time improve?

7 What is an optical illusion? Start a collection of optical illusions. Try them out on others and make a record of people's reactions.

8 Try this activity on "afterimages" with others to explore one aspect of how your eye works. The spot you see after a flash picture has been taken is an example of an afterimage. Draw a one-inch square on a clean piece of white paper. Blacken the square with paint, ink, or crayon. Now for your afterimage test, place another blank piece of white paper alongside the one with the square. In bright light, stare at the black square for 30 seconds and then quickly shift your gaze to the blank paper. In a few seconds you will see an afterimage. Now try this with squares of different colors. Make a record of the square color and the afterimage color. Try this with other people and make a chart of each person's reaction.

9 Develop your own crossword puzzle. Make certain you have at least ten clues across and ten clues down. Use graph paper to help you lay out your puzzle.

Measure the small figures in the picture above. Did they appear to be the same size?

Stare at this picture. You can see a young woman or an old woman.

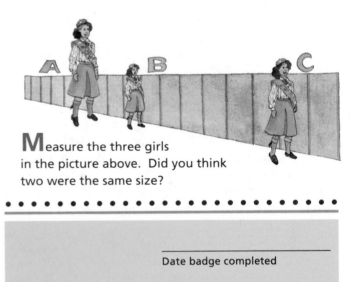

Measure the three girls in the picture above. Did you think two were the same size?

· ·

_____
Date badge completed

_____
My signature

_____
Leader's signature

· 118 ·

READY FOR TOMORROW

DO SEVEN ACTIVITIES, INCLUDING THE ONES STARRED.

*1 Go on a global product hunt in your household. Make a list of all the things in your house that come from outside the United States. This might include such items as clothing, footwear, electronics, food, cosmetics, art, and games. On a map of the world, find the countries that are part of your daily life. Share this information with the rest of your troop or group.

or

Make a collage from magazines or newspapers using pictures of products and resources that come from different parts of the world. These should be things that you or your family and friends use, or depend upon. Share your collage with your troop or group.

2 Use the sun's energy for cooking! Construct a solar oven (see pages 242–243 for instructions) and use it to cook a simple meal or purify water (for instructions, see *Outdoor Education in Girl Scouting*). Can you think of some reasons that you might use this solar cooker in your family and with your troop/group?

*3 Design an "Earth Matters" seal of approval that you could award to products and services in your community. Make up a checklist of important considerations that must be met before receiving this award, such as "not using wasteful packaging," "not polluting water," or being "energy-efficient." Find resources in your library or community that might give you additional information on products and the companies that make them. Share your findings with others in a product fair, or by using your power as a consumer to purchase products that do not harm the environment.

4 With help from your family or troop/group, for a minimum of one month, collect all of the appeals in mail, magazines, or newspapers that ask for financial help for social or environmental action projects. Pretend that you have a budget for "giving" by setting aside a dollar in pennies. Decide how you would divide your pennies among the different organizations that you choose to help. Discuss the reasons why you chose the organizations you did.

5 Adopt an endangered species that lives in a different part of the world and learn more about it. Find out why this species is endangered and what you might do as an individual to help preserve it. If possible, view a video or TV show, observe the species at the zoo or in an arboretum, or keep a scrapbook on it. Share your knowledge with others through an environmental fair, display, or forum. Find out how you can help through an organization that works to preserve this species.

or

Participate in a project that improves the habitat for wildlife in your community.

6 Trees are one of the most important renewable resources on the earth. They are essential in removing the carbon dioxide from the air and adding oxygen to the air we breathe.

Unfortunately, we are cutting forests down faster than they are being planted worldwide. Work in your community on a tree-planting project. Care for the trees after they have been planted.

or

Find out about an organization that is helping people in other countries to plant trees in order to fight pollution, to prevent soil erosion, or to add oxygen to the earth's atmosphere. Share this information with others and find out what you can do to help.

*7 The word "credo" means a group of beliefs or principles that you live by. Write a personal credo that tells how you feel about the environment. (See page 244 for some assistance.) Share your credo with others in your troop or group. Make a list of actions that you might do to live with your environment, use recycled materials, celebrate your special place on the earth, and save water, air, and soil. Adopt these actions in your daily life and share them with others.

Many American Indian cultures have great respect for the earth, its plants, animals, and all things, living and not living, that are a part of the land, sea, and sky. They see all things as being related. If you destroy forests or pollute a river, you are also harming all other living and nonliving things. Think of ways that the American landscape has changed over the past 200 years.

Which changes have been positive?

_____

_____

_____

Which changes have been negative?

_____

_____

_____

What changes can you predict for the next 20 years?

_____

_____

Will they be positive or negative?

_____

_____

_____

8 Learn about an issue in your community that affects the environment. This might involve water, land use, landfills, recycling, toxic waste, land development, open space, use of chemicals, transportation, or energy. Attend a public hearing sponsored by a government agency or city government that is addressing one of these issues. Find out how an informed individual can be a part of this process.

or

With your troop or group, stage a mock public hearing about a real issue concerning the environment in your community. Role-play different groups and their concerns. Make some recommendations based on the needs of the people and the needs of the environment. Are they the same?

or

Interview an elected official and find out how she/he feels about the environment. Discover what kinds of actions have been taken that affect the environment in your community, state, nation, or the world.

*9 Participate in an environmental action project that has a positive impact on the quality of life in your community.

• •

_____

Date badge completed

_____

My signature

_____

Leader's signature

SCIENCE IN ACTION

1 Invite a firefighter, police officer, or emergency medical technician to your troop/group meeting or visit one or more of them at work to find out how they use science and technology in their jobs. Share what you discover with others.

2 Find out how two or more of the following communications devices work: cellular telephone, picture phone, TDD beeper, cable TV reception box, or communication satellite.

3 Find out ways in which your community is using technology to meet the needs of people with disabilities, such as TDDs for people who are deaf or lifts on buses to accommodate wheelchairs. (TDD, or telecommunications device for the deaf, is a generic term referring to any mechanical or electronic device that enables people to send typed messages over the telephone network.) Talk to people in the community who have disabilities to find out about their needs. Then talk to local engineers, scientists, and community leaders to find out what they are doing to meet those needs.

Share what you find out with your troop or group. Make some suggestions for future community efforts and try to carry out one of your ideas.

4 Design a transportation system or type of transportation for a city or country in the year 2050.

or

Design something using science and technology that you would like to have in your community in the near future to improve the quality of life.

5 Read about "Sharpening Your Observational and Investigational Skills" in Chapter 7 of your *Junior Girl Scout Handbook* and try the "Science and Technology Hunt."

6 Visit a factory in your community. Find out how science is used in manufacturing.

or

Visit a farm or other agricultural business to find out how science is used in growing its crops.

7 Look up "engineer" in the Yellow Pages of the telephone book and make a list of all the different kinds of engineers listed.

or

Ask people what kinds of engineers there are until you find at least five different kinds.

For either choice, find out what at least three kinds of engineers do in their jobs.

CAN YOU DRAW A LINE FROM THE FAMOUS BRIDGE TO ITS NAME?

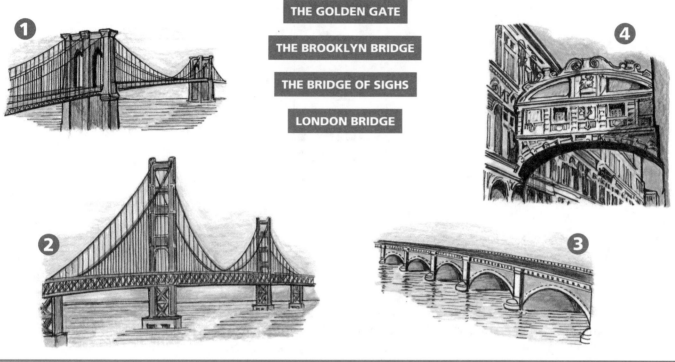

THE GOLDEN GATE

THE BROOKLYN BRIDGE

THE BRIDGE OF SIGHS

LONDON BRIDGE

Answers: 1-the Brooklyn Bridge, 2-the Golden Gate, 3-London Bridge, 4-the Bridge of Sighs (Venice)

8 Find out about a bridge in your community. What kind of bridge is it? When was it built? How much weight can it safely support? How much traffic does it usually have? Make a chart with your findings and share it with your troop or group. You may want to also share it with your local government leaders.

or

Build a model of a suspension bridge, using rope, twine boxes, chairs, or other materials. Share it with your troop or group.

Date badge completed

My signature

Leader's signature

SCIENCE
SLEUTH

- -

COMPLETE SEVEN ACTIVITIES.

1 With the help of a police officer, private investigator, or other source, dust for and lift a fingerprint, or measure a footprint or tire track. Find out how police departments use these signs in solving crimes. Find out what other pieces of evidence can be used to identify a person or vehicle. With the permission of your parent/guardian, take part in the child identification program in your local community.

2 Make a simple musical instrument that you can tune. Listen to the pitch of the sound and try ways to change the pitch.
- Try to explain how the sound is made.
- Play a simple melody.

3 Grow crystals out of sugar, salt, or another substance. Find out the chemical names and formulas of the substances you are working with. Look at the crystals with a magnifying glass and describe what you see. Compare your home-grown crystals with some natural crystals.

Fingerprint patterns are unique. No fingerprints from two different people have ever been discovered that are the same. There are some characteristics that people inherit that make them unique. See if you or any of your family members or friends can do the following: roll your tongue, have a double-jointed thumb, wiggle your ears.

What did you discover?

DOUBLE-JOINTED THUMB

ROLL YOUR TONGUE

WIGGLE YOUR EARS

• 124 •

4 Look around your home, school, and community to find at least one example of each of the following six machines: inclined plane, lever, pulley, screw, wedge, and wheel and axle. Make a drawing, take pictures, or act out your examples to help you explain to others how these simple machines work.

5 For two days, make a list of all the things you use that are electric. Look at your list and think about which appliances you might be able to live without. From your list, pick three appliances and look back in history to see where they came from. Try to predict how these appliances will change in the future.

6 Figure out how to do two of the following and show someone else how to do them:
- Move water from one jar to another without pouring.
- Make a fire extinguisher and put out a fire.
- Show that air exerts pressure.
- Send and read messages written with invisible ink.
- Make something float that is heavier than water.
- Move an object by rolling it rather than pushing it.

7 Discover how newspapers, posters, or paper are made by doing one of the following:
- Visit a place that uses a printing press. Have the operator explain how the process works.
- Visit a place where paper is made and learn about the process.
- Make your own paper. Then write a letter to a friend using your paper.

8 Find out what happens to different kinds of metals when they are left outside. Compare iron, silver, copper, and brass. Find at least eight examples of metal that has undergone some changes. Learn what can be done to restore the finish.

9 Find out how to hook up a VCR to a TV, or stereo components such as stereo speakers, turntable, CD player, or tape deck. Find out how the machines connect and what each one does.

Date badge completed

My signature

Leader's signature

SCIENCE IN EVERYDAY LIFE

DO ONE ACTIVITY IN EACH CATEGORY

Science, Health and Fitness

A.1 Read about "Changes in Your Body" in Chapter 2 of the *Junior Girl Scout Handbook* and take the "Get the Facts Quiz."

A.2 Interview a doctor or dentist and find out about the different ways science and math are used in her or his work. Try to arrange a demonstration of science at work—for example, having your blood pressure taken.

Science in the Lives of People

B.1 Learn about the life of a woman who was or is a scientist. She could be a historical figure such as Marie Curie or someone living in your community. Find out what special problems she may have faced in reaching her goals. List three important lessons that you learned from her achievements.

B.2 Find out about nuclear energy. How is it used in this country and in other countries? What are some of the main concerns about the use of nuclear energy? What are some of its benefits? Plan and hold a debate on the pros and cons of nuclear energy.

B.3 Look for examples of science at work in your community. Make a list and share your findings with others.

Notice a spider web. What kind of pattern does a web have? Look for other spider webs. Notice their patterns. Try drawing one of the patterns you see on a blank piece of paper. Color your web in different colors to make a beautiful design.

Science and the Arts

C.1 Make a design using geometric figures or lines. Use paint or another medium for your artwork—for example, needlepoint, cross-stitch, embroidery, knitting, crocheting, or patchwork.

or

Make a string design that gives the feeling of curves but uses only straight pieces of thread. Mount your string design on a board using nails that have small, flat heads.

C.2 Learn about primary and complementary colors. Start with liquid paints in the three primary colors, plus black and white. Experiment with different color combinations. Keep track of which color combinations give a particular result. Then do a painting that has at least 15 different colors that you have mixed.

Science and Technology

D.1 Write a science fiction short story, skit, or musical about life in the year 2050. What will life be like? What will have become better? Worse?

or

Read a science fiction story about life in the future. Decide what you think is realistic and what you think won't happen.

Can you match the writer to her or his prediction?

Science fiction writers have made many predictions that have already come true. Draw a line connecting the writer with the prediction.

Satellites	**Mary Shelley**
Submarines	**George Orwell**
Interactive television	**Ray Bradbury**
Heart transplants	**Jules Verne**
Mechanical body parts	**Arthur C. Clarke**

Answers:
Satellites-Arthur C. Clarke, submarines-Jules Verne, interactive television-George Orwell, heart transplants-Mary Shelley, mechanical body parts-Ray Bradbury

D.2 Select an item of technology that you use. Find out how it has changed over the past 50 years. Then imagine what it might be like 50 years from now. Draw or make a model of the futuristic version describing all its new features. Some items to consider are a car, a telephone, stereo equipment, a wristwatch, a calculator, or a television set.

Science and Nature

E.1 Use a simple identification book or field guide to find the names of seven different species of a group of living things that you can observe in your area. You might choose a group such as birds, mammals, reptiles, amphibians, flowers, or trees. Learn the key characteristics of each species that can help to identify it. These might include what it looks like, where it lives, and how it behaves. Share your knowledge with your troop, a younger person, or a friend.

E.2 Go on a geology walk! Find evidence of a changing earth brought about by water, wind, weather, plants and animals, and gravity. Look for:

- Erosion on a hillside.
- Plants that grow on rocks.
- Plants that are splitting rocks with their roots.
- Loose rock at the bottom of hills.
- Smooth and jagged rocks.
- Sand deposited by water.
- Buildings, statues, or gravestones that show weathering.
- Signs of things left by moving water.
- Evidence that people can change the face of the earth.

_____
Date badge completed

_____
My signature

_____
Leader's signature

SKY SEARCH

*1 Learn how to use a star map. Be able to point out to others what the different symbols on the map mean. Obtain a star map for your stargazing location and the appropriate time of year to help you complete this badge. Many local newspapers have a star watch map, or check with your library.

2 Learn which of the nine planets are visible to the naked eye. Try to locate at least one of these during your stargazing adventure.

3 Look at a star map and choose six constellations. Note any distinguishing features such as size, shape, number, and brightness of the stars. With the help of a star map, locate the constellations in the sky, then point these out to others.

4 Find out why being able to locate the North Star is important. Help others in your troop to locate the North Star. Learn how to use the stars to find directions.

5 Learn the stories from two or more modern or ancient cultures, such as Greek, Norse, American Indian or Chinese, that were used to explain what was seen in the sky.

Coyote Became the Moon

In the past there was no moon. People couldn't see at night. They didn't like having to move around in the dark. So they discussed the problem. "We must have light at night. We must have a moon. Who could be a moon?" "I'll do it," said Yellow Fox. He went in the sky, but he was so bright and made things so hot that everyone became upset. "We need a different moon. Who could be our new moon?" Coyote said, "I'll do it," because he knew that he could look down and see everything and know everyone's secrets. At first, Coyote was a good moon. He made enough light for people to see by, but not too much heat to be uncomfortable. But, there was one big problem. He could see everything and he made a comment about everything he saw. People who were doing things that they did not want other people to know about were very upset. They had a meeting and said, "We have to get a new moon. Coyote makes too much noise!" Coyote lost his chance to be the Moon, but he still sneaks around and tries to discover what everyone is doing.

6 Learn why some stars appear to be brighter or bigger than others. Find out about the different colors stars appear to have. For example, the constellation Orion contains stars that are bluish white and reddish, as well as all white. Find stars that change in brightness.

7 Some constellations are only visible during certain times of the year. Make a schedule of which ones are seasonal and when they would appear. Explain why this happens.

8 Explain to your troop/group or others what a solar system is. Be able to describe the differences among planets, a sun, a moon, and stars.

or

Learn which planets, asteroids, moons, and sun make up our solar system. Create a scale model or display of our solar system. Share it with younger girls.

9 Learn about meteors, meteorites, meteor showers, and comets. Find out when meteor showers will be visible in your area. Arrange a meteorite sighting excursion. Make certain everyone in your group knows what a meteorite is and in which part of the sky to look. Have the group count how many are seen in an hour. Make sure you have arranged for an adult to be present.

10 Learn how to tell time using a simple sundial.

or

Learn how to use the sun to find directions.

11 On nights of a first quarter or last quarter moon, use a moon map to help you look for the valleys, ridges, and mountain ranges that pattern the moon's surface. Try using a small telescope or binoculars to observe these features.

or

Find out answers to the following questions:
- How long does the moon take to complete an orbit around the earth?
- What causes the phases of the moon?
- How does the moon's orbit affect the tides on earth?
- How do the features of the moon get their names?
- How old is the moon?
- How were craters formed?
- Who were the first American astronauts to walk on the moon?

12 Visit a planetarium. Take part in one of their school workshops. Share what you learned with others.

or

Talk with a person who is in an astronomy-related profession. Find out what she does and what education she needed. Find out why or how she chose her profession.

13 Plan an evening of astronomy activities with your troop on your next camping trip.

14 Organize a neighborhood astronomy club or help to set up an astronomy program that can be used at your council campsites by all troops/groups. Ask a local astronomy club for their guidance. If an astronomy club already exists in your area, ask what you might do to add to the program.

Date badge completed

My signature

Leader's signature

WATER WONDERS

If you live in an area where salt water is not available, go to your local aquarium or contact a science teacher or science department in a college to learn how to make salt water to use in some of the following activities.

*1 Demonstrate your understanding of how the water cycle functions by sharing your knowledge with other members of your troop/group. Develop a poster, slide show, or take a walk around the neighborhood to get ideas to help you with your demonstration. Discuss with the group why we study the water cycle, how we use it, why we try to control it, and how people and industry pollute it.

2 Change the temperature of water to show how water acts in its three states: solid, liquid, and gas. Show how you can get water to: push, become invisible, flow uphill, and form a cloud and float things.

3 Water is a valuable resource. Today we need to conserve it as much as possible. Discover three ways you and your family can conserve water. Practice using these methods of water conservation.

4 Find out where your drinking water comes from. Is it ground water, spring water, river water, reservoir water, or does it come from another source? What is done to the water to make certain it is safe to drink?

5 Collect water using a solar still.

or

Purify water from a source other than a faucet.

6 Observe things that live underwater. Visit a place like an aquarium or a pet store. Set up your own aquarium or make a water scope to help you observe a water habitat. Find out what adaptations enable fish and other animals to live underwater. How could people live underwater?

7 Compare salt water and fresh water. Do at least two experiments to find out which:
- Boils first.
- Freezes first.
- Yields salt crystals.
- Makes better soapsuds.
- Makes floating easier.

8 Do one activity about the food chain in the ocean or in fresh water.

- Trail a plankton net through the water and look closely at what you collect. (See "Helps and Resources," page 244.) Find out where plankton fits in the food chain. Imagine how much plankton it takes to feed a whale.
- Catch, dig, or buy food that comes from the ocean or fresh water. Clean the food and make a tasty dish using fish, seaweed, watercress, or other such delicacies. Be sure your food is from unpolluted water!
- Set up and keep up an aquarium. Balance the numbers and kinds of living things with a healthy food and water supply.

9 Find out about working in the world of water in one of the following ways:

- Visit a place where water has been put to work, such as in a sewage or water treatment plant, an irrigation control center, a mining operation, a power plant, a fish hatchery, or a physical therapy center. Show that you know where the water comes from, how it works in the place you visit, where it goes, and what the water is like at the end of the process.
- Tour a work boat, such as a ferry, barge, research vessel, tugboat, cargo ship, commercial fishing boat, dive boat, Navy vessel, or Coast Guard cutter. Ask people on board, if possible, to compare their jobs on the water with similar jobs on land.

- Find out what it means to be an oceanographer (a person who studies oceans), hydrologist (a specialist in the study of water on the surface of the land, in the soil and underlying rocks, and in the atmosphere), or limnologist (a specialist in the study of fresh waters, especially ponds and lakes). Look for ways that these jobs are like any other scientist's job and ways that the water setting makes them special.
- Visit an aquatic center (community pool, YWCA, health club, etc.) to learn about the different types of jobs that are available. Find out what training is needed for these jobs.

10 Take a hike along a shoreline to discover what happens when water meets land. Observe the varieties of animal and plant life. How might the land affect the water quality?

11 Find a quiet spot by a body of water, then use all of your senses to observe what is happening. Write a poem, draw a picture, choreograph a dance, or create a song to describe your awareness of water. Share this with others.

12 Compare at least two bodies of water and explain the differences you found.

13 After a rainstorm, compare the erosion in two areas which are alike, except that one has plants and the other does not. Discuss with your group what this means. How do plants help stop erosion?

• •

Date badge completed

My signature

Leader's signature

WEATHER WATCH

1 Interview a weather reporter or meteorologist about weather forecasting. Find out about what kind of equipment is used, how the data are interpreted, and how accurate predictions usually are.

2 For one week, keep a record of a television or newspaper's daily weather forecast. Make a chart that compares the weather forecast to actual weather conditions. Share the result with your troop or group. What was the percentage of accuracy?

3 Read "Safety Tips for Weather" in Chapter 3 of the *Junior Girl Scout Handbook*. Make a weather safety rule checklist for your area. Be sure to note seasonal changes.

4 Find out ways in which scientists and others have tried to change the weather. What are some of the reasons why we would want to change it? Share your findings with your troop or group.

5 Keep a chart for one month that shows how weather affects your activities. How often did you change your activities because of the weather?

6 Make a game about weather. You can make a card or board game, a word game, or an active game. Share your game with others.

7 Become a cloud watcher. Each day for a week, record the types of clouds you see. Find out what type of weather is common with each type of cloud. Make notes about the weather and try to predict how the weather may change based on the clouds you see.

8 Find out about weather-related emergencies that your community might face, such as hurricanes, tornadoes, or flash floods. Learn what types of safety measures you should be prepared to take. Develop a plan for educating others.

Build Your Own Barometer

Cut a large section from a balloon and stretch it tightly over the mouth of a large baby food or similar size jar. Wrap a heavy duty rubber band around the balloon so that it stays in place. Cut the end of a drinking straw into a point. Glue the non-pointed end of the straw to the center of the balloon. Fold a piece of cardboard so that it stands next to the jar. Mark where the pointed end of the straw touches. Draw a line and mark the line with number 5. Make 5 lines counting up from 5 and 5 lines counting down from 5. The marks should be 3 millimeters apart. Write the numbers 0-10 on the lines. Make sure your straw is pointing at number 5. Now watch what happens to the straw for a week. Try to look at the barometer at the same time every day. What is the weather like when the barometer points to lower numbers? What is the weather like when the barometer points to higher numbers?

CARDBOARD

STRAW

RUBBER BAND

BABY FOOD JAR

BALLOON

9 With your troop or group, make your own weather station. Measure wind speed and direction, rainfall or snowfall, barometric pressure, humidity, and temperature. For many of these, you can make your own simple equipment. (This counts as two activities.)

Date badge completed

My signature

Leader's signature

Arts Around the World

What do you think this girl is doing? What do you think this girl is feeling? Choose a piece of music that makes you feel happy. Invent some dance movements to match the music.

Art can be part of ceremonies and religions. Art can be part of holidays and celebrations. Art can be beautiful paintings in museums. Art can be a window to discover what is beautiful and valuable in other cultures. Take a large piece of paper.

Draw a window, like this [// //] or this [▯] . In the window, draw, paint, or make a collage that would show others looking in the window what is beautiful and valuable to you.

Name this tune.

You can use words to describe how you feel or what you see. You can keep your writing secret or you can share your creations with others. Sit in a quiet place, indoors or outdoors. Choose an object that appeals to you. Examine it. What makes this object different from all others? Look at it closely. Use your senses. Now close your eyes and imagine how it would feel to BE this object. What would your skin be like? your voice? What would you think about? How would you see the world? What things would be important to you? Try writing a short poem or story from this object's point of view.

What do these letters stand for?

Actresses make the audience believe that their characters they portray are real. Try being an actress. Look in a mirror and practice facial expressions that show emotions. Can you show joy, happiness, sadness, fear, surprise, boredom, excitement, and anger?

DABBLER

COMPLETE ONE ACTIVITY IN SIX OF THE GROUPS, INCLUDING THE ONE STARRED.

A.1 Create a model of a building in which you would like to live, study, work, or play. Use inexpensive or scrap materials to create your model.

A.2 Decide what works of art help make a community more beautiful, such as fountains, statues, or murals. Choose one type and draw an original design that you feel would look good in your community.

B.1 Create a work of your own design that is intended to hang on a wall. This could be a painting, drawing, print weaving, stitchery, macramé, or mixed media project. Display your piece at a troop/group or patrol meeting or someplace else where it may be seen by others.

B.2 Create a work of your own design that is meant to be seen from all sides. This could be a sculpture, a piece of pottery, a mobile, or other design. Use clay, wood, plaster, plastic, metal, paper, or fibers. Display your piece at a troop/group meeting or to others.

C.1 Learn about two different kinds of instruments from the four families (string, percussion, wind, and brass); how they sound, where and when they are played, and so forth. Make a simple instrument that you can use to accompany singing at your troop/group meeting or other gatherings.

C.2 Learn a new song and practice it with your friends until you know it well. If possible, tape your song and play it back to hear how you sound. Practice until you like the sound that you hear.

D.1 Write a story or poem about something you know—yourself, your family, your favorite season of the year, your favorite holiday, a special place you like. Then write an imaginary story or poem. Share what you have written with your troop/group or with others.

D.2 Read a book. Then describe it to others in a newspaper review, a poster, or a play so that they will want to read it.

E.1 Design a room—a playroom, a bedroom, a dining room, or a living room. Show your design in a painting, a drawing, or a diorama.

E.2 Make an item that would make your home more beautiful. This could be a picture, a pillow, a wall hanging, or other decorative item.

F.1 Make plans to see a play, a movie, or television drama in a group. Afterwards, discuss with your group the kinds of things that made the performance interesting, dull, good, or bad.

F.2 Take part in a dramatic skit, play, mime, musical, or dance performance either as a performer or as a part of the backstage operation.

G.1 Design one of the following:

- A greeting card.
- An advertisement to sell something.
- A poster or leaflet.
- A symbol or logo that would be your trademark.

G.2 Draw your own design for something new that would be useful—a car, a train, a plane, a can opener, a tool, a pot for cooking, a telephone, etc.

Whichever activity you choose, share the results with others.

H.1 Find out about some of the folk art created in your area. If possible, talk to someone who knows about an art that was popular many years ago—quilting, wood carving, scrimshaw, toy making, egg decorating, lace making, embroidery, etc. Ask the person to explain it to you and show you how it is done.

H.2 Choose a holiday that is celebrated in your community or in another country. Find out the different ways in which this holiday is celebrated. Learn about and demonstrate any special songs, games, decorations, clothing, or other art forms that go with this holiday.

Fiestas Patrias

September 16th is Mexican Independence Day (Fiestas Patrias). People celebrate with fireworks, dancing, parades, games, and special foods. Some streets are hung with green, red, and white lights—Mexico's national colors. Why not make some nachos with an adult to celebrate? Arrange tortilla chips, corn chips, or taco pieces on a cookie sheet. Slice Monterey Jack cheese or cheddar cheese in very thin slices and put one slice on each chip. Open a can of mild jalapeno peppers and cut the peppers into little pieces. Put the pepper pieces on top of the chips and cheese. Broil in the oven for 2-3 minutes. OR Heat cheese sauce that has been made especially for nachos in a microwave oven. Pour the sauce while hot over a bowl of tortilla, corn, or taco chips.

I.1 Design and make something for someone as a gift. Keep in mind the person's interests, likes, and dislikes. It could be a special box for a collection, a piece of jewelry or clothing, a plant holder, a toy, or a game. Show your design to others and explain why you made it for the person.

I.2 Look through a catalog, newspaper, or magazine and choose several articles of clothing for girls your age for different occasions. Cut them out or draw them and make posters of the clothing that is comfortable and attractive for different kinds of weather or different occasions: for example, sunny, cold, or snowy days; parties, troop meetings, camping, school, religious services, traveling, sports. Explain why you chose the different outfits for each occasion.

J.1 Attend or watch a performance on television of a type of dance you have not seen before. Afterwards, learn as much as you can about that dance form and present it to others in some manner.

J.2 Perform or participate in a dance recital, an ethnic dance festival, or a neighborhood, troop, or Girl Scout council folk or square dance.

*K Read the section, "Exploring the Arts" in Chapter 7 of the *Junior Girl Scout Handbook*. (You do not have to do the activities in the section, just read them.)

• •

_____

Date badge completed

_____

My signature

_____

Leader's signature

ARCHITECTURE

COMPLETE FOUR ACTIVITIES, INCLUDING THE ONE STARRED.

*1 Plan and take a walk in your community (or a city, town, or village you are visiting) to find examples of beauty in objects made by people, such as buildings, statues, fountains, and fences. Also identify the objects or areas that are unattractive. Tell why you feel some are beautiful and some are not. Make a list and compare notes with others.

2 Design a school that you would like to attend. In your design, consider the number of teachers and students, the types of activities that would happen in different rooms, ways to save energy in the building, and activities that would take place outdoors. Draw your school to scale on graph paper or make a model of your school with simple, inexpensive materials. (Drawing to scale means drawing an object smaller than its real size, but keeping its proportions accurate.)

or

Design a house of the future. Decide where it will be—floating in space, on a planet, at a space station, under the ocean, etc. Draw the house to scale on graph paper or create a model of it and a plan for the transportation to get to it.

For either activity, show your scale drawing or model to others and explain why you designed it the way you did.

3 Design a garden—perhaps a kids-only garden, a maze garden (see example on next page), a storybook garden, or a garden that might be in another country. Think about what will go into your garden—kinds of flowers and/or trees, sculptures, walkways, waterfalls or fountains, and places to sit. Plan the entrance and center of your garden. When plans are complete, draw it to scale on graph paper or make a model of the garden using inexpensive materials.

or

Together with three or four other girls, design a neighborhood zoo. First, decide what animals will live in your zoo. Cut out or draw pictures of the animals. Find out what each animal eats and what else it needs to keep happy and healthy. Plan spaces for the animals, buildings, walls, pathways, plantings, water, and fun places for animals. Decide how visitors will see the animals. With your team, make a model and give your zoo a name.

Whichever activity you choose, show your model to others and explain your plans.

START →

ENTER GARDEN ↓

CAN YOU MATCH THESE FAMOUS BUILDINGS TO THEIR COUNTRIES?

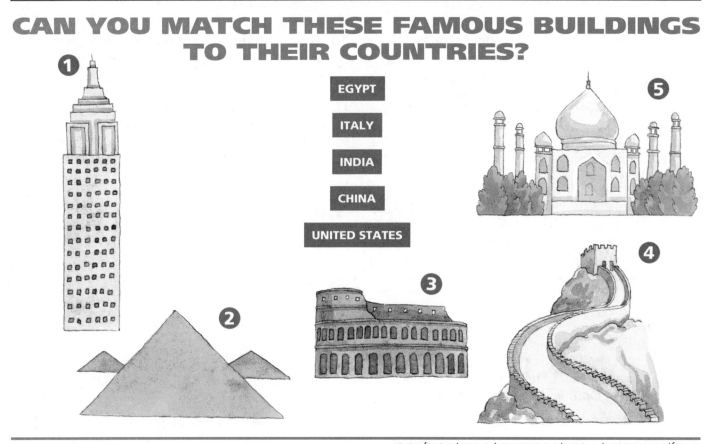

EGYPT

ITALY

INDIA

CHINA

UNITED STATES

Answers: 1–the United States, the Empire State Building; 2–Egypt, the Great Pyramid; 3–Italy, the Colosseum; 4–China, the Great Wall; 5–India, the Taj Mahal

4 Show that you have learned about architecture throughout the world by creating a game, poster, exhibit, or mural that shows buildings in other parts of the country or other parts of the world. Include examples of at least four of the following types of buildings:

- One where there is a season with heavy rain and a season with some dry spells.
- One where there is cold weather most of the year with many forests.
- One where there is cold weather with few trees.
- One built on a river or other waterway.
- One where there are many mountains.
- One where the weather is hot and dry all year.
- One built for the religion of the people.
- One that is unique and different from any other you have seen.

Prepare to explain to other people where the buildings are located and why they are built the way they are.

5 Create a plan for your community based on your list from Activity #1. Include things other than buildings that would make your community more beautiful as well as a better place to live, work, and play. Make certain the space you design can be used by people with disabilities. Make a drawing or model of your plan and explain why it would be appropriate.

6 Find out in what ways the following careers contribute to the beauty of buildings, parks, and towns: architect, landscape architect, sculptor, designer, urban planner. Arrange to interview at least one person in one of these careers. Ask about such things as: how the person decided on the career, what training or education is required, what kind of work is involved, what materials and tools are needed, how laws and building codes make a difference in designs. Present your findings to others in an interesting way.

7 Create an exhibit of pictures or actual samples of building materials and a drawing or picture of buildings made from these materials: cardboard boxes, sheets of cardboard, corrugated board, wrapping paper, wallpaper samples, contact paper, pebbles, stones, bits of brick and concrete, plastic, balsa wood, and/or wood scraps. Explain why the material is right for each building shown.

8 Learn how to create floor plans to scale. Measure a room and the furnishings to scale on graph paper, indicate the scale (for example, 1 inch = 1 foot), and display your scale drawing at a Girl Scout meeting or to others.

9 Create a structure that is pleasing to you out of twigs, small pieces of driftwood, toothpicks, coffee stirrer sticks, or a combination of such small sticks. Use glue, string, and tools appropriate to the materials.

10 Using pictures from magazines and your own artwork, construct your ideal living space.

11 Using what you have learned in other activities, plan, design, and construct with actual building materials and supplies a small structure, such as a dollhouse, bird feeder, or pet house.

_____
Date badge completed

_____
My signature

_____
Leader's signature

ART IN
THE HOME

1 Make a collection of pictures of different rooms showing different styles of furniture, rugs, wall coverings, decorations, lighting, and colors. Pictures can come from newspapers, magazines, or catalogs. Using your collection, do three of the following:

- Look over the different furniture styles and decide which you like best and why.
- Look at the patterns in the rooms in the pictures. How many patterns are there—on the floor, walls, windows, furniture? How do they go with each other? What mixture of pattern and plain color do you like best?
- Look at the colors and how they are used. Do different colors give different feelings? How are colors used together? Decide which three color combinations you like.
- Look at the lighting arrangements. How many different lighting fixtures can you find? What light is best for different activities in the home—reading, dining, cooking, sewing, etc.?
- Look at the decorations in the rooms in your pictures. Are there pictures, wall hangings, baskets, ceramics, collections, plants? Decide which type you like best and why.

2 Measure a room in a house. Draw it on a large piece of paper in scale, 1 inch = 1 foot. Indicate doors and windows. With paper of another color, cut shapes to scale for furniture, rugs, storage units, etc. Place these on the scale drawing, trying different arrangements that fit the size, shape, and purpose of the room. When satisfied, glue the shapes in place.

3 Find a large box. Collect samples of wallpaper, rugs, fabric, and paint colors. With your group, troop, or others using the box as an experimental room, decide which wallpaper, rug, fabric, and color combination each of you likes best. Then look through the magazines and cut out pictures of the kind of furniture that would look good in your room. Plan how you would arrange the space of the room and what the room would be used for.

or

Using a cardboard or wooden box, create a dollhouse room, complete with rugs, wall covering, window treatment, and cardboard or wooden furniture.

In Ukraine, located in southeastern Europe, bordering the Black Sea, people dye eggshells with many different colors and designs. This art is called Pysanka. You can try your own Pysanka egg decorating. Take an egg and make a small hole in the narrow end with a pin. Move the pin to make the hole a little bigger. Now make a hole in the fat end of the egg with your pin. Move the pin to make a bigger hole on this end. Take the pin out and hold the egg so that the fat end is over a bowl. Blow gently through the narrow end. The white and yolk of the egg should come out of the hole and you should have an empty egg shell. Then take a white or light yellow crayon and draw a design on the egg. Using Easter egg dyes or food coloring, dip the egg in one color of dye. Blot it dry and color more of the egg with crayon. Then dip the egg into another color of dye. Blot the egg, cover more parts with crayon, and dye the egg again in a third color. Have an adult help you with the next part. Light a candle and hold the egg near the flame. The crayon wax will start to melt. Wipe the wax off with a tissue. You will see all the different colors appear as the wax melts.

4 Visit a store that sells plants and flowers. Study your pictures again to see how flowers and plants help decorate a room, or add plants or flowers to a box room you make. Create a floral arrangement or an arrangement of fruit or natural materials for a home, or pot a plant to give as a gift.

5 Create something that would beautify your home or someone else's home. Examples could be a basket, bookbinding, placemats, napkins or tablecloth, pillow, wall hanging, picture, baby's quilt, etc.

6 Learn about a decorative art that is used in the home, such as stenciling, wood staining, paint antiquing, marbelizing, or wallpapering. Visit a paint, hardware, or home decorating store. Study the types of paints, colors, finishes for wood, wallpapers, and the tools for applying these materials. Then complete a small project using one of these decorative arts. For example:

- Paint or stencil a small piece of furniture.
- Finish or refinish a wood object or piece of furniture.
- Wallpaper something large enough so you can gain an understanding of the technique (a box, the inside of a bookcase, etc.).
- Help someone wallpaper or paint a room.

7 Find out something about the influences of other countries on furniture design or interior decoration. Collect magazine or newspaper pictures of three rooms containing furniture, rugs, or wall hangings that show the influence of another country. Be able to identify the country.

or

Find out how people from a culture other than your own decorate their homes for one of their holidays. Make or demonstrate how to make one decoration or craft you have learned.

8 Visit a store that sells furniture, rugs, china, table linens, curtains, and other household items or look through mail order catalogs. Select items that you think you would like to have in your home someday. List them and find out the prices. Then make two plans for a room for your own use, including the essentials you need for sleeping, storage, relaxing, homework, hobbies, etc. Make one plan if you had an unlimited budget, the other plan if you had very little money to spend.

9 Visit model homes or apartments, dollhouse exhibits, restoration or historical homes, friends' homes, model rooms in stores or museums, or take a house and garden tour or go to an open house. Make notes or sketches of the things you like—the furniture, decorations, rugs, quilts, windows, china, paintings. After you return, do a painting from memory of your favorite room. Be able to explain to your group why you made your choices.

10 Design and make or assemble a creative arrangement for storage. This might be a place to keep your things, a way to provide space for a hobby, or a way to display a collection.

11 Read about "Tying Knots" in Chapter 7 of the *Junior Girl Scout Handbook* and create a macramé wall hanging or plant hanger.

• •

_____
Date badge completed

_____
My signature

_____
Leader's signature

ART IN
THE ROUND

1 Create a figure out of available materials, such as cardboard boxes or rolls, glue, string, paint, and assorted bits of scrap material.

2 Create a three-dimensional design in wire, by twisting, cutting, and/or coiling. (A three-dimensional object is one that has height, width, and depth.) Use tools appropriate to the heaviness of the wire and your design. Add other materials as needed for your design.

3 Create an abstract piece of sculpture using boxes, crates, pieces of wood, cardboard, or polystyrene. Include negative as well as positive space in your design. (In a sculpture, the positive space is the solid part of a sculpture and the negative space is the air space that is still considered a part of the design.)

4 Carve a sculpture in soft wood. Finish it and be able to explain the tools and equipment used in wood carving.

5 Know the meaning of "in the round" and "in relief." Find examples of these in your community and draw or photograph them.

6 Mix plaster of Paris to be sculpture material. Pour into a mold. When the mold is ready, carve a design in the round.

7 Create a relief design in plaster and sand using natural materials as part of your design. (A relief sculpture is one in which figures or forms stand out from a flat background.)

8 Find out about three different kinds of wood that can be used for carving, and experiment with carving them. Be able to explain which ones you feel are best and why.

or

Create a sculpture in a sculpture material other than wood or plaster.

9 Visit a museum, gallery, studio, art show, crafts fair, sales shop, or other place where sculptures in various materials are on display. Be ready to explain what you liked best and why.

10 Collect pictures and read about some outstanding pieces of sculpture in the United States or another country; know about the artist and the kind of work she/he did or does.

ORIGAMI is the ancient Japanese art of paper folding. The crane is a symbol of peace and hope. Follow these introductions to make your own crane. Use a square sheet of origami, typing, or copy paper. Construction paper would be too heavy and tissue paper would be too light. You could make a mobile out of cranes or use them as decorations or gifts.

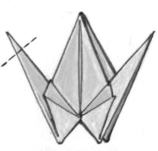

9.

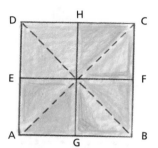

1. Fold square as shown; solid lines form peaks, dotted lines form valleys.

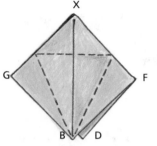

2. Bring ABCD together to form small square. Bring F and G to center fold. Repeat on other side. Fold down top to form triangle.

3. Unfold to small square. Pull B up over center point X, pulling in G and F. Repeat with D on other side.

4. Fold outside points to center on dotted line. Repeat on other side.

5. Make diagonal creases on neck and tail.

6. Fold up neck and tail.

7. Unfold tail. Push into wing, reversing center fold at the same time. Repeat for neck.

8. Fold head on dotted line. Push into neck, again reversing center fold.

9. Spread wings gently, holding bottom and pushing down on X.

11 In a craft or art book, read instructions for making papier mâché and then complete one of the following:

- Create a decoration for a party or holiday from cardboard or paper.
- Create a papier-mâché mask to be worn as part of a play or festival or to be used as decoration.
- Create a sculpture in papier-mâché over wire, boxes, or other forms.
- Create a useful object from papier-mâché.
- Using stiff paper, create sculpture-like designs by cutting, folding, coiling, rolling, glueing, and taping.

_____
Date badge completed

_____
My signature

_____
Leader's signature

ART TO WEAR

For definitions of special terms, see "Helps and Resources," pages 244–245.

*A.1 Design an outfit for yourself or for someone else. Complete a full-color sketch of your outfit and list or show types of fabrics on your sketch. Choose an outfit for school, camping, sports, or a party.

A.2 Learn to sew a simple garment for yourself or someone else using a pattern and sewing machine, if possible.

A.3 Create a poster of traditional dress of countries from three continents. Explore libraries, museums, magazines, or talk to family and friends to find out how the garments or decorations reflect the culture and lifestyle of the people.

*A.4 Read about "Clothes That Fit and Look Good" in Chapter 4 of the *Junior Girl Scout Handbook* and make a sewing kit.

A.5 Find three different types of fashion illustrations in magazines and/or newspapers. Use these as a rough guide to make fashion sketches of three outfits you have or would like to have.

In fashion illustration, the human body is not drawn accurately. Compare the figures above. Why is one better for showing clothing?

A.6 Find pictures of fashions from four periods of history, approximately 20 years apart (example: 1750, 1770, 1790, 1810 or 1900, 1920, 1940, 1960). List the similarities, differences, and trends that may show up in different periods.

B.1 Find out about the kinds of decoration that may be added to clothing to beautify or make it more personal. Learn one of the following and create a small decorative item for yourself or someone else.

- Embroidery or crewel.
- Crocheting or knitting.
- Finger or other belt weaving.
- Macramé.
- Lacework or tatting.
- Quilting.
- Appliqué.
- Braiding of yarn, threads, or ribbon.
- Wrapping (using yarn over a cord).
- Tassels, fringe, pompoms.

Add other decorative touches if you wish, such as beads, natural materials, or buttons.

B.2 Fabric and fashion go together. Weave at least two small squares of fabric on a simple loom. Use different colors and textures of fibers in your design.

or

Make a poster, display cards, or booklet showing eight different fabrics. Label each fabric and give some information about it. Choose from these:

- Weaves, such as twill, tabby, tapestry, brocade, pile.
- Knitted.
- Nonwoven.
- Natural fibers.
- Manufactured fibers.
- Combinations of natural and manufactured fibers.
- Printed and woven designs.
- Water-repellent or other finish.

B.3 Many designs or patterns are created in fabric by means other than weaving—batik, stencil, tie-dye, and silk screen are a few of these. Select one method and create a simple design or an all-over pattern. Use it on a shirt, or other clothing, or a plain piece of fabric.

B.4 Look in stores, magazines, newspapers, craft shows, and fairs to find examples of jewelry and ornaments that have been handmade or could be handmade. Make a list of techniques, such as crocheting, warp wrapping, knotting, weaving, or working in metal, clay, beads, or natural materials. Learn one technique and create your own piece of jewelry or hair ornament.

C.1 Find out what looks best on you. With friends, make full-size silhouettes of each other by drawing around the outlines of your body. Cut from plain paper different shapes of dresses, skirts, pants, jackets, and blouses, and place them against each silhouette. Decide which looks best on each silhouette.

or

Measure your own face, then draw your face in actual size on a piece of paper. Make several different styles of hair out of heavy paper and try them fitted around the drawing of your face. Decide which ones look best on you.

or

In front of a mirror, place several large pieces of colored paper or fabric under your chin and around the drawing of your face. Decide which colors are best for your skin, hair, and eyes.

C.2 Create a clothing accessory for yourself, such as a jacket, a vest, a belt, a scarf, or a hat, in a technique that you have learned: sewing, knitting, crocheting, or embroidering.

• •

_____
Date badge completed

_____
My signature

_____
Leader's signature

• 149 •

BOOKS

1 Explore your local library's resources. Prepare a brochure about the library for new residents, a poster to encourage greater use of the library, or an advertising flier to let the community know what the library has to offer. Be sure to include information on the kind of books, tapes and records, exhibits and special programs, newspapers, magazines, and audiovisuals available for children and adults. Find out what help is available and what you can borrow from the library besides books.

2 Find out about the folktales, stories, poems, plays, and/or writers of a culture other than your own. You may discover this information by talking to someone from that culture, by looking in the library, or by watching a special television show. Share what you have learned by acting out one or more of the stories or folktales; telling about one or more of the writers of that culture; reading one of the stories, poems, or folktales to your Girl Scout group or another audience; or creating puppets for one of the tales and putting on a puppet show for a group.

3 Read a book especially for this badge. After reading, find a way to let others know about the book.

or

Write up an annotated list of at least ten books you believe a girl your age would like to read. (An annotated list includes title, author, publisher, and a short description of each book.) Include different kinds of books in your list. Be sure you have read them.

4 Write one of the following:
   • An original short story.
   • A different ending to a story or play you already know.

5 Design a set of book covers for three books or stories.

or

Create illustrations for a familiar story, folktale, or poem.

6 Ask your school or community librarian to show you books illustrated by five children's artists, particularly Caldecott Medal winners.

INTERNATIONAL CHILDREN'S BOOK DAY

April 2nd is International Children's Book Day. This day was chosen because a very famous author of children's fairy tales and stories was born on this day in 1805. Two of his most famous stories are "The Ugly Duckling" and "The Emperor's New Clothes." Can you unscramble his name below?

SHAN SCHARTINI DREANNES

_____   _____   _____

Answer: Hans Christian Andersen

What can you do to celebrate International Children's Book Day?

_____

_____

Borrow the books and make a troop display, if possible.

or

Look at the illustrations of three or more nursery rhymes or ABC books to see which ones you think a little child would enjoy. Create your own illustrated ABC book for a child.

7 Collect books, paperbacks, and magazines appropriate for one age level. See if you could give them to a library at a camp, nursing home, youth shelter, well-baby clinic, day-care center, or veterans' hospital.

or

Make an audiotape of books, magazine articles, jokes, riddles, poetry, or short stories that you can give to someone who may not be able to read at the present time.

8 Set up a schedule with other Girl Scout members to bring books from your local library in large print, braille, or on tape to someone who will enjoy them.

or

Volunteer to work at your local library.

9 As a project, collect books that are appropriate for children and young people and set up a lending library for your own troop or group or for several troops in your area. Work out a plan for girls to take turns being librarian. Volunteer to help someone learn to read better.

10 Find out about careers with books. You might visit with an author, poet, illustrator, editor, or book publisher. Draw a diagram of how a book gets from the idea stage to the printed page. Visit a publishing house, if possible.

11 Read a variety of stories, poems, or folktales that reflect life in the United States in the past. What do these stories tell you about the way people lived, what kind of houses they lived in, what they wore, and what they ate? Try to discover whether the stories give an accurate or a fictionalized picture of the past. Draw a large map of the United States and place drawings, authors, and books in various parts of the country to make a diorama of what you've read.

12 Read a long poem and a short poem that you like. Then do one of these activities.

- Find a piece of artwork, do a floral arrangement, or select a piece of music that would go with one of the poems.
- Read several other poems by the same poet.
- Write your own poetry and identify the form you are using: limerick, jingle, haiku, narrative, etc.

There once was a Junior Girl Scout,
Who only knew how to shout,
She started a riot,
'Cause she couldn't be quiet,
So now all she does is pout!

Try writing your own limerick!

13 Find out from your local librarian or school librarian a list of Newbery Award–winning books. If you have not read any of these books, read at least one. Then, make a decorative bookmark, book poster, or promotional flier about Newbery books.

or

In a newspaper or other source from your community, read reviews of new books for your age level. Check one of these books out of the library, read it, and review it yourself. Was your review similar to or different from the review you read?

14 Learn how to mend books and do a simple bookbinding of something you have written for this badge.

15 Write your own book about Girl Scouting for someone who is a new member. Let girls who want to learn about Girl Scouts read it. Base some of your information on Chapter 1 of the *Junior Girl Scout Handbook*.

16 Ask your leader for a copy of the Contemporary Issues booklet, *Right to Read: Literacy*, look through the activities and plan what you can do to encourage reading.

_____
Date badge completed

_____
My signature

_____
Leader's signature

CERAMICS
AND CLAY

. . . .

COMPLETE SIX ACTIVITIES.

1 With a lump of clay, demonstrate the difference between modeling and carving.

2 From a plaster block, create a three-dimensional figure, or a bas-relief. Be able to demonstrate or explain how plaster is mixed and poured into the mold.

3 Learn about various types of ceramic clay and glazes. Find out how an unfinished piece of pottery is kept damp and how it is cared for between working periods.

4 Learn about kilns, the ovens used for hardening clay. Fire a clay piece you have made in a kiln or oven.

or

Help build a simple outdoor kiln for troop, camp, school, or community use.

or

Learn how a kiln is stacked, and if possible, help stack one.

5 Make a piece of pottery, using the coil method, and finish it with a glaze.

6 Make a tile or pottery piece (box, etc.), using the slab method. Apply a design in slip, graffito, incising carving, or painted design. See page 245 for definitions. If possible, glaze and fire it.

7 Make a figure or form in clay. If possible, glaze and have it fired. Be able to explain the difference between ceramics and pottery.

8 Visit a studio where you can observe a potter at work, such as a commercial pottery, or a professional potter's studio. Ask questions about the kind of work being done, and also about the way the people became involved in this career and the kinds of training they received.

9 Collect pictures of pottery or ceramics, read about these works or the artists who created them, and be able to explain something about the items and why you selected them.

10 Find pictures or examples of pottery that is used today. Select some that you feel are both beautiful and useful. Be able to tell something about the different kinds of pottery in use today.

11 Find examples of folk sculpture or folk pottery. Look for pictures in magazines and books, or sketch what you see in museums or exhibits. Choose three different examples to show your troop or group, to display at another Girl Scout gathering, or to show to your friends. These examples can be from three countries outside the United States, three regions within the United States, or a combination. Label each as to where it is found and the material used.

Date badge completed

My signature

Leader's signature

COMMUNICATION ARTS

COMPLETE ANY SIX ACTIVITIES.

For definitions of special terms, see "Helps and Resources," page 245.

1 Through words, images, and/or colors, communicate an idea you want to get across. Show or read your piece to others. Did they get your message? If not, what could you change so that they do get your message?

2 Put together a collage or poster with examples of communications, such as semaphore, braille, sign language, signal flags, international road signs, distress signals, or referee's signals. Learn one set of the above examples and teach it to someone else.

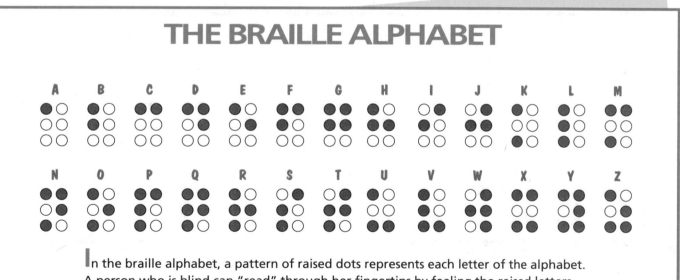

THE BRAILLE ALPHABET

In the braille alphabet, a pattern of raised dots represents each letter of the alphabet. A person who is blind can "read" through her fingertips by feeling the raised letters. Above is an alphabet written in braille. The colored dots represent the raised dots. If you poke a pin or pen point through the back of each of the colored dots, you can "raise" the letters. Try feeling the pattern with your fingers. Now try to write your own coded message in the braille alphabet.

3 Write a short news story about an event in your school or troop. Submit it to the school newspaper or your Girl Scout council bulletin.

4 Participate in a debate, or prepare and give a two-minute speech on a favorite subject.

or

Develop a publicity campaign for a candidate of your choice in a make-believe election.

5 Read a play to discover how plays communicate differently from stories or poems. Write a short play, puppet show, Girl Scouts' Own, radio show, or other dramatic performance.

6 With a still, movie, or video camera, take pictures that tell a story without the need for words. Select two different stories to tell. Some ideas are:

A rainstorm, snowstorm, or other event in nature; an example of pollution or other environmental concern; or something that makes you feel happy or that makes you laugh.

7 Make a list of a variety of advertising and commercial designs you see in a week. Include such things as billboards, posters, signs, and packages. Look at them to see how they use color, lettering, and space; decide which are best. Choose a theme and make a poster that gets its message across without many words.

or

Take photographs that can be used to advertise something. Try at least two of the ones listed below. Do several views of each and decide on the one that you think will most likely sell the item.

• A house, farm, store, or business for sale.
• New or used carpentry, plumbing, or kitchen tools.
• A spot to visit or a site to see.
• A used car, bicycle, motorcycle, trailer, camper, or motorbike.
• A handmade item.
• Shoes, boots, sneakers, moccasins, or sandals.

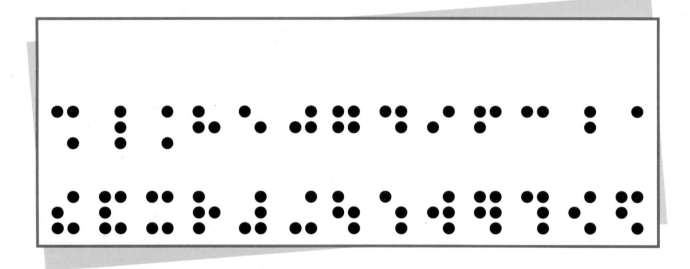

8 Collect examples or draw familiar symbols and logos that immediately convey a message. Arrange these in poster form. Design a logo for yourself, to print on your stationery, book covers, etc.; for your troop, as an identifying symbol; or for a special event that is happening in your school or Girl Scout council.

9 After looking through several magazines, put together your own magazine of at least 16 pages showing how magazines use words and pictures together.

10 Look through several books that combine pictures with words. Decide which books must have both pictures and words, and which ones could have used only pictures or only words. Create one of the following: a travel book, an art book, or a child's beginning reader.

11 Movies, television, and slide shows also use words and pictures. Tell how your favorite movie, television show, or slide show combines words and pictures to get the message across. Do a storyboard (a plan showing a drawing of each picture and words that go with it) for a two-minute movie, television short, or slide show that shows how you would use pictures and words together.

12 If possible, visit a radio or television station. Visit the studios and find out how a show is produced. Listen to several radio shows. Create the script, sound effects, and format for a news program, a disc jockey program, an interview talk show, or another kind of program you choose.

or

Investigate ham radio and how it works. Learn how to get a license. If possible, see a ham radio in operation. Prepare a short broadcast for a ham radio operator to give when seeking help in a disaster.

13 After doing some of the other requirements for this badge, find out about careers in communications. Choose one and explain why it could be an interesting job.

14 Show that you have discovered the kinds of communications needed in public relations promotional work by outlining what you would plan for one of the following:
- A party at the opening of an art exhibit to introduce a new artist to the community.
- A tour of your community to encourage business people to open shops in the area.
- A workshop to show parents and children the new facilities at the science center.
- A ceremony for an awards presentation in your troop or group.
- A conference for international visitors, to introduce them to your community.

Date badge completed

My signature

Leader's signature

DANCE

. . . .

COMPLETE SIX ACTIVITIES.

1 Select two different kinds of music and dance to them.

2 Demonstrate in body movements at least two of the following:
   • The feelings that a particular piece of music brings out in you.
   • The ways people move (athletes, waiters, young people, old people, conductors, cooks, traffic directors, etc.).
   • An expression of nature, such as trees moving in the wind; a story; movements of machines; or a dramatic situation, such as missing a train, saying goodbye to someone, or meeting old friends.

   Then make up a dance by yourself, with a partner, or with a group, using these movements.

3 Attend a dance concert or a dance class. Make an appointment first, and after the concert, talk to the performers or the teachers about their work, using questions you prepared before going.

4 Participate in a dance program either as a soloist or as part of a group. Share your experience with others.

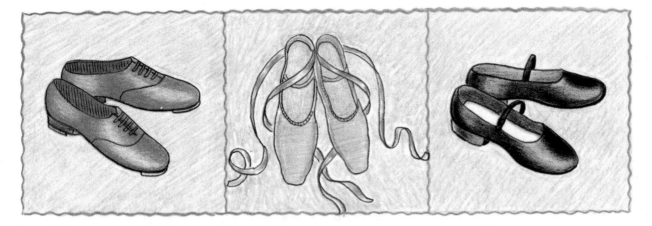

5 Learn about three different types of dances and demonstrate to your troop/group or to others how to do them.

6 Explore the dance of three countries other than your own. Choose at least one country in another continent. Investigate what the dance means in that culture, and something about the costumes, seasons, or festivities that might be associated with it. Demonstrate what you have found out.

7 Listen to several recordings of dance music. Using steps you know, create a new dance to go with at least two types of music. You may want to use percussion instruments, such as tambourines or drums, with one of the dances.

8 With your troop/group or others, hold a party that includes dancing. You may teach a new dance, or plan well-known dances. Try to include most of the guests in the dancing.

9 Find out more about careers in dance. Invite someone to visit your troop/group or visit a dance studio or theatrical production. Some possible careers to investigate are dance instruction, choreography, costume design, and aerobic dance instruction or the business side of theatrical or dance company management and accounting.

Date badge completed

My signature

Leader's signature

DRAWING AND PAINTING

1 Explore different types of media: paints, crayons, pastels and chalk, felt-tip markers, colored pencils, and charcoal. Choose three from this list and make three different pictures of the same thing using a different medium each time. How does the use of different media change the picture?

2 Learn the primary and secondary colors. Practice mixing primary and secondary colors to make new colors. Make a picture that uses only the colors you have created.

3 Experiment with two different painting techniques. You can choose from the following: finger painting, where you use your fingers instead of brushes; sponge painting, in which you use sponges or pieces of sponge instead of brushes; string painting, where you dip string in paint and make a design on your paper with the wet string; or spatter painting, in which you put a toothbrush in paint and knock it against a small screen or hard edge to "spatter" the paint on paper. Try making a painting using a technique that you invent. Show your paintings to others.

4 Make two pictures that show different uses of line. Experiment with pencils, felt-tip markers, crayons, or chalks to get different kinds of lines: thick or thin, straight, curved, broken, horizontal, vertical, and diagonal. Color in between the lines if you choose.

5 Use shapes to make a picture. Look at an object or scene and try to find the basic shapes: triangle, circle, square, rectangle, etc. What shapes would you use to make a human being? What shapes would you use to make a flower?

6 Create two pictures in which you show many shades of the same color. What do darker shades do? What do lighter shades do? How can you use color to make something appear closer or farther away in your picture?

7 Find out about perspective. Look at something far away. Measure it with your fingers or a ruler. How big is it? What happens if you move closer to the object? How can you show this on paper? Draw or paint a picture in which you use perspective.

8 Murals are pictures painted on walls. Murals usually tell a story in a series of scenes and may be painted by groups of artists. You can try making a mural using a long roll of white or butcher paper. Cover the floor with newspapers. Stretch your paper on top of them. Decide with your Girl Scout troop or group or others what the design of your mural will be. Then, start painting. Each painter may be responsible for her own section or painters can work together on each part before starting on the next.

*9 Create your own work of art using all the different things you have learned in the activities in this badge. Share your work with others, or create a gallery or art show where you can display your work and those of others.

• •

_____

Date badge completed

_____

My signature

_____

Leader's signature

FOLK ARTS

For definitions of special terms, see "Helps and Resources," page 245.

1 Draw or paint a picture of yourself or of your whole family, as it might have been done by an artist before cameras were invented. Put some things in the background that are very special about you or your family.

or

Look at some old photographs of your family or groups of people. Compare them with some recent ones of yourself, your friends, or other people. Are there differences in the poses, the clothes, the expressions? What kinds of feelings do you get about the people in the pictures? Write a short story about what the pictures tell you.

2 Learn something about the tradition of storytelling. If possible, get together with someone who is a good storyteller and learn some of the special ways to make your audience want to keep listening. Read a fairy tale, myth, or legend that you like and be able to tell it to a group, perhaps as part of a ceremony or special event.

3 Learn a folk dance from your part of the country or one from a country that interests you. Teach it to some friends. Put together a simple costume or part of a costume and find an opportunity to perform your dance for someone else.

or

Learn a folk song or ballad that tells a story about people, a place, or events. Be able to explain the story behind the song and teach the words to your friends, patrol, troop, or group. If you like, design actions to match the words and perform for someone.

4 Find out how to make a whistle, drum, or other folk instrument. Make one and demonstrate its use to your troop or friends.

or

Learn about folk instruments and the people who made them. Tell others about the traditional ways people have used the instruments. Show pictures or drawings of the instruments during your presentation.

In the 1700s, silhouettes were a popular form of art. A silhouette is a shadow portrait, usually of someone's profile. Ask a friend to help you make your own silhouette. Attach a sheet of white paper to a wall or door. Stand or sit between the paper and a lamp or flashlight. Your profile should appear on the paper. Ask your friend to carefully trace the outline of the shadow. Do not move while she is tracing. Carefully cut out the outline. Now you have your silhouette. You can attach this silhouette to dark paper or trace around this silhouette onto black or dark paper and attach the dark silhouette to light paper.

5 Choose a section of our country and find out about the folk toys made there long ago and today. Make a folk toy or game and plan to share it with a special child or friend.

or

Find out about puppets from several countries. Design and make a puppet. Plan a puppet show and have your puppet act out a folktale or legend or your own play.

6 Look for examples and pictures of traditional folk arts from at least three countries. Try a project for which you can find the instructions or which someone could teach you. Some ideas might be: quilling, origami, pysanky eggs, piñatas, ceremonial masks, jewelry, traditional foods, and ceremonies.

7 Learn how to do a folk art well enough to teach others, such as a group of younger Girl Scouts. You might learn how to make quilts or baskets or learn how to paint traditional designs on fabric or wood or some other craft. Or try working on a large project that requires lots of helping hands, such as a taffy pull, kite flying festival, or a troop/group quilt.

or

Create your own new folk art project.

8 Many useful and decorative things that are now machine-made and easily found in stores were once all handmade. Some examples are dishes, pottery, brooms, baskets, candles, soap, paper, thread, cloth, and dyes for clothing. Add other things you can think of to this list and think about the materials it would take to make each. Are these materials easy to find? Would using them be harmful to the environment? Would making some of these things involve special health and safety procedures today?

Make one of the items from your list.

9 Find some articles belonging to your family that have been passed along from person to person. Share these in some way with your friends, troop, or group, explaining what the articles are and where they came from.

or

Visit a place near you where antiques, historical crafts, or collections of folk art are on display. You might visit restorations, museums, or places designated as historic landmarks. Find out how one or two of the items you see were used in the past.

10 Find directions and recipes for some of the following:

- Dried fruits.
- Herb teas.
- Traditional sourdough or herb breads.
- Apple dolls.
- Dried flower arrangements.
- Holiday decorations.
- Wok cooking.

Perhaps an older friend or adult might enjoy working with you. Try at least one project.

_____
Date badge completed

_____
My signature

_____
Leader's signature

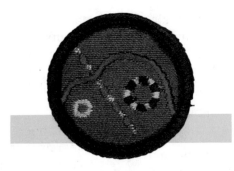

JEWELER

COMPLETE FIVE ACTIVITIES, INCLUDING THE ONE STARRED. SEE "HELPS AND RESOURCES," PAGE 245, FOR FURTHER IDEAS ON HOW TO DO THE PROJECTS.

*1 Make two pieces of jewelry using materials that are not precious metals or gems. Some ideas are:

HANDMADE BEADS Form beads from papier-mâché, handmade clay, colorful magazine pages, wrapping paper, or aluminum foil.

HARDWARE Use bits of hardware such as screws, nuts, washers, wire, and chains.

MACRAMÉ Knot string and other cords into decorative patterns. Interweave beads, sanded pieces of wood, and shells to create unique macramé jewelry.

PAPER Paint or draw designs on pieces of paper. Several pieces can be glued together.

Protect and harden the finished designs with a clear varnish. Safety pins can be glued to backs to make pins, holes can be punched to attach the pieces to necklaces, and hair pins or barrettes can be attached to make hair ornaments.

or

Create and carry out a jewelry project of your own.

2 Learn about the jewelry of four different cultures—for example, an American Indian culture, one of the cultures within an African country, a European culture, or a South American culture. Describe the materials used, the styles, and their customs and traditions for wearing jewelry. If possible, find pictures of the type of jewelry worn in each culture. Deliver a brief presentation on your findings.

3 Learn about the different jewelry-making techniques of soldering, casting, hammering, and molding. If possible, talk to a jeweler who uses one or more of those techniques.

4 Visit a museum or gallery exhibit of jewelry. Take an organized tour of the exhibit or ask the curator to explain it to you.

5 Make a piece of jewelry out of organic material (something found in nature). You can combine a variety of colors, shapes and textures by using shells, stones, seeds, and other material you find on an outdoor scavenger hunt.

6 Create a piece of jewelry out of clay. When the clay dries, you may paint it or bake and glaze it if you like.

7 Make a jewelry box for your jewelry. You can decoupage a cigar box or other small wooden box, make a box out of papier-mâché, or decorate a small basket with pieces of discarded jewelry, pearls, beads, or shells.

8 Learn about the different kinds of stones and minerals that are used in jewelry. Select one to learn more about. For example, you might learn more about your birthstone.

9 Find out about the symbolism of different kinds of jewelry, such as wedding bands or friendship bracelets. Make a piece of jewelry to give to someone else as a symbol of your friendship.

Date badge completed

My signature

Leader's signature

MUSICIAN

COMPLETE SEVEN ACTIVITIES, INCLUDING THE ONE STARRED.

1 Writing music is an art that requires much skill and training, but you can start in fairly simple ways.

If you play an instrument, write a simple melody for that instrument of at least eight measures. Try to notate your piece using symbols for key, tempo, and dynamics and teach it to someone else.

or

Make up words and music for a nonsense song about something funny that happened in your troop or at camp.

or

Do your own variation of a popular song.

2 Finding out about the background of a piece of music helps us appreciate the music today. Do one of the following:

• Find out about the life and works of a living composer or performer. Using tapes or records, give a 30-minute program to tell others about the musician.

• Learn about early singing groups—minstrels, troubadours, minnesingers, and meistersingers. (See "Helps and Resources" Section, page 246, for definitions.) Sing at least one song from this period, and explain about the group, the time, and the country where it was found.

• Listen to a musical composition that tells a story. Find out all you can about the music and the composer; then try to sell the recording to your leader or another adult by a simulated television commercial or movie advertisement.

3 Listen to and watch an opera or operetta on television. Listen for the story idea, how much is sung, or spoken, and in what language, how the voices are related to the characters, who the composer was, and when she or he lived. Be able to tell the story of the opera or operetta to a group. Illustrate your talk in some manner.

or

Learn to sing a ballad. Dramatize it or make a shadowgraph or puppet show of it.

or

Listen to and see a ballet or concert, live or on television. Choose several other pieces of music that you feel would be appropriate as dances and create a dance for one of them.

*4 Expand your knowledge of songs by learning at least three new songs well enough to perform them. Be able to tell something about your songs.

5 Do a poster for a Girl Scout or other group to show the arrangements of instruments in an orchestra. Identify the instruments and the section to which they belong.

or

Make a bulletin board display or exhibit depicting a famous composer, an era in musical history, or the history of your instrument.

6 Participate in a musical performance using your musical skills in at least one of the following: a Girl Scouts' Own, an individual instrument or voice recital, a group performance, a musical extravaganza, or a neighborhood or community musical event.

7 Share your musical knowledge. Learn three action songs suitable for young children. Teach them to younger Girl Scouts or to a school or church group.

or

Teach the children how to make simple rhythm instruments and play them.

8 Have a musical sharing afternoon or evening with a senior citizen's group, where you and other people share favorite songs or instrumental favorites.

9 Program music is orchestral music with a theme or story. Pretend that you are selecting the music for a concert for people who like one of the things listed below. Give the

name of the music and the composer, and possibly a recording of your selections.

• The sea or rivers.
• Urban cities.
• Woods or mountains.
• Fields or meadows.
• A circus or festival.
• Marches or parades.

10 Choose three pieces of music heard in concerts or on radio, television, or recordings that show the influence of a country outside the United States. Play or sing them for your troop or group and be able to explain what these influences are.

11 Many folk songs have a message or a story. Listen to some folk songs and share their stories with your troop/group.

• •

_____
Date badge completed

_____
My signature

_____
Leader's signature

MUSIC
LOVER

• •

COMPLETE FIVE ACTIVITIES.

1 Choose a favorite piece of music and create a rhythmic beat to go with it. Use a rhythm instrument you have made or select a variety of items that will give you the tone and sound you want. If possible, tape a performance of your piece with its accompaniment and see if others can guess the materials used for the sound.

2 Listen to several records and choose one you feel is good for dancing. Create a dance that you and a group can do in time with the music.

or

Learn two singing games and play them with your troop or teach them to others.

3 Listen to a piece of music and explain what the music says to you by doing one of the following:

• Create a design or picture with paint.

or

• Create a poem that the music inspires.

4 Learn three songs well enough to sing them to a group or to teach others.

5 Learn folk songs from five different countries on three different continents. Learn as much as you can about these songs. Create an illustration that you feel might go with two of the songs in a songbook.

Take a stick or ruler and tie a cord around one end. String the cord with items that make sounds when shaken: beads, shells, pieces of metal, bottle caps, small bells, or other small hard things. Use this as a rhythm instrument. Try adding objects or taking some away to make different sounds.

6 Interview a musician (or a music teacher). Find out why that person chose music as a career. Learn what preparation was necessary and what the person enjoys about her/his career. Write up a career interview with drawings to tell about that career.

7 Find three songs on records or in a music book that were popular music in another period of history and that tell something about that period.

8 Have listening sessions, alone or with others, to hear records or tapes, a concert on television or radio, or a live concert. Listen to at least two of the following: a symphony, musical comedy, opera or operetta, chamber music, jazz, rap, blues, popular or rock music, country, or gospel. Try to get a variety of large and small orchestras, single instruments, voices, choruses.

9 Participate in a performance as a soloist or as part of a group in a vocal or instrumental concert or performance. After the concert, share with others what you know about one of the pieces performed or what is special about your instrument.

10 Read about tools in Chapter 4 of the *Junior Girl Scout Handbook* and make an instrument that works.

Date badge completed

My signature

Leader's signature

PHOTOGRAPHY

*1 Select a camera that you will be able to use to do this badge. Learn everything you can about that camera. Read instructions carefully or have someone familiar with the camera show you how to work it properly. Learn what it can and cannot do. Be able to explain its use to someone else.

2 All cameras require film. Find out about types of film available for cameras today. There is black and white film, color film for slides or prints, Polaroid film, disk film, fast film, slow film. After studying the factors involved in each type, find pictures that would illustrate the kind of photo you might take with at least three types of film.

3 Light is the key element in photography. Try this to see how reaction to light leaves an image. Do this with light-sensitive paper that you can get at a crafts supply store. Follow the instructions on the paper.

   a Create a sun print using natural forms and sunlight. To do this, put a flat object on light-sensitive paper. Place a sheet of glass over the object. Expose to sunlight until the paper turns dark.

b Create a photogram design using cut-outs or shapes of miscellaneous items that will create a good composition. A photogram is similar to a sunprint except that you make an arrangement of objects in a design on the photographic paper. Often this is exposed to indoor light.

4 Photography helps us learn to see things we might otherwise overlook. Take four pictures that illustrate each of these:

    a Shape.

    b Lines.

    c Rhythm.

    d Texture.

5 Like painting, good photography is based on principles of art: of balance, proportion, scale, line, planes, etc. Take three pictures that use some of these principles.

6 Colors can create a mood or feeling. Some people say that reds and oranges are exciting and shades of blue are soothing. Take color pictures that create the mood of four of the following:

Happiness

Loneliness

Sadness

Pride

Fun

Anger

Confusion

Boredom

Fear

7 Take at least four pictures that tell a story, or illustrate a children's book or poem. Set them up in an exhibit for others to see, or prepare a slide show to share with your group.

8 Make a pinhole camera and give a demonstration of how it works (see page 246 for instructions). Share this with a group of younger Girl Scouts.

or

Visit a film developing lab to see how film is developed and how enlargements are made. Share this information with your group.

9 Look for the work of some famous photographers. Attend a photography exhibit if you can. Select two of your best photographs, have them enlarged, and mount them and display them in an exhibit in your troop, neighborhood, or council.

10 Learn how to maintain, clean, and store your camera.

11 Do one of the following activities:

    a Pick a tree, a building, a monument or other outdoor object in your community and take a series of photographs at different times of day or in different types of weather. Notice what happens to light and shadow in your photographs.

    b Pick a shape—a triangle, square, circle, and take a series of photographs of everything you can find outdoors in your community that contains this shape. Mount your photographs and see if others can find the common theme.

_____

Date badge completed

_____

My signature

_____

Leader's signature

POPULAR ARTS

1 Find seven examples of symbols, such as the American eagle. Draw some simple shapes that could be used for symbols of things familiar to you. Design your own coat of arms using symbols to depict yourself or your family. See if others can guess the meaning of your symbols.

or

Look for pictures of symbols/designs and find out all you can about the people for whom these symbols were or are important. Here are some things to look at: American Indian jewelry, Early American crewel work, West African basket designs, Norwegian rosemaling, Pennsylvania Dutch hex signs and quilts, Chinese brush painting, stained glass windows, masks and headdresses, holiday ornaments, rugs, and tapestries. Create a poster that shows the symbols you have collected and where they originated.

2 Look around your home, school, stores, or community to see how many things you can find that have been decorated by hand. Find, through pictures or actual examples, several items, such as decorated tinware (tole painting), scrimshaw, painted furniture, painted wooden objects (boxes, etc.), decorated chinaware or pottery, stenciled walls and floors, decorative carvings for interior walls or windows, or decorated textiles. Choose one to learn more about. If possible, find someone to teach you. Create one work of art with your decoration.

or

Visit a folk art museum or restoration where you can see examples of the folk arts listed above. Learn from booklets or demonstrations and create one art piece.

3 Learn about quilting terms and techniques. What are patchwork or pieced designs, appliqué, trapunto, tufting, embroidery, and quilting? Learn how to cut out shapes for pieced designs and appliqué, and how to plan and transfer designs onto fabric for other processes. Do samples and diagrams so that you can teach others.

4 Make a sampler to demonstrate your skill in one of the following. Find someone to teach you the skill if you need help.

• Needlepoint.
• Crewel work.
• Knitting.
• Knotting (macramé).
• Cross-stitching.
• Crocheting.

5 Look for examples of woven materials and pictures of looms from different areas of our country and other parts of the world, such as Africa, South America, Asia, Europe, Australia, and the Pacific Islands (Oceania). Notice the patterns and colors, and, if you can, the texture. What do the colors and designs tell you about the way of life of the people? How do the looms relate to the finished fabric? Create a small, handmade loom and weave something.

or

Visit a place where you can see weaving and looms. Find out about simple looms you can make yourself. Learn about several types of weaving and the terms used to describe weaving. Here are some to start thinking about: warp and weft (or woof), tabby weave, pattern weaving, tapestry weaving, shuttle, loom, heddles. Add others that you can find. Get together with your patrol or badge group and find a way to make, or have someone help you make, a loom you can share and add to the troop equipment.

6 Learn tales and legends from three countries. Using these tales and legends, create a puppet show, illustrate a booklet, or conduct a storytelling hour for younger children.

7 Find out about careers in arts and crafts. Find out if your community contains apprenticeship or guild programs in woodworking, stained glass, decorative painting, furniture refinishing, decorative tile and ceramics, or other crafts. Visit a studio or workshop, or have a professional visit your troop/group to demonstrate her craft.

8 Draw or find pictures of five instruments that accompany folk music of another country. Be able to demonstrate or play recordings of some of these instruments, or imitate the sound with your own instrument.

9 Learn five additional folk songs from five countries on three different continents and be able to explain something about them and what they mean in that culture.

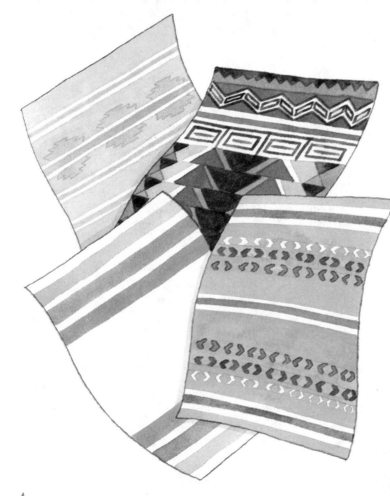

Date badge completed

My signature

Leader's signature

PRINTS AND GRAPHICS

1 Make two transfer prints with leaves, stones, bark, or other natural materials.

2 Make four rubbings of something raised or engraved, such as carved wood, a coin, a design on an iron gate, a leaf, a brick, a stone, a manhole cover, or a rubber floor mat.

3 Make a relief print by cutting a design into an eraser, potato, or turnip, or by gluing a felt, rubber, or cardboard design to heavy cardboard or a block of wood.

4 Create a design and cut a stencil for it. Demonstrate the safe way to use a stencil knife. Print your stenciled design on paper or fabric.

5 Learn about silk screening. Create a design that can be silk screened, and print your design on paper or cloth.

6 Learn how to do a linoleum block print. Create the design; cut, and print one for a greeting card, bookplate, gift wrapping, or other project of your choice.

7 Experiment with at least two kinds of prints, such as: stamp or impression, spatter prints, sun prints. Try to create a border design, an all-over design, and a design in two colors. Make one finished print to use for some purpose.

*8 Make a scrapbook of the different prints you have made, label each, and choose a suitable mat and frame for one of your prints to use in your home or give as a gift, or use one of your print designs as a wall hanging.

9 Visit an exhibit that includes several kinds of prints. Try to visit a printmaker and see her at work. Ask about the kind of work she does and why she chose this occupation.

10 Use your printmaking skills to carry out a service project, such as making notepaper, cards, or bookplates for a church or other organization, programs or posters for some event, curtains for a day-care center, or some other project of your choice.

11 By searching through books, magazines, newspapers, or through museum, print, or art collections, discover five different examples of how prints are used in countries outside the United States. Be able to explain the technique and something that makes the designs unique.

or

Find out how stenciling was used by the earliest European immigrants in this country.

Be able to explain and illustrate at least two examples, such as Hitchcock or other stenciled furniture, wallpapers, floors, textiles, or tileware.

or

Collect pictures made by five historical or contemporary printmakers. Arrange an exhibit and give the artists' names, periods or dates, and the techniques used.

12 Explore the printing processes as they apply to the printing of books. Find out about type and how it was used in the early days of the printing press. Find four different styles of typeface in magazines or newspapers. Compare them to see in what kinds of books, advertisements, or posters they would work best. Choose one you like best and design a page of a book, including the typeface, an illustration (line drawing or photograph), and borders—or choose one and design three slides that might open a filmstrip or slide show giving title, credits, and some line design.

_____
Date badge completed

_____
My signature

_____
Leader's signature

TEXTILES
AND FIBERS

COMPLETE FIVE ACTIVITIES: ONE ACTIVITY IN SECTION A, THREE ACTIVITIES IN ONE CATEGORY OF SECTION B, AND ONE ACTIVITY IN SECTION C.

There are many different kinds of textile arts that use yarns, threads, and fibers. For definitions of special terms, see "Helps and Resources," pages 246–247.

A.1 Gather samples or pictures of five types of weaving, embroidery, crewelwork, needlepoint, hemstitching, or printed batik-dyed fabric. Make a display of your collection and label each example.

or

Learn about five distinctive types of textiles, weaving, and needlework from other countries. Show samples or pictures and share your knowledge with your troop or friends.

A.2 Visit a museum, a historical restoration, or an exhibit and identify at least five types of needlework or textiles in clothes or household articles of previous years. Are they different from what we use today? How?

or

Attend a needlework or textiles show or demonstration. Talk to the people who do the weaving or needlework. Think about what you would like to make and what you would need to learn beforehand.

A.3 Visit a textile mill and see how fabrics are produced. Discuss the differences between handmade and machine-made fabrics. Find out about five different fibers from which textiles are made and be able to explain something about each.

B.1 Weaving—do at least three of the following:
- Weave something on a cardboard loom.
- Do a tapestry weaving on a cardboard or other type of loom.
- Make and thread a simple loom (such as a back-strap or flat frame). Demonstrate how to use it and weave something on it.
- On a simple loom, experiment with different textures, using various materials for warp and weft.
- Make a belt with finger weaving tube weaving, or some other type of narrow weaving.
- Create a basket in a woven, coil, braided, or twining technique.

CONNECT THE KNOT WITH ITS NAME

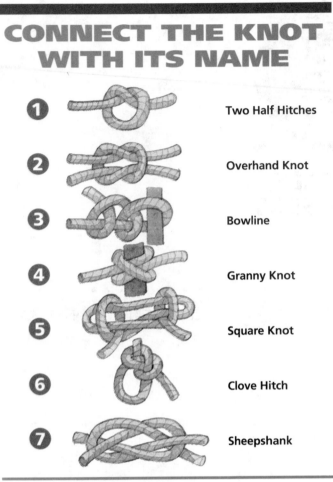

1 Two Half Hitches

2 Overhand Knot

3 Bowline

4 Granny Knot

5 Square Knot

6 Clove Hitch

7 Sheepshank

Answers: 1-Overhead knot, 2-Square knot, 3-Two half hitches, 4-Colver hitch, 5-Sheepshank, 6-Bowline, 7-Granny knot

B.2 Knitting, crocheting, or macramé — do at least three of the following:

- Demonstrate the following knots: overhand, square, two half hitches, clove hitch, lark's head, sheepshank, bowline, taut line hitch, sheet bend, granny knot. Make a macramé sampler experimenting with colors, beads, textures, and several knots.
- Macramé a flat item, such as a place mat, doormat, or wall hanging.
- Do a simple macramé project, such as a belt or bookmark, using only square knots in an even and precise pattern.
- Create your own macramé, knit, or crochet design for a gift, an item for your home, or for camp equipment.

- In knitting, learn to cast on, bind off, knit, purl, and yarn over. Select a suitable yarn and pattern and knit a small garment or accessory.
- In crocheting, learn to start, finish, and do chain, single crochet, double crochet, and afghan stitches. Select a suitable thread or yarn and pattern, and crochet one small article.

B.3 Printed textiles — do at least three of the following:

- Create two simple border designs for a piece of fabric.
- Design and cut a stencil, and using one color, decorate some useful item.
- Cut a linoleum block and print a one-color design on some household item or garment.
- Learn about commercial dyes. Use one to dye or tint an article. Learn about textile paints.
- Make a tie-dyed article, using at least two kinds of tying but only one dye bath.

B.4 Hooking, braiding, or quilting — do at least three of the following:

- Learn something about hooked rugs and their history.
- Hook a small article, such as a chair seat or a pillow top.
- Learn something about making braided rugs from a variety of materials. Make a small braided piece for a chair, a bench, or a footstool.
- Gather several pictures or samples of quilts, including pieced, embroidered, appliquéd, or ornamental quilting.
- Make a quilt square of any type.
- Find out about different types of quilts. Compare old and new quilts. Make a small quilted article.

B.5 Embroidery and needlepoint — do at least three of the following:

- Learn to do eight of the following stitches and create a sampler to display your accomplishments: outline stitch, chain stitch, cross-stitch, back stitch, blanket stitch, satin stitch, darning stitch, French knot, lazy daisy, couching.

- Using five stitches you know, create your own picture or wall hanging, or decorate a garment or a household article.
- Work out a design on graph paper for counted thread work. Use the design to make a small piece of needlepoint or cross-stitch.
- Convert a design or your initials to graph paper and show four ways that graph designs can be used (such as cross-stitch).

C.1 For whatever technique you choose, learn about the kinds of tools, fibers, equipment, thread, needles, scissors, and hoops you would need for your own equipment kit.

C.2 Find out about artists or specific styles in the technique you choose. Visit artists and see their work in progress if possible.

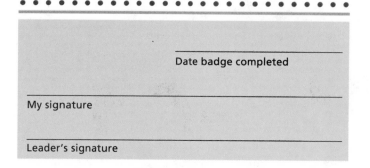

Date badge completed

My signature

Leader's signature

THEATER

1 Read a play. Choose one character and describe:

- The character's personality.
- The character's behavior.
- What other people think of your character.
- What goals the character has.

2 Take a trip to a makeup center or to a place where theatrical makeup is sold. Watch a demonstration. If possible, watch the makeup being applied the night of an amateur or professional performance in your town. Learn how to identify different types of stage makeup. Make up one complete face for a special character (old man, clown, animal, etc.).

or

Create a mask to be used in a skit based on a story you like.

3 Using basic materials (pieces of fabrics, yarn, newspapers, sheets, old clothes, costume jewelry, etc.), design your own costumes and props for a performance.

4 Attend a play, a theatrical performance, a children's theater, a puppet show, a dinner theater, or a school, church, or community play. Make an appointment ahead of time to talk with the performers after the show. Prepare your questions before you go to the theater.

5 Find out about choral reading and choose a piece to rehearse; perform this for your troop/group, for another troop, for a group of friends, or for a council occasion.

*6 Create some puppets, a shadowgraph, or marionettes and prepare appropriate stage sets and lighting. You might make up an original play, act out a folktale, or act out a story that is on a record or tape. Perform for another group.

7 Try at least two of these creative dramatic techniques:

- Try to "mirror mimic" with someone else. While facing each other, one person must copy everything the other person (the leader) does. Take turns being the leader. Don't talk; try to express a feeling.

- Say "I did it" five times, expressing a different emotion each time: for example, pride, guilt, fear, happiness, surprise, horror.
- Create a pantomime based on a reaction to something: taste something delicious/bitter, touch something hot/cold, see something beautiful/horrible, smell something sweet/rotten.
- Use pantomime to show at least five different ways a person can feel—for example, lazy, sad, energetic, happy, sick, athletic.
- Pretend to have a conversation on the phone with an imaginary person.
- Do an improvisation with a small group based on suggestions from your audience.

*8 With others, choose a familiar story. Make a list of the important events in the story. Decide which events you'll show in a scene and how many scenes you'll have. List the characters. Decide who will play each part. Make up the dialogue, movements, voices, and gestures that suit the characters. Use a narrator to present your scenes. When you're ready to act out your story scenes, try using simple costumes.

9 Prepare a pantomime performance using costumes, makeup, and/or props if possible.

*10 With your troop/group, or with a small group of friends, choose a written play or scenes from a play. Produce the play with your group. Rehearse and put on your play with an audience. Each girl should do two or more of the following:

- Learn and perform the part of one character or be an understudy.
- Be the play director, stage manager, set or costume designer, part of a directing committee, or the prompter.
- Draw a model of the stage set.
- Work out the stage directions for every action and movement.
- Create the actual stage set with backgrounds and furniture.
- Collect properties, list when they are to be used, and be ready to present them on cue. Set up a prop table behind stage.
- Prepare the costumes.
- Do the makeup.

- Design and make the programs, invitations, posters, or fliers for the play and distribute them.

11 Find out about the historical or modern theater, drama, comedy, or puppet theater in two other countries. Find pictures, make drawings, prepare a booklet, or do a dramatic presentation to demonstrate to others what you have learned.

12 Find a short mystery thriller or science fiction play, or write an original one that needs several sound effects. Put on your play with all the sound effects. Figure out and gather the props to make at least ten of these: rain on a window, thunder, dog barking, rocket launch, ocean waves on rocks, horn of an old car, car door slamming, feet on a fire escape, horses galloping, truck climbing a steep hill, helicopter in flight, foghorn from a distance, attic door opening, people running, communications from outer space (or make up your own sound effects to fit your story). The sounds can be taped ahead of time if equipment is available.

13 Read a "Decision-Making Story Maze" in Chapter 2 of the *Junior Girl Scout Handbook* and create a play with multiple endings from which the audience can choose.

14 With a group, perform a short original play or skit. Either audiotape it as a radio play or videotape it as a movie. Share your performance with others.

Date badge completed

My signature

Leader's signature

TOYMAKER

1 Create a toy of your own design in one of the following categories:

  Rolling toy
  Spinning toy
  Balanced toy
  Stuffed toy
  Mechanical toy
  Musical toy

2 Find out about toys in other countries and in several cultures in the United States. Prepare a short booklet on how these are the same as or different from toys you know. Use pictures or drawings. Create one of the toys that you discovered. Share with your troop/group or others.

3 Investigate the history of toys. What kinds of toys did your grandparents and great grand-parents have? If possible, visit a museum or historical society to see a collection of toys. Find out what materials they were made from. Learn how to make one of these toys and construct it.

4 Dolls, dollhouses, and doll furniture have been a large part of the history of toys. Dolls have been made using socks, wool, cotton, felt, wood, papier-mâché, corn husks, bread dough, apples and other dried fruit, or clothespins. Make a doll from one of these materials.

or

Make a dollhouse and doll furniture. Use wood or heavy cardboard for the house, and use found items of wood, clay, or papier-mâché for the furniture.

or

Create a piece of furniture and clothes for a doll you have.

5 Visit a toy store and make notes about the kinds of toys you find there. How many of them have something to do with violence, war, or fighting? Talk with friends your own age and with some adults you know and discuss how they feel about these toys. Find out if you can have some influence on manufacturers of toys.

6 Create a physical game that you and your friends can play. If it requires construction, such as a ring toss, make the equipment. If it involves materials already made, collect these. Make up rules for your game, teach it to others, and play it.

7 Find out about board games played in other countries and cultures, such as chess, checkers, Go, Chinese checkers, or backgammon. Construct a board game based on one that you have studied. Play the game with your friends. Learn something about the history and use of the game.

8 Create an educational game: (a) to help someone learn something, or (b) for someone who can't see, or (c) for someone who can't read.

9 Create a game, toy, or puzzle to challenge the imagination. For example, it could be a mechanical puzzle, a mathematical game, a string game, a puzzle composed on a computer, or a game that involves remembering trivia. Describe your game and play it with others in your troop/group or with other people.

or

Study the history and worldwide use of kites. Try to visit an exhibit that shows a variety of kites. Determine what sizes, shapes, and forms would make a kite fly well. Design and construct your own original kite. Decorate it with your own artwork. You could hold a kite-flying festival with a group of friends.

Date badge completed

My signature

Leader's signature

VIDEO PRODUCTION

1 Visit a video store, school, library, cable TV station, or other place that has video equipment. Have a technician, a salesperson, or an instructor demonstrate how to use the various pieces of equipment. Learn what accessories are available plus when and why you would use them.

2 Become familiar with the basic language of video production. Discuss with your group what these terms mean—panning, boom, dissolve, trucking.

3 Review the operating instructions manual for the video equipment you will be using. With the manual and your camera, go over the major operating controls and their functions.

4 Learn three basic types of video camera shots, such as a long shot, medium shot, and close-up. Demonstrate your skill at these by taking several different shots of the same object, keeping the camera on a tripod (a three-legged stand). Practice these shots until you can handle the camera with ease. Then try the same shots while holding the camera in your hand instead of putting it on a tripod. A test for steadiness might be to compare shots taken using a tripod with those taken while hand-holding the camera.

5 Learn how to use your camera creatively so you can get the visual effects you want.

- Set up a session at which you practice unusual shots such as extreme close-up or extreme long shot.
- Learn about shots taken from different angles (low, high, side, etc.) and how and why to use them. Pick out some angle shots used in your favorite television show or movie and try those that are appropriate.
- Experiment to find out how you can make your camera move sideways without changing the distance from it to the subject. Then set up a practice session using the techniques of panning, tilting, and trucking. With a partner, review your work.

6 Visit a video edit facility (where parts of a video are put together in final form). Learn about cuts, dissolves, wipes, cut-aways, and special effects. Look at samples of these and learn why and when each would be used. Present your findings to your troop.

7 Have a video specialist come to your meeting and demonstrate how to artistically arrange subjects and props and put shots in order so that they go together well in the edit. Then, using the storyboard technique, develop a sequence of shots demonstrating what you have learned.

SHOT 1

SHOT 2

SHOT 3

SHOT 4

SHOT 5

SHOT 6

8 Do a storyboard (a plan showing a drawing of each key shot and words that go with it) that includes a sequence of six shots illustrating a short scene with a beginning and an end.

9 With friends, take some time to watch a few children's programs on television. Discuss your observations, the purposes of the shows, the types of set designs that were used, and the kinds of performers seen. What types of edits were done and why?

10 As a final project, put together a short video presentation. Share this presentation with your troop/group.

_____
Date badge completed

_____
My signature

_____
Leader's signature

VISUAL
ARTS

1 Find out about primary and secondary colors. Make a color wheel and explain it to others. What are complementary colors? Practice mixing colors to make new ones. Create a picture using all the colors on a color wheel and some of the new colors that you created.

2 You can make many shades of the same color. Look at something that is mostly one color. Notice that light and shadow can change the basic color into different shades. Make a picture of something that is mostly one color. Some examples are a hill full of trees that are many shades of green, buildings in a city that are many shades of brick red or gray, snow on fields that are many shades of gray and white, or curtains on a window that are different shades of blue.

or

Look through magazines and catalogs. Get permission to cut out shapes in different shades of the same color. Make a one-color collage.

3 Make a design or picture using only black and white. Look for examples of drawings, advertisements, and photographs that are in black and white instead of in color. Share some of these with others. See if you can figure out why the artist or photographer chose to use black and white instead of color.

4 Look for design in everyday objects. List 15 different designs you can find in nature and 15 different designs that are man-made. Make a drawing of one of the designs you see.

5 Look through a new catalog or fashion magazine, or visit a department store when the new fall or spring clothes appear. What special colors are considered "new" for this season? Look at the different colors in one outfit. What colors "go together"? With a group of friends, have a "mix and match" party. How many different combinations of tops and bottoms, dresses and accessories can you make from the clothes you already own? How can you update the clothes you already have with something in a "new" color?

6 Visit one or more places where you can see many types of visual arts. You could visit a museum, an art exhibit, an art gallery, a gift shop, a department store, a card shop, an art collector's home, an artist's studio, an art show or festival, a ceramic studio, a class in weaving, embroidery, or crewel work, or an advertising agency or graphic design studio. If possible, visit a place where you can see the artist at work.

7 Create at least three visual works that show different feelings or emotions. Try to use color to show happiness, sadness, calmness, joy, excitement, or any other emotion.

8 Collect a variety of objects that have unusual shapes. Place them on a blank piece of paper and trace around them to make an interesting design. You can trace your design in black and white or color it in to make an abstract picture. Try moving the objects to make a different picture. Share the result with others.

Date badge completed

My signature

Leader's signature

Exploring the Out-Of-Doors

Learn to make a s'more

Show 3 ways to use a bandana

Learn 3 ways to use a square knot

Use a map to get from one place to another

Fly a kite

Find 3 examples of change in the outdoor environment

Go on a field trip to a park or nature center

Learn how to pitch a tent

Plant a tree

Learn first aid for a blister

Learn to protect yourself from sun, wind and cold

Sleep outdoors

Observe wildlife in your community

Can you do 5 in any direction?

Make some gorp for an outdoor expedition

Learn some outdoor hiking songs

Go on a color chip hike

FREE

RELAX IN A FAVORITE OUTDOOR SPOT

Leave an outdoor place cleaner than you found it

Play a compass game

Write a poem or story about a horse

Take some pictures of the outdoors

Find the Big Dipper

Cook a meal in the outdoors

Take a walk in your neighborhood

Learn to put on a personal flotation device (P.F.D.)

DABBLER

PICK FIVE GROUPS FROM THOSE BELOW. WITHIN EACH OF THE FIVE GROUPS, COMPLETE ONE ACTIVITY.

A.1 Select a plant, such as a tree, a weed, or shrub growing in your community. Learn how this plant gets food and water. Find out what living things depend upon this plant for food and shelter. Use drawings, poetry, photographs, or some other method to tell about the plant and all the living things that depend on it.

A.2 Make an environmental discovery tool or select a piece of equipment you can use to explore nature. Learn how to use it. Teach someone else how to use it to make her own discoveries.

B.1 Observe birds, insects, or other wild animals during different seasons around your home and notice how they live and what they eat. Keep a log of your discoveries to share with your troop.

B.2 With other girls, help plan a Girl Scout's Own to share your feelings about the freedom of being in the out-of-doors.

C.1 Learn the following outdoor skills well enough to show someone else: how and when to tie a square knot, half hitch, and overhand knot; how to handle a knife; how to make a bedroll.

C.2 With your group, plan one meal or snack that needs no cooking, or one that lets each person cook, or one that serves the whole group. Know how to build and put out a fire or use a camp/backpacker's stove. Help plan, buy, carry, prepare, serve, and eat food. Help clean up.

D.1 On a map of your community, mark places where you can do outdoor activities and sports.

D.2 Locate the camping sites your council owns or uses on a map. Find out what types of activities are available, and learn how and when you can use them. Share this information with your troop/group.

E.1 With your troop/group, take a hike to a favorite spot. Use a compass and map to help you make a sketch map. Share your sketch map with another troop so they can find your favorite spot.

E.2 Make something you can use when hiking, biking, camping, riding, or boating.

F.1 Put on a skit, make a video, or prepare a photo story that shows you know the buddy system, the safety rules, and how to dress for outdoor trips in different kinds of weather.

F.2 Put on a demonstration or show to help younger Girl Scouts learn how and when to use a personal flotation device (PFD). See page 248.

G.1 Make a list of things happening in your community that hurt the environment. Do a project with your family or troop to improve your community's environment.

G.2 Find out what kinds of environmental activities are going on in the camps in your Girl Scout council. Ask what kinds of projects need to be done by girls. Pick one of these projects to do the next time your group goes to camp.

H.1 With a small group, start a walking program that has you walking at least one mile a day four times a week for one month.

H.2 Go to a local facility that has a fitness walking trail. Use the trail at least five times in a one-month period.

I.1 With your group, visit a marine/boat store or have someone come to your meeting to talk to you about safety when using a small craft.

I.2 Ask a Water Safety Instructor (Red Cross or YMCA) to come to your troop meeting to talk about what you can do to help yourself if you're in trouble in the water, what you can do to help others even if you can't swim, and the safety "common sense" rules for participating in water-related activities.

• •

_____
Date badge completed

_____
My signature

_____
Leader's signature

ECO-ACTION

COMPLETE FIVE ACTIVITIES, INCLUDING THE FIRST STARRED ACTIVITY AND AT LEAST ONE ACTIVITY FROM ACTIVITIES 6–9.

*1 Develop a list of personal "eco-actions" you can take that will have a positive effect upon the environment. Include actions that conserve water and energy resources, actions that cut down on waste, actions that do not abuse or overuse environmental resources, and actions that minimize pollution of the environment. At least three things on your list should represent a change in your personal lifestyle. That means a real change in the way you do something or view something. Compare this list with other girls' lists. Share it with your family, adopting at least one of the changes.

or

Discuss with your group/troop or some friends a way to change the way people live with the environment. Find a way to change a negative ecological behavior (such as littering at a park site, picking wildflowers, not recycling) that is often seen in your school or community.

2 Find out how to read your electric meter. Compile a list of the items in your home that use electricity. Which appliances use electricity at a faster rate? Find out where your electric power comes from and how many people are served. Learn what a brownout is and when this is most likely to occur. Visit your local electric company or ask for materials to learn how to cut down on energy consumption.

or

Develop an energy conservation plan for your home or school and put it into effect.

3 Find a safe corner in your community where you can make a traffic survey. Count the number of vehicles that pass by in 30 minutes at three different times of day. Keep track of how many vehicles carry only one person. Evaluate the way you and your family use transportation. Keep track of everyone's travel for a week. Decide if there might have been alternative ways to travel or ways of consolidating trips. Discuss personal and environmental reasons for seeking alternatives to the automobile and what these might be in your community. Make a poster to remind you and your family to consider alternative transportation, consolidation of trips, or car pooling.

4 Find out if your community or state has regulations that require automobiles to be checked to maintain air quality. Visit an inspection station to find out how auto emission pollution is monitored.

or

Contact the department of health in your community and find out if acid rain is being monitored in your own area. Learn what causes acid rain and how it affects the environment around you.

or

Visit a weather station. Learn what conditions lead to an "air pollution alert" and what steps can be taken to reduce air pollution.

5 Interview someone who has a career in environmental action. Find out what she or he does on the job and what issues are considered most important in dealing with the environment. Discover what kind of training and education were necessary for the job.

Although people are a part of the ecosystem, they often do things that damage or endanger their environment. Such things as pollution, erosion, loss of habitat, overcrowding and overuse, and poor waste disposal are people-caused problems. Activities 6–9 have to do with identifying specific environmental problems in your community and working with others to change them. When doing one of these activities:

- Learn all you can about the problem.
- Evaluate the possible solutions.
- Develop a plan of action.
- Act on your plan.
- Evaluate what happened.

6 Look for examples of soil erosion in your community, camp, or recreation areas. Find examples of water and wind erosion, as well as erosion caused by people. Find a site that is eroded that would benefit from a soil conservation project. You may want to consult a local agency such as the Soil Conservation Service to assist you in evaluating an area or in planning the project. Use any or all of the following to help maintain the soil on the site:

- Planting vegetation.
- Educating property users.
- Blocking short-cuts on hillsides.
- Installing drainage ditches, culverts, or waterbars (erosion-prevention devices used on trails).
- Terracing.

7 Locate a place in your community where you think trees are an important part of the environment. Do they provide shade, beauty, a wind and sound barrier, or protection from soil erosion? Remember that trees are also an important part of the oxygen cycle, absorbing carbon dioxide and producing oxygen which we breathe. Can you think of any other reasons trees are important? What difficulties do trees have in growing in your area?

Participate in a project in which you plant trees in an area that needs reforestation, or plant a tree in a treeless area and be responsible for providing the things it needs to grow.

8 Participate in a project that helps to conserve water or clean up a water resource, such as:

- Distributing water savers for showerheads in the community.
- Working with your community to mark storm drains to prevent chemical and waste dumping into streams and rivers.

- Planting streamside vegetation to make shade and to prevent erosion.
- Cleaning up water or a shoreline area.

9 Identify a specific environmental problem in your community and work to change it.

_____
Date badge completed

_____
My signature

_____
Leader's signature

ECOLOGY

COMPLETE SIX ACTIVITIES, INCLUDING THE THREE STARRED.

Ecology is the study of plants and animals and their environment. Together plants, animals, and nonliving elements, such as soil, air, and water, make up an ecosystem.

*1 Visit a natural area near where you live, a park, or an area at camp. Mentally mark out a study area for yourself that is no larger than 20 paces square. This will be your ecosystem to study.

- List the plants and animals you observe in your ecosystem. If you do not name them, count the variety of species present.
- Determine if you have different levels of plant life in your ecosystem, such as an under-story, middle-story, and upper-story. If there is more than one level, how do you think the different levels affect each other?
- Dig a small hole into the soil or study an exposed bank and note the different layers of soil. Feel to determine if there are differences in composition (what it is made of) and texture (how it feels).
- Using a thermometer or your hand, take or feel the temperature at ground level and chest level in at least three different places in your ecosystem. Where is it the warmest, the coolest? What causes differences in the temperature?

- Decide how soil, water, sun, and wind interact with the plants and animals in your ecosystem. Find examples of these actions.
- Find examples of decomposers at work in your ecosystem.
- Draw or create a simple food chain using plants and animals from your ecosystem.

*2 Lead your group/troop or others (or a younger troop) in understanding relationships within an ecosystem by playing a game that shows how plants and animals depend upon each other. This might involve predator-prey relationships, food chains, or a simple food web.

3 Ecological succession is a natural process of change, when one community is replaced by another over a period of time. A pond might fill in to become a meadow, or a meadow might become a forest. Think of yourself as a time traveler. Draw what your camera might record in the future for two of the following sites:

- A lake or pond that has a marshy area at one end.
- A rock or lava flow that is barren.
- A fallen tree.
- A vacant lot or a meadow.
- A burned forest.

4 Find an example of how animal or plant populations change. Make observations over a period of time, if possible.

Using an insect net, sweep through a grassy area and count the kinds and numbers of insects captured. Do the same thing several weeks later. Are there any differences?

• Keep track of the kinds and numbers of birds coming to a feeding station or special spot over several months. Are there differences?

• Visit an area where you can see migrating animals or fish returning to spawn. Learn about their journey and changing numbers.

• Visit an area that has been changed by fire, volcano, or another natural disaster. How were the plants and animals affected? How long did it take for the animals to return or reestablish themselves?

5 Look for some examples of ways that plants or animals have developed or adapted in order to survive in their habitat. You might consider environments with little water or lots of water; those that are very hot or very cold; or even those environments that have been changed by humans.

or

Choose an ecosystem that is familiar to you. Design an imaginary creature with adaptations suited for survival in this ecosystem. Compare your results with those of a friend.

6 Learn to identify ten tree species in your area, using leaves, seeds, fruit, and bark as means of identification. Describe the kind of ecosystem where each is likely to be found.

7 Find a tree stump where you can read the growth rings. A year's growth consists of a light and a dark ring. To find out how old the tree was when it died, count each dark ring and add five to the total. Look for years of rapid growth (the wider rings) and years of slow growth. What might have caused this?

8 Learn to identify ten wild plants in your area. Learn the habitat where each is most likely to be found. Find out whether your wild plants are used by animals or insects in the ecosystem, and if your wild plants were used by American Indians for food or medicine. Find out what plants are protected by law in your state.

*9 Investigate how two or more of the following might affect the earth as a balanced ecosystem and yourself as a part of that ecosystem:

• Factories emitting pollutants into the air in the eastern United States.
• Trees being cut down in South American rain forests to create grazing land for cattle to be eaten by people in North America.
• An oil spill in coastal waters.
• Running out of landfill sites for garbage in major cities.
• A person who refuses to recycle or to turn off lights when not in use.

Design a way to share what you learn with others. Commit yourself to an action that you can do to improve or protect the environment.

_____
Date badge completed

_____
My signature

_____
Leader's signature

FINDING YOUR WAY

*1 Collect several different types of maps or charts that include the place where you live or an area you would like to visit. Be able to explain what maps are and the information each gives about the area.

2 Find out how long it takes for you to walk one mile comfortably over fairly level ground. Then figure out how long it should take you to walk the distance between two points you have marked on your map. When calculating your walking time, don't forget to consider the type of terrain and your walking speed. Walk the distance and see if your estimate was correct.

3 Draw a sketch map of your route to school, to a shopping center, or to a favorite spot. Ask someone to test your map by following it. Draw a second sketch map from your home to some place of interest, based upon the description someone gives you. Together, follow your map to see if it is correct. In both maps, include a legend (key) which explains the symbols you used and the compass direction. Read the section, "Reading a Map," in Chapter 7 of the *Junior Girl Scout Handbook*.

Try to lead your Junior Girl Scout group through the park

*4 Draw a map to scale of a campsite or of your neighborhood locating major landmarks, streets, paths or trails, bodies of water, and other important features. Include a legend (key) which explains the symbols you used, a scale, and a compass direction.

*5 Show that you know how to use a compass by:
- Explaining how to adjust a map for the difference between true and magnetic north.
- Taking a compass bearing from a map and following it.
- Sighting on an object, walking to it, and returning to your starting point.

6 Learn to read an orienteering or topographical map. Teach someone else.

7 Show how to find the four cardinal directional points by using the sun, stars, or other natural signs.

or

Describe what natural signs lost hikers could use to find their way back to camp.

8 Learn and teach a game that could help other girls in your troop to use a map and a compass.

9 Make a three-dimensional model of a portion of a topographical map to show contour intervals of the hills and valleys.

10 Use an orienteering or topographical map to plan a hike to at least six stations. Plot your route and what you will see along the way. Take the hike and see if your interpretation of the map was correct.

11 Take part in a map and compass clinic or orienteering meet in your area.

• •

_____

Date badge completed

_____

My signature

_____

Leader's signature

FROSTY FUN

DO SIX OF THE FOLLOWING ACTIVITIES, INCLUDING THE TWO THAT ARE STARRED.

*1 Find out the proper attire for winter outdoor activities. Tell why layers and head coverings are important. Learn about fabrics that repel water and those that help to reduce perspiration.

*2 Learn how the human body reacts to cold. Find out about the purpose of shivering and goose bumps. Describe the symptoms of hypothermia and frostbite and what first aid to use for each. Know what weather conditions should signal the cancellation of an outdoor wintertime activity.

3 With a group, plan and carry out a winter outdoor fun day. You might include activities like games, hikes, a snow sculpture contest, skating, or a cookout. Invite another troop to join you.

4 For a winter outing, plan and take a nutritious snack and a hot beverage. Take along plenty of liquids to replace body fluids lost as you perspire and exhale.

5 Learn how the ice thickness on a pond or lake is tested for safety. Show how you would rescue a person who fell through the ice. Show that you know how to report an accident and summon a rescue squad or police help.

6 With a group, plan and carry out an ice skating party or ice fishing trip.

Find the Don'ts

7 Learn about the equipment used for downhill skiing, cross-country skiing, or snowshoeing. Learn how to choose equipment for your size and skill level. Learn three basic skills and the etiquette of your chosen sport.

8 Check out the snow! Use a thermometer to find out the air temperature and the temperature inside a layer of snow. How do they compare? Fill a large can or bucket with snow. Melt the snow to find out how much water it contains. Estimate how many cans (or buckets) of snow you would need for all the ways you use water each day.

9 Catch snowflakes on a dark cloth and look at them with a magnifying glass. Describe their shape and symmetry.

10 Take a discovery hike and test to find where the soil is frozen and the snow is deepest. Make predictions first and then see if they are right. Check the snow depths on a slope that faces north and one that faces south. Which will melt off first? How does wind seem to affect the snow cover? Look for the footprints of animals, humps left by animals burrowing underneath the snow, marks left by objects blowing across the snow. Where are animals most active?

● ●

_____
Date badge completed

_____
My signature

_____
Leader's signature

HIKER

COMPLETE EIGHT ACTIVITIES, INCLUDING THE THREE STARRED.

1 On a map of your area, locate three hiking trails or walking paths within 25 miles of your home. Find out what permission is required to hike on them. Plan to take a day hike on one of these trails or paths.

*2 With others in your group, learn about hiking health and safety. Make a list of the most important things to remember. Know how to get emergency help on a hike.

3 Know how to give first aid treatment for common hiking problems such as blisters, sunburn, and insect bites. Also, be able to give first aid for serious bleeding, hypothermia, frostbite, heat stroke, shock, and heat exhaustion. Prepare a first aid kit.

*4 Give a demonstration of how to dress and what to take along on a day hike or a one-night backpacking trip. Be able to explain the advantages and disadvantages of the various types of clothing and equipment. Take part in a wide game or act out a situation where you and others in your group must make a shelter for the night and improvise bodily protection from heat, cold, wind, rain, or snow.

5 Use a compass and topographical or orienteering map to lay out a cross-country hike. Help a group follow the route you have selected.

6 Find a way to share the fun of hiking with others. This might be by taking some other group on one of your hiking adventures, or by finding or writing a poem, story, or picture to describe how you feel. Read "Useful Skills for Outdoor Adventures" in Chapter 7 of the *Junior Girl Scout Handbook* for more ideas.

7 Organize or take part in a trail-building project. This might be an urban trail, an interpretive nature trail, a jogging path, a physical fitness trail, or a wheelchair route through your community.

8 Find out about the Appalachian Trail, the Pacific Crest Trail, or a scenic or historic trail located in your area. Find out if you can help with the upkeep and repair of one of these trails.

or

Help others become aware of good hiking practices and the need for trails in your community.

9 On a day hike or a backpacking trip, carry a day or backpack containing nutritionally balanced meals, snacks, drinks, clothing, your share of group equipment, and anything else you need and can carry comfortably. Show your appreciation of the outdoors by leaving things cleaner than you found them.

*10 Help your group plan and go on two all-day hikes or an overnight backpacking trip to a council-approved site. Plan where to go, what to wear, and what to take. Find out about hiking, camping, and fire regulations you must observe and why. Get the necessary permissions; arrange for an at-home emergency contact and transportation.

_____
Date badge completed

_____
My signature

_____
Leader's signature

HORSE LOVER

COMPLETE SIX ACTIVITIES, INCLUDING THE TWO STARRED.

*1 Find out where you can ride in your community. Ask each group or facility how much it charges for membership, riding, or riding lessons. Find out whether its specialty is English or Western riding and which groups provide instructions, which require you to own your own horse, which have indoor and outdoor rings, and which have riding trails.

2 Visit a stable. Find out from the owner or manager what is involved in the care of a horse. Find out how much and what kind of food a horse needs daily, acceptable treats for horses, everyday care for a stable, how often a horse needs to be shod and why. If possible, watch while a farrier pulls and resets a shoe.

3 Examine the tools used to groom a horse. Discover the purpose of each. Learn to use the brush and currycomb. Learn how to brush a horse before and after saddling. Practice safe stall and barn behavior.

4 Make an illustrated booklet about the history and development of the horse. Be able to point out and name the principal parts of a horse.

or

Collect or take photographs of at least four breeds of horses that interest you. Tell or write about their distinctive features and uses.

5 Take riding lessons to learn the basics of riding: lead a horse before and after riding, mount and dismount, start, stop and back up, ride at a walk, and trot, guide a horse while riding and with supervision, lead a horse to the stable.

or

Demonstrate to others how to mount and dismount, ride at a walk and a trot. Show others how to groom a horse and how to care for a horse after exercising.

6 Find out the type of training and experience your instructor needed before she or he could begin to teach others.

or

Explore the different careers that are involved in the field of horsemanship.

7 Be a safer rider. Develop a horse safety poster or display. Include safe riding rules, good ring manners, safe clothing and gear for Western or English riding.

*8 Review the "Staying Safe" section of Chapter 3 of the *Junior Girl Scout Handbook* and then develop safety guidelines that your group will follow while earning this badge. Use your leader's copy of *Safety Wise* as a model.

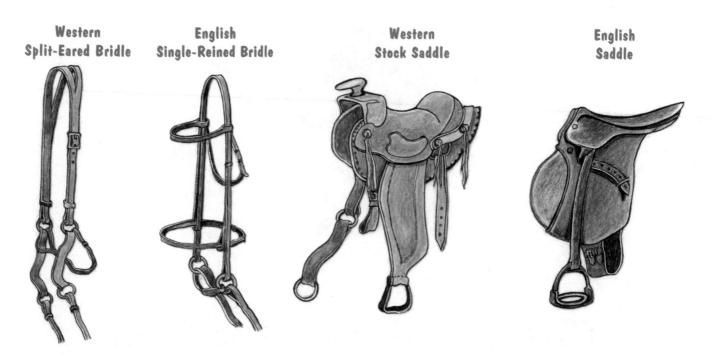

Western Split-Eared Bridle **English Single-Reined Bridle** **Western Stock Saddle** **English Saddle**

9 Learn the parts of a saddle and a bridle. Find out how each part contributes to the comfort of the horse and rider. Learn how to take care of a saddle and a bridle to keep them in good repair.

10 Watch or assist with the saddling and bridling of a horse. Be able to explain to someone else what is being done and the use of each piece of equipment.

or

Saddle and bridle the horse you are going to ride.

11 Find out how to use your natural aids—your hands, your legs, your weight, and your voice—to tell your horse what to do. Know how to get along with horses in the stable and in the ring or pasture.

12 Read one or more books about horses. These might include books on horsemanship, information on related careers, stories about famous horses, or stories of adventure on horseback.

13 Attend a horsemanship event at camp or watch a live or televised performance by show riders, such as a rodeo, a local horse show, or a draft horse pulling contest.

14 Find out about the breeding and training of horses used in your community, such as police horses, cavalry horses, race horses, or dray horses.

Date badge completed

My signature

Leader's signature

HORSEBACK RIDER

COMPLETE SEVEN ACTIVITIES, INCLUDING THE TWO STARRED.

1 Saddle and bridle a horse by yourself. Explain the care and use of each part of the tack and the importance of correct fitting. Hitch a horse at the correct height when bridled, using a halter or rope, a suitable knot, and the correct length of rope.

2 Visit a harness or tack shop or obtain a harness catalog and become acquainted with different styles of saddles, bridles, and bits. Find out the advantages of each type and know the approximate cost. Teach someone else how to clean and care for tack.

*3 Demonstrate that you can do the following in good form: mount and dismount correctly; turn and stop a horse, at walk and at trot, on command; post at trot; back up, circle, and canter in good form either from the halt or the walk.

*4 Explain to your troop the safety regulations for riding and equestrian etiquette. Show how to give proper hand signals when riding on public roads and how to do an emergency dismount at halt and at walk. Tell what to do if your horse rears, trips, bucks, stops, or bolts.

5 Illustrate by demonstration or pictures the correct and safe clothing for horse shows, Western trail rides, and your group's own equestrian activities. Point out to others the safety features to look for in the footwear, pants, jackets, and safety hat you wear when riding.

6 Find out where there are suitable trails for horseback riding in your area. Help with the care and maintenance of one of these bridle paths.

or

Name the tools used for grooming a horse. Demonstrate the use of each one. Learn how to care for a horse after exercising.

7 Help someone you know to feel comfortable around horses and understand the need for safety precautions on the trail or in the ring, stable, or pasture.

or

Help someone earn her Horse Lover badge.

or

Help become an active partner in mainstreaming by helping a person with a disability earn the Horse Lover badge.

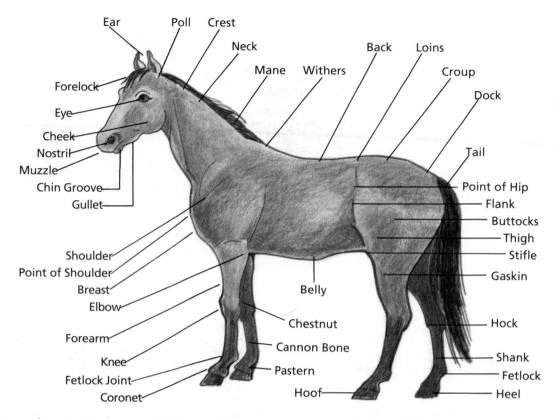

Ear   Poll   Crest
Neck   Back   Loins
Forelock   Mane   Withers   Croup
Eye   Dock
Cheek
Nostril   Tail
Muzzle
Chin Groove   Point of Hip
Gullet   Flank
  Buttocks
  Thigh
Shoulder   Stifle
Point of Shoulder   Gaskin
Breast
Elbow   Belly
  Chestnut   Hock
Forearm   Cannon Bone
Knee   Shank
Fetlock Joint   Pastern   Fetlock
Coronet   Hoof   Heel

8 Name the principal parts of a horse. Find out from the veterinarian or horse trainer what can be done to prevent the common ailments or diseases of horses.

9 Collect cowboy ballads and teach one to your troop.

or

Learn about famous or legendary horses. Tell a horse story to your troop or another group.

10 Plan and take part in a trail breakfast, a supper ride, a troop demonstration of riding skills, or a short cross-country ride.

or

Take a trip to a state or county fair to see the horse show. If possible, enter a show class that is right for you and your horse.

or

Attend a local horse show. If possible, serve as an usher, runner, or in some other capacity that will help the show run smoothly.

or

Attend a class on how to mainstream people with disabilities into a horseback riding clinic. (Refer to the section, "Other Kinds of Prejudice and Discrimination," in Chapter 5 of the *Junior Girl Scout Handbook*.)

11 Plan and carry out a gymkhana (a program of games on horseback) for your troop. You may also wish to invite another troop or other riders to participate.

Date badge completed

My signature

Leader's signature

OUTDOOR COOK

COMPLETE EIGHT ACTIVITIES, INCLUDING THE FOUR STARRED.

*1 With a group, help plan, prepare, and serve four different outdoor meals, using a different cooking method and fuel in each meal. Help do at least two of the following for each meal: plan the menu, make shopping and equipment lists, shop, pack, take care of the food at the site, establish an eating area, prepare and serve the food, or clean up including dishwashing. Read the sections, "Using a Camp Stove," and "Making a Fire," in Chapter 7 of the *Junior Girl Scout Handbook* for some helpful hints.

2 Using a common food, such as beans, rice, or potatoes, find a few recipes from your own region or recipes from at least three different cultures or countries. Prepare at least one of those recipes during a cookout. Save the other recipes for future trips.

*3 Learn to use charcoal as a fuel for cooking. Explain the advantage of using charcoal, when not to use it, differences in cooking time, methods of starting and extinguishing a charcoal fire, and the safety precautions necessary when using charcoal.

4 Demonstrate your ability to maintain a cooking fire in windy or wet weather.

5 Demonstrate how to use a backpacker's stove or camp stove safely by preparing a meal on it for yourself and your group. Read the "Cooking in the Out-of-Doors" section in *Outdoor Education in Girl Scouting* to help you. Discuss the environmental impact of using stoves rather than fires for your cookouts.

*6 On one of the cookouts, take the lead role in the cleanup process. Show that you can instruct and supervise others in how to put out a fire, remove the ashes, or extinguish the camp stove; wash, sanitize, and store the dishes; and dispose of the trash, wet garbage, tin cans, and glass without endangering the environment.

7 Help collect or make items for a troop, group, or patrol kitchen box or kit. Pack the equipment in a container/carrier so that one or two people in your group can easily transport it.

Menu

APPETIZER •

SOUP •

MAIN COURSE •

VEGETABLE •

SALAD •

DESSERT •

SERVES •

EQUIPMENT NEEDED •

INGREDIENTS •

COOKING DIRECTIONS •

NOTES •

8 Help plan and package a tasty, easy-to-pack, lightweight, high-energy dinner for hot weather or emergency use that requires no cooking fire or refrigeration.

9 With one or more friends, check out your local stores for tasty, inexpensive, light-weight foods that do not need refrigeration or long cooking time. Develop a list of these items and where they can be found for future trips. With your troop/group, taste-test a few of these food items.

or

Experiment by preparing and packaging your own dry mixes for use on your next camping trip.

or

Sun-dry or oven-dry some fresh fruit, vegetables, or seasonings to use on a cookout.

10 Try your hand at a little gourmet cooking. Bake something in a cardboard box oven.

or

Learn to bake something over a backpacking stove.

11 Practice measuring dry, liquid, and solid ingredients until you can judge amounts with and without standard measuring tools.

12 In camping areas where the water has not been tested and approved by the local health department, you will need to know how to purify the water before using it for drinking or cooking. Demonstrate your ability to purify water using one of the following methods: commercial water purification kit, water purification tablets or boiling.

*13 Share your skills with others. Teach someone or some group how to use a backpacking or camp stove. Be sure to include safety practices and some repair tips. Have the group use the stove to prepare, cook, and clean up.

••••••••••••••••••••••••••••••

_____
Date badge completed

_____
My signature

_____
Leader's signature

OUTDOOR CREATIVITY

1 Use nature as an inspiration for your artwork. Find a special subject, such as a pleasing vista or an object that you can study up close. Draw with a pen and ink, make a charcoal sketch, do a water color, or take a series of nature studies photographs in the outdoors.

or

Visit a museum or library and study some of the great painters or photographers whose specialties were landscapes or wildlife. Look for ways that they show light and texture, and different styles. Choose a subject in the outdoors and try some different approaches in the way you depict your subject.

2 Look at the outdoors with different eyes. Find beauty in things that you normally would pass by. Pretend that each object you focus upon is a work of modern art. Look at texture, play of light and shadow, color, shape, patterns. Play with distance and perspective. Use a still or video camera to record your images and create a photo exhibit to share with others.

3 Create a flower or herb garden that is pleasing to the senses. If you do not have space for a large garden, consider making planters. When planting, consider colors that go together, height of flowers or herbs, length of flowering, shade or sun required, scent, etc.

Rain falls softly now
a thousand tiny rivers
as I look outward.

4 Use the outdoors as an inspiration for a poem. Try writing a cinquain or a Japanese haiku about something that you see or feel while in the outdoors. See page 247.

Use your poem in a ceremony or with a card or picture, or as a gift.

5 Use natural materials as an inspiration for a craft or artwork:

a Use natural clay to create a piece of pottery. You might even want to experiment with outdoor ways of firing your pottery under supervision.

b Dry or press flowers and leaves to use in a pressed flower project (such as notepaper or special cards) or a dried arrangement. Remember not to pick wildflowers.

c Weave a wall hanging using natural materials.

d Use leaf prints to decorate an article of clothing or something for the home. (Use water-soluble fabric paint.)

6 Keep a nature journal for several months. Find a special spot where you can return on a weekly or daily basis. Record what you are able to observe in the natural environment over a period of time. Keep track of changes in the environment. Record any thoughts you have about your special spot and your relationship to that spot. Find a way to share what you have learned or experienced in writing, song, or dance.

or

Pretend that you are a traveler from outer space visiting earth for the first time. Your assignment is to find a special spot and de-

scribe it so that it can be reproduced on your own planet. Using a tape recorder or notebook, record your impressions. You only have one hour. Your mission is not to startle the inhabitants or interfere with the ecosystem. Report on shapes, colors, textures, movements, sounds, smells, and the interactions of things.

7 Be a creative cook in the outdoors. Try some gourmet cooking using a vagabond stove or use another method of cooking a new recipe. Read the sections on "Using a Camp Stove" and "Making a Fire" in Chapter 7 of the *Junior Girl Scout Handbook.*

8 Help plan an outdoor evening program. Include audience participation, activities, songs, and a legend about nature. Consider the moods that are created when planning your program.

9 With your troop or group, plan a Girl Scout's Own that takes place in the outdoors, celebrating your relationship to or appreciation of nature. You might use music, poetry, and personal thoughts to express this. Make sure that each person has an opportunity to contribute.

10 Participate in a night watch when your troop or group is on a camp-out. Choose a special spot in the outdoors. Arrange one-hour shifts throughout the night, signing up in pairs. Let yourself become a part of the night by being silent. Write in a journal about what you hear and how you feel. The next morning, meet as a group and share your thoughts. What kinds of sounds did you hear? How is the night world different from the day world? How did you feel?

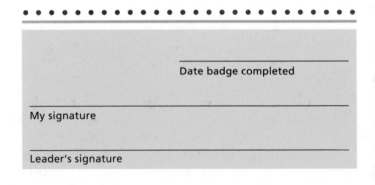

Date badge completed

My signature

Leader's signature

OUTDOOR FUN

- -

COMPLETE FIVE ACTIVITIES, INCLUDING THE TWO STARRED.

*1 Help your troop, group, patrol, or family plan and carry out three different outings. They should each be one-half day or longer. Plan activities specific to the sites. Find out what types of equipment and facilities are already on each site. Then make a list of additional group and personal equipment you will need to take.

2 With others, help plan, buy, pack, carry, prepare, and serve a different meal or snack for each of your three outings, such as one that requires no cooking, one that lets each person cook her own food, and one in which you cook for the group. Prepare a kaper chart for each meal or snack; include cleanup chores.

   For information on how to make sun tea and sun jam, see pages 247–248.

3 Show that you can build a basic fire, prepare food on it, put it out, and leave the fire site "without a trace" of use. Remember to use only enough wood or charcoal to get your task done.

4 Help to plan, assemble, and pack a first-aid kit that is appropriate for your outdoor activities. Demonstrate your knowledge of the uses of the items in the kit. Know first aid and prevention practices for burns and cuts.

5 Plan games, songs, and activities for each outing that are especially suitable for the season and the site.

6 Know how to dispose of waste water and garbage without damaging the environment. Learn how to sanitize and keep your dishes clean in the outdoors.

7 Demonstrate several ways in which knowing how to tie a square knot may be useful to the group on one of your outings. Learn a new knot, like the bowline, that will be useful when you go on troop camping trips. See "Tying Knots" in Chapter 7 of the *Junior Girl Scout Handbook*.

OUTDOOR EMERGENCY CHART

Emergencies:

Prevention:

_____   _____

_____   _____

_____   _____

_____   _____

_____   _____

_____   _____

_____   _____

_____   _____

_____   _____

_____   _____

_____   _____

*8 Develop a chart showing what to do in outdoor emergencies and how to prevent or avoid them. Keep the chart and use it for other outings. Demonstrate what a lost camper should do to help others find her.

9 Help to unpack, clean, and store your group's equipment after each outing. Talk over how your trip went, the things you learned that will be useful when you go out again, the things you would do differently another time, and some new activities you want to try next time.

• •

_____
Date badge completed

_____
My signature

_____
Leader's signature

OUTDOOR FUN
IN THE CITY

· ·

COMPLETE SIX ACTIVITIES.

1 Compile a directory of outdoor recreation activities in your city to use as a resource for yourself, your troop, or your family. List activities by season. Use a city map to show where activities take place. List activities that are free as well as those that cost money. Try at least three activities with your troop, your family, or a friend.

2 Participate in a sidewalk city recreation:

• Look at pages 12 and 13 in this book. Learn how to jump double-dutch jump rope. With friends, work up a routine that you can demonstrate to others.

or

• Learn two ways of playing hopscotch. Organize a tournament within your troop or group of friends.

or

• Learn the rules for playing outdoor handball or paddleball.

3 Decorate your personal kite or Frisbee and investigate a safe area for flying objects. Host a kite day or Frisbee clinic. Invite a kite flyer or an accomplished Frisbee thrower to demonstrate to your group. Before taking to the air, discuss safety tips that are specific to each sport.

4 Organize a roller skating or bicycle safety clinic and skills session for younger girls, for your troop, or for anyone in your neighborhood who wishes to attend.

5 Use the city sun to create some healthy snacks.

Find out how to make a simple solar food dryer and prepare some fruit to be dried in the sun. Try different fruits and vegetables when they are in season.

or

• Make some sun tea. See page 247.

or

• Make some sun jam. See pages 247–248.

6 Participate in or help organize an outdoor walking or running activity for fun and exercise in the city. This might be an orienteering meet, a walk-a-thon, a running competition, or a Volksmarch (guided walk with a group).

7 Find out what kinds of animals live in your city and where they live. Look for different habitats and spend some time observing wildlife in more than one habitat. Look for parks, vacant fields, trees, roof gardens, and schoolyards. Is there wildlife that lives year round in the city? Are there birds that pass through your city during the fall or spring migration? Is there wildlife in your city that can be harmful to your health? Is there a problem in your city with domestic animals that have been abandoned to become feral animals? Do a project to benefit wildlife in your area.

8 Find a place in your city to go fishing safely or enter a city fishing derby. If you have never fished before, learn from someone who has. Learn how to clean a fish and cook it for eating. Be sure that you are fishing in unpolluted waters so that you can eat the fish that you catch.

9 Get involved in city gardening. Help with a community garden plot, a rooftop garden, window boxes, or planters that brighten up your neighborhood. Make a commitment to tend your garden throughout the growing season. Share your crop or bouquets with a neighborhood food bank, shelter for the homeless, community center, or someone special.

10 Find four different jobs where people work in the outdoors in the city. Talk to people in these jobs; at least two of the four people should be women. Find out why they chose their job, what kind of training is needed for the job, and what kind of salaries and benefits come with the job.

11 Participate in a community service project that tackles a community environmental problem, or help with a community event that involves outdoor recreation. For example, you might be sprucing up a city park or working at an aid station at a city-sponsored marathon.

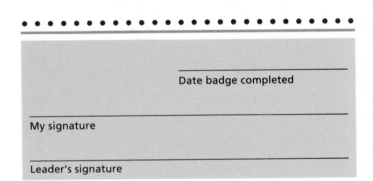

Date badge completed

My signature

Leader's signature

SMALL CRAFT

COMPLETE SIX ACTIVITIES, INCLUDING THE THREE STARRED.

*1 Show that you can select, use, and care for a PFD (personal flotation device).

- Tell when PFDs should be worn and who should wear them (see page 248).
- Tell from the label if a PFD is Coast Guard-approved, the correct size, and the right type for the craft.
- Adjust a life jacket or life vest to fit.
- Know if a PFD is in good condition.
- Throw a buoyant cushion or life ring.
- Float, swim, and do HELP (Heat Escape Lessening Position) and Huddle in a PFD. See page 248.
- If you are a swimmer, put on a PFD while in water that is over your head.

2 Be able to trim your craft (maintain a balanced position of a boat in the water by moving around passengers and gear). Show that you can:

- Tell how to determine your boat's maximum load capacity in good weather.
- Stow things and move weight around safely.
- Change places safely.

3 Show that you can handle a small craft safely. In a rowboat, rowing shell, canoe, sailboat, or motorboat:

- Board.
- Get underway.
- Make turns and go straight.
- Speed up, slow down, and stop.
- Land.
- Secure the craft.

4 Keep a sharp lookout. Show that you practice boating rules-of-the-road as you:

- Keep away from swimmers, divers, and people fishing.
- Look out for other craft, floating objects, or hazards under the surface.
- Spot landmarks or navigational aids such as buoys or lights.
- Help someone in distress, or signal for help yourself.
- Cross wakes correctly.
- Treat the water habitat with care.

5 Do your share to keep a boat shipshape. Do at least three of the following:

- Unload or stow gear or rigging.
- Wash down, bail out, or sponge off.
- Sand, scrape, chip.
- Paint, patch, or fix up.
- Tie knots, splice, or whip lines.

*6 Be ready for boating emergencies. Discuss what to do if:

- You fall overboard.
- Someone else falls overboard.
- The wind rises (or, if sailing, dies).
- You are caught in a storm.
- The boat swamps or capsizes.
- It gets dark or foggy.
- There is a fire on board.

7 Be a water and weather watcher. To tell if it is safe to be out in a boat, show you can take clues from:

- Wind direction and speed.
- Waves, tides, currents, and water releases from dams.
- Cloud formations.
- Weather reports and signals.

8 Take care of your comfort afloat. Model what you should wear to prevent harm from:

- The sun.
- The wind.
- Hot or cold temperatures.
- Wet conditions.

9 Show that you know how to recognize and treat someone who:

- Is not breathing.
- Has sunburn, heat stroke, or heat exhaustion.
- Has hypothermia.
- Is seasick.
- Is in shock from an injury.

Read the section on "Staying Safe" in Chapter 3 of the *Junior Girl Scout Handbook* for more information.

10 Ahoy! Be an "old salt" by doing at least two of the following:

- Use the nautical terms for the major parts of the boat.
- Point out different types of craft for different uses.
- Tell time from ship's bells or a 24-hour clock.
- Find out some everyday phrases that have nautical origins.
- Learn your name in international code flags.
- Use a chart to plot a course.
- Swap sea stories or chanteys.

11 Learn about people who work on board ships.

- Find out what life at sea was like before 1900.
- Look into what it is like to be a crew member, a scientist, or a captain at sea today.
- Imagine life on a ship in the future.

*12 Add at least three important items to this safe boating checklist.

- Have a PFD available for each person.
- File a float plan.

- _____

  _____

  _____

- _____

  _____

  _____

- _____

  _____

  _____

13 Launch a day-long adventure by a small craft, or be in a parade, regatta, or race. On a chart or map, determine:

- What course you will follow or what landmarks you can expect to see.
- How far you will travel.
- How long it will take.
- Where you could find refuge in an emergency and get help.

_____
Date badge completed

_____
My signature

_____
Leader's signature

SWIMMING

COMPLETE SIX ACTIVITIES, INCLUDING THE TWO STARRED.

*1 Go over ways to help yourself in case you accidentally fall in or get into trouble in the water. Show that you know when and how to:

- Select and wear a PFD (personal flotation device). See page 248.
- Keep afloat with clothing and other flotation devices.
- Cooperate with someone who is trying to rescue you.
- Use good sense in cold water, in deep water, in a current, and in rough waters.
- Tread water.

*2 Use the buddy system every time you swim. See page 248.

- Use a checkboard system. See page 248.
- Pair off with a swimmer of equal ability.
- Practice buddy calls until every pair of buddies gets together instantly.

3 Show that you can breathe with a regular rhythm. Try one of these exercises for two minutes. Take breaths while you bob up and down in water over your head. Or, in shallow water, hold onto the side of a pool or dock and turn your head to breathe while you float face down.

4 Look at ways other living things move through the water. Watch for creatures that are jet-propelled or tails that act as rudders, feet that paddle, fins that flutter. Imitate animal actions in a water game that you make up.

5 Show that you can swim:

- Glide six feet.
- Kick 25 yards.
- Swim doing the crawl for 25 yards.
- Do two of these strokes—crawl, elementary backstroke, sidestroke, or breaststroke—for 50 yards each.

6 Show that you can help another swimmer who:

- Has a cramp.
- Is shivering from hypothermia.
- Has a sunburn or heat exhaustion.
- Is tired.

Read the section on "Staying Safe" in Chapter 3 of the *Junior Girl Scout Handbook* for more information.

7 Make a water safety checklist that includes ways to avoid:

- Underwater hazards.
- Falling through ice.
- Falling in accidentally.
- Overestimating your own swimming ability.
- Polluting water that you swim in.
- Swift currents.

8 Swim under the surface. Show that you can do a surface dive, a deep dive, or a jump, then swim underwater and bring up something from the bottom.

9 Perform two different dives from a low board or deck. Be sure to check the water depths and look for hazards first.

10 Get involved in a swimming competition.

- Join a swim team to build your speed and endurance.
- Learn about swimming stars and their records.
- Be able to follow the rules in competitive swimming for starting, turning, timing, and scoring.

11 Participate in a water show, synchronized swim meet, play day, competitive swim meet, or pageant on the water. Or, organize your own event with a group.

12 Learn to snorkel. Show that you can choose a mask that fits your face, put it on so it won't fog, and know how to clear the mask. Show that you can breathe through a snorkel and clear it. Practice your snorkeling skills by swimming 25 yards along the surface parallel to the shore. Show that you can surface dive, swim 15 feet underwater, resurface, and clear your snorkel and mask.

_____
Date badge completed

_____
My signature

_____
Leader's signature

TROOP CAMPER

COMPLETE AT LEAST EIGHT ACTIVITIES, INCLUDING THE THREE STARRED.

*1 Help plan and carry out a camping trip to a troop house, cabin, tent unit, or cottage for at least two nights. Be sure to include a budget, source of finances, menus, equipment needs, personal gear, and plans for activities, transportation, and emergencies. Check with your leader and council to find out what types of sites are available and what permissions are needed to use the site you select.

*2 When you start planning the camping trip, make a list of the disturbances to the environment that might be caused by your activities. Discuss how you will change the activity (e.g., changing from wood fires to a camp stove for cooking) to lessen the impact. Make all the changes that will help you to "walk softly" on this earth. See page 248.

3 Plan well-balanced menus that fit your budget. Include at least one meal that requires cooking. With your group, help shop, pack, carry, store, prepare, and serve the food. Demonstrate your knowledge of environmentally sound sanitation practices.

4 Develop a list of troop and personal equipment to take with you on your trip. Help to pack and carry the equipment and supplies.

or

Make something for your own or group use at camp, such as a day pack, a stove sack, a water bottle with a holder, a food sack, or a fire starter.

5 Discuss what you and the group will do in case of an emergency. Review the fire and evacuation plans posted at the site. Learn what you should do. Practice one of the drills posted.

6 Learn to recognize hazards such as cliffs, poisonous plants, animals, or rock slides on the camp site that may be harmful to you, and decide what you might do to protect yourself.

and

Demonstrate to the group what to do if you get lost and some preventive measures that you might use. Read the section on "Staying Safe" in Chapter 3 of the *Junior Girl Scout Handbook* for more information.

☀	🪣	🧻	🔥	🪵	🧹	🍲	☕
MORNING	Susan	Rachel	Mary	Ayisha	Toni	Lee	Sarah
AFTERNOON	Toni	Ayisha	Lee	Sarah	Mary	Susan	Rachel
EVENING	Lee	Sarah	Toni	Susan	Rachel	Mary	Ayisha

7 Before you go, make a schedule for activities, meals, cleanup, free time, setting up and closing camp. Make a kaper chart that gives each girl a turn at the different jobs.

8 Make or take resources, such as a camera, sketch pad, notebook, tape recorder, magnifying lens, compass, waterscope, star map, or nature guide, to help you find your way, to make discoveries, and to record what you discover at camp.

9 With a buddy or patrol/group, be responsible for a flag ceremony, a quiet game, an evening program, a stargazing evening, a Girl Scout's Own, team-building activities, an environmental awareness activity, something to do while traveling to and from the campsite, or an activity to do when an unexpected change in the weather keeps you under cover.

or

Lead a tour or hike to locate points of interest and boundaries of the site.

10 Learn a skill to use at future camping events such as pitching a tent, orienteering, backpacking, purifying water, or cooking in a way new to you.

11 Leave the site in good condition, unpack and store troop or patrol equipment properly, return borrowed items, pay bills, and write thank-you notes to those who helped make the trip possible.

12 While on your troop camping trip, have someone who has been to resident camp come and share her experiences with you. Discuss some of the differences between troop camping and resident camp.

*13 (Do this activity last.) Make a list of camping tips to share with new campers and to help you the next time. Write down what you discovered about yourself and the outdoors and what you hope to do when you go camping again.

_____
Date badge completed

_____
My signature

_____
Leader's signature

WALKING
FOR FITNESS

*1 Learn three stretching exercises to do before walking. Practice warming up before you walk and cooling down after your walk. For more information on exercise and physical fitness, read the section on physical exercise in the Contemporary Issues booklet, *Developing Health and Fitness: Be Your Best!*

2 Develop a personal walking program for at least one month. Walk at least two miles a day three times per week. Each week, try to increase your speed and distance. Keep a diary of the length of your walk, the time spent walking, the weather conditions, and anything else you would like to record.

3 Visit several stores that sell walking shoes. Ask a salesperson what to look for in a walking shoe. Compare several brands of shoes. Be able to explain which brand you would buy and why.

4 Prepare a simple first aid kit to take on walks. Know how to care for sunburn, insect bites, heat exhaustion, heat stroke, and blisters.

5 Plan and take a well-balanced, easy-to-carry snack for an extended walk. Know what foods and drinks cause thirst and know which ones quench thirst.

*6 On a walk, use a street or road map to arrive at a new destination. Know which side of the road to walk on and how to walk safely in a group.

7 Take part in a project to clean up a walkway or trail in or near your community.

8 Help make a list of interesting places within a two-mile radius of your troop meeting place or school. Write down the directions for reaching each site. Include information on fees, hours open, nearby picnic and toilet facilities. Share this information with other Girl Scouts in your area.

9 Find out about the organized groups in your community interested in walking. Attend one of their meetings or ask someone from one of the groups to come tell your group about their activities. Find out if you can join them for a walk or take part in any of their special projects.

10 Show that you can dress for the weather when you walk. Know the importance of dressing in layers.

● ●

Date badge completed

My signature

Leader's signature

WATER FUN

COMPLETE SIX ACTIVITIES, INCLUDING THE TWO STARRED.

1 Increase your awareness of different water habitats by doing three of these:
 - Listen to the sounds of moving water by the ocean, along a lakeshore, or by a swiftly running stream.
 - Watch waves in salt or fresh water.
 - Watch a leaf float in running water.
 - Smell salt air.
 - Feel a breeze under sail or fly a kite at the beach or lakeshore.
 - Watch changing colors in the water during different times of the day.

 Then express your own feelings or enjoy music, art, or words that others have created about water.

*2 Show how to use a PFD (personal flotation device). See page 248.
 - Put it on, adjust it to fit, and fasten it securely.
 - Jump into the water with it on.
 - Float and swim with a PFD on.
 - Practice the HELP (Heat Escape Lessening Position) and the Huddle position to keep warm. See page 248.

*3 Make up and play a game in the water to show you understand and can use the buddy system.

4 Without making a swimming rescue, demonstrate ways to assist someone in trouble in the water. Safely practice:
- Reaching with a towel, pole, arm, or human chain.
- Tossing a ring buoy and line, inner tube, or other buoyant object to help keep someone afloat.
- Rescuing someone who's fallen through ice.

5 Without disturbing the natural environment, search for four signs of life along the water's edge.

6 Show how to get in and out of a small craft safely. Keep the boat in trim (balanced) as you:
- Load gear.
- Stow things.
- Sit down and stand up.
- Move around and change places.

7 Live a bit of a sailor's life. Do at least two of the following:
- Tie a fancy knot.
- Sail a model boat.
- Walk the deck of a historic ship or visit a maritime museum.
- Learn and teach a sea chantey.
- Launch your own nautical lore activity.

8 Keep yourself comfortable even when you are wet or perspiring. To see how you can keep warm when it is cold and wet or cool when it is hot, try out the following:
- Clothing made of wool, cotton, or synthetic materials.
- Clothing in dark and light colors.
- Different kinds of hats.
- Different kinds of foot gear.

9 Show that you care about clean water. List at least five ways that you can save water and not add to pollution. Then make it an everyday habit to be a clean-water-saver.

10 Show how well you can swim:
- Float on your back for one minute.
- Demonstrate two different swimming strokes.
- Tread water for two minutes.
- Pick your best stroke and swim 50 yards.

11 Attend a water event such as a canoe or kayak race, swim meet, surfing competition, fishing derby, game, parade of sail, synchronized swimming show, or water ski show. Get someone to go along who will point out special things to look for and help you share the excitement.

12 Tour a place where people go to have fun on the water, such as a marina, pool, cruise ship, party boat dock, or boat landing. Talk to someone who works there and find out what they do that helps others enjoy and be safe on the water.

● ●

_____
Date badge completed

_____
My signature

_____
Leader's signature

WILLDLIFE

1 Find out which bird, tree, and flower have been chosen to represent your state. See if your state has any other wildlife symbols, such as a state insect or a state fish. Discover why each was chosen.

2. Learn to identify the poisonous plants in your locality and where each is most likely to be found. Know what to do if a poisonous plant is touched or eaten. Learn about poisonous animals and insects in your area, and what to do if you see a poisonous or sick animal.

3 Visit a wildlife refuge, a nature center, a Girl Scout Lou Henry Hoover Memorial Sanctuary, or a wildlife management area. Investigate how this area is providing habitat for wildlife. Find out if there are ways the area is being managed for wildlife and why.

*4 Find out if there are any endangered plants and animals in your state. Find out why they are endangered and what is being done to protect them. Learn about an organization that works to protect endangered species in your area, the United States, or the world. Participate in a project that improves or establishes wildlife habitat in your community, state, or another country.

POISON SUMAC

POISON IVY

POISON OAK

*5 Focus on at least one of the following wildlife groups and complete the activities for that group as outlined below:

Amphibians
Birds
Fish
Insects
Mammals
Reptiles

Learn to identify at least five species of this particular wildlife group by a combination of how they act (behavior), how they sound, how they look (field marks), or where they live (habitat).

Describe the characteristics that are shared by species of this wildlife group. For example, how do they give birth to their young; are they warm- or cold-blooded?

6 Visit a park, zoo, stream, aquarium, wildlife preserve, or perhaps your own backyard, where you can observe a species from your wildlife group. Observe how it interacts with its environment and with other creatures. Does it have any special adaptations, such as teeth or color, to do this? How does it eat, move, and relate to others of its own species?

Learn which species in this group are protected by law.

7 Find out about careers related to wildlife by talking with someone who is in wildlife management, works for a zoological society, or is a wildlife biologist.

Date badge completed

My signature

Leader's signature

THE COOKIE CONNECTION

COMPLETE FIVE ACTIVITIES, INCLUDING THE ONES STARRED.

1 Find out about the different ways your troop or group has sold Girl Scout cookies in the past. Then, with the help of your Girl Scout friends, create five new ways. Can you sell them at a community fair? neighborhood recreation center? holiday parade? Maybe you can meet with officials in your town who can help you with the project.

2 Imagine asking a salesperson for information about a product and she doesn't know the answer. Good salespeople know all about their merchandise. Find out about Girl Scout cookies. What are the ingredients? How many calories do they contain? How long have Girl Scouts been selling cookies as a way to earn money for activities? Also, be prepared to tell your customers what your troop or group plans to do with the money earned.

3 Knowing how to deal with the public is an important part of being a salesperson. You should always be polite and say "thank you," even if someone doesn't buy anything. With your troop or group, think of several situations that might come up when you are selling cookies and how you will handle them. For example, someone wants ten boxes of trefoil cookies delivered to his daughter's birthday party; someone tells you she is tired of always being asked to buy things; a little boy says he would like to buy a box of cookies for his mother but doesn't have any money.

INGREDIENTS: ENRICHED FLOUR (WHEAT FLOUR, NIACIN, REDUCED IRON, THIAMINE MONONITRATE, RIBOFLAVIN, FOLIC ACID), SUGAR, VEGETABLE SHORTENING (CONTAINS ONE OR MORE OF THE FOLLOWING PARTIALLY HYDROGENATED OILS: PALM KERNEL, SOYBEAN, COTTONSEED), COCOA (PROCESSED WITH ALKALI), CARAMEL COLOR, LEAVENING (SODIUM BICARBONATE, MONOCALCIUM PHOSPHATE, AMMONIUM BICARBONATE), HIGH FRUCTOSE CORN SYRUP, SALT, WHEY, SOY LECITHIN (EMULSIFIER), PEPPERMINT OIL, NATURAL AND ARTIFICIAL FLAVOR.

4 With your troop or group, design a giant poster or display for your cookie campaign that is suitable for a mall, a public building, or other place where many people will see it. (In most cases, you have to get permission from store owners or public officials to do this.) Think about the ways advertisements get your attention. Is it the bright colors, pictures, or what it says? Consider a design that includes information about the cookies, how the money earned is used, and what Girl Scouts are all about.

or

Have a cookie party and see how many adjectives your group can come up with to describe Girl Scout cookies. Maybe you can use them for an advertisement.

5 If you have a computer and know how to use the Internet, see what information you can find about selling Girl Scout cookies and then share it with your troop or group.

* 6 With your troop or group, develop a plan for what to do with the money you earn from cookie sales. Think of several projects or activities. Estimate the costs of each activity by finding out about admission fees, transportation, etc. Based on the amount the troop will earn from the sale of each box of cookies, figure out how many boxes you would need to sell to reach your goal. Work out a plan for reaching your goal and chart your progress.

or

Read pages 105–109 in your *Junior Girl Scout Handbook* and make a troop or group budget for an activity that you would like to do with the money you have all earned selling Girl Scout cookies.

7 Be a good neighbor. Buy several boxes of Girl Scout cookies with your troop or group money and wrap them in pretty paper to give as gifts. You might take them to senior citizens in a nursing home, someone in the hospital, or maybe a couple who just got married. Use this as an opportunity to make a new friend and share experiences.

8 With your troop or group, think about the different jobs connected to food products, such as farm grower, baker, advertiser, artist, nutritionist. With help from your leader, make plans to talk to two people about their jobs and what the jobs involve.

* **9** Make a list of safety rules for selling Girl Scout cookies. Get ideas from your leader, parents, teachers, and other adults. Then put them on a poster where everyone can see them. Review them from time to time.

MORE

Read pages 17, 52, and 171 in the *Junior Girl Scout Handbook* to find out more about selling Girl Scout cookies.

Safety Rules

1. Always sell cookies with an adult.

2. Never leave money from cookie sales lying around where it can get lost or stolen.

3. _____

_____

4. _____

_____

5. _____

_____

6. _____

_____

7. _____

_____

_____
Date badge completed

_____
My signature

_____
Leader's signature

OUR OWN
TROOP'S BADGE

There are a lot of activities in this book and many badges from which to choose. But, you and the girls in your troop might have developed an interest in an activity for which no badge is listed. Or, while you were doing a badge, one of the activities may have been so interesting that you want to work on it more. Maybe you've completed all the badges on the same subject but want to go further. Or, your community might be famous for something unique and you want to learn more about it. That's why Junior Girl Scouts have an Our Own Troop's Badge. As a troop, you decide on the activities, the name, and the symbol of the badge. This badge then becomes special for your troop.

What Do We Do?
• Check that the subject is not the same as any other Junior Girl Scout badge, including the ones in the *Junior Girl Scout Handbook*.
• Your badge should be on a topic that is consistent with the Girl Scout Promise and Law.
• Your topic should be broad enough so that you can do from four to eight different activities.
• Your topic should be interesting to all the girls in the troop.

How Do We Create Our Activities?
Brainstorm with the other girls in your troop and your leader to think of as many activities as you can on your topic. Think of these things when making up activities:

• Are we learning something new?
• Do all the activities show respect for the Promise and Law?
• Can all the girls in my troop do this activity?
• Does the activity help others, the community, or the environment?
• Are there any people or organizations in the community who can help us with our badge?
• Are there enough activities to include something fun or interesting for everyone in the troop?
• Are the activities safe?
• Are the activities free or affordable?
• Are the activities challenging and not too easy or too boring?
• Will we have enough time to finish the activities?
• Do the activities respect the differences in values, tradition, and culture of the girls in my troop?
• Are the activities original? (They should not repeat activities in this book.)
• How are the activities related to Girl Scouting?
• How will we know we have completed the badge? What will we have accomplished?

Then What Happens?
Your Girl Scout council must approve your badge topic. After your troop designs a symbol, and chooses a title, your leader sends a copy to your council. Some Girl Scout councils will also want to see your activities. Once your Our Own Troop's Badge is approved, have fun completing your very special set of activities.

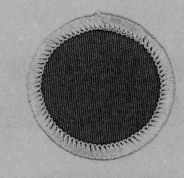

OUR OWN
COUNCIL'S BADGE

An Our Own Council's Badge reflects what is special about your community and your area. Your leader can find out from your council office if your council has its own badge.

Some topics for an Our Own Council's Badge would be a special or unique resource located in the council, such as a science museum, a space exploration center, a historical site, or an ecological feature, such as the seashore, a mountain range or desert, or an endangered or unique species of plant, animal, or insect.

An Our Own Council's Badge is different from a patch you would get for attending a council event. An Our Own Council's Badge requires the same kind of activities and learning as other badges do. The activities should follow the same guidelines as those for an Our Own Troop's Badge.

THE JUNIOR AIDE PATCH

Help Brownie Girl Scouts bridge to Junior Girl Scouts and earn your Junior Aide patch. Junior Girl Scouting is different from Brownie Girl Scouting. You have the opportunity to learn so much about yourself, your community, and the World of Girl Scouting. You have new badges to earn, new activities to try, and new skills to learn. Brownie Girl Scouts might not know what Junior Girl Scouting is all about. The Junior Aide patch gives you the chance to prepare them for new fun and challenges.

How Do We Do It?
Talk with your leader about doing the Junior Aide patch. With help from your leader or council, find a troop of Brownie Girl Scouts where girls are bridging.

If you have decided to earn the Junior Aide patch by helping Brownie Girl Scouts in bridging activities, make a plan. Chapter 6, "Leadership in Action," in your *Junior Girl Scout Handbook* will help you plan and evaluate your activities.

What Do We Do?
Do four of the following with girls in their last year as Brownie Girl Scouts, including the two activities starred.

*1 Visit at least two different Brownie Girl Scout meetings. Talk about Junior Girl Scouting with the troop. Lead the Brownie Girl Scouts in a song or game that is new to them or demonstrate camping skills you have learned as a Junior Girl Scout.

*2 Invite Brownie Girl Scouts to one of your troop meetings. Let the Brownies ask you any questions they have about being Junior Girl Scouts. Discuss the activities your troop has planned for the year.

3 Help Brownie Girl Scouts choose and complete an activity from the *Junior Girl Scout Handbook*.

4 With Brownie Girl Scouts, plan a sports or multicultural festival or other event where activities from the *Junior Girl Scout Handbook* are emphasized.

5 Meet with a Brownie Girl Scout troop and their leader. Plan an overnight camping trip, backyard campout, or other trip with the girls and their leader, or invite them along on one of your troop's trips if your leader agrees. Review any rules or safety tips the Brownie Girl Scouts should learn before the trip.

6 Invite Brownie Girl Scouts to help plan and participate in a service project your troop is doing.

7 Help a Brownie Girl Scout do a Dabbler badge.

8 Assist a Brownie Girl Scout leader at a council-sponsored wider opportunity.

9 Find out which Brownie Girl Scout Try-Its the girls have earned and have most enjoyed. Show them which activities from the *Junior Girl Scout Handbook* or which badges from *Girl Scout Badges and Signs* would give them more opportunities to explore these subjects.

10 With Brownie Girl Scouts, plan a special ceremony for Thinking Day, for the birthday of Girl Scouting in the United States, for Girl Scout Leader's Day, or for Juliette Gordon Low's birthday. Or, plan a Girl Scouts' Own.

You can change activities or add activities as long as Brownie Girl Scouts are learning more about Junior Girl Scouting. The most important thing to remember is to have fun and to do the activities you and the Brownie Girl Scouts most enjoy.

_____

Date badge completed

_____

My signature

_____

Leader's signature

 Choose one badge from Health and Fitness and do the activities. When you have finished the activities, draw the badge or write its name in the circle and color in the red section of your rainbow.

 Choose one badge from Science and Technology and do the activities. When you have finished the activities, draw the badge or write its name in the circle and color in the orange section of the rainbow.

Choose one badge from Exploring the Out-of-Doors and do the activities. When you have finished the activities, draw the badge or write its name in the circle and color in the yellow section of the rainbow.

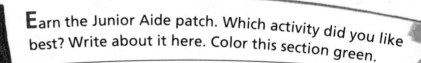 Earn the Junior Aide patch. Which activity did you like best? Write about it here. Color this section green.

Earn the Girl Scouting in the U.S.A. and the Girl Scouting Around the World badges from World Citizens. Draw the badges or write their names in the circles and color in this line blue.

Choose one badge from Arts Around the World and do the activities. When you have finished the activities, draw or write its name in the circle and color in the purple section of the rainbow.

236

Sign of the Rainbow

Where do rainbows end? Following rainbows can lead you to new discoveries and new worlds. When you do the activities in the Sign of the Rainbow, you'll explore the five worlds of interest in Girl Scouting. You'll also share your experiences and adventures in Girl Scouting with younger girls.

Organize a display, slide show, video production, or other activity that introduces the five worlds of Girl Scouting to others.

Record what you did in this space

_____

_____

_____

_____

and color the trefoil gold.

Sign of the Sun

Develop a personal exercise plan and record your participation for one month. Choose from activities like: aerobics, biking, dancing, jogging, swimming, walking. Rate how you feel using ☹ ☺ each day as part of your record.

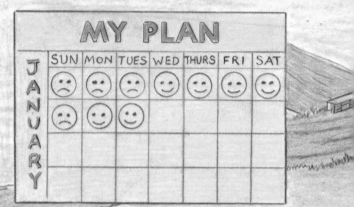

MY PLAN

JANUARY	SUN	MON	TUES	WED	THURS	FRI	SAT
	☹	☹	☹	☺	☺	☺	☺
	☹	☺	☺				

START HERE

Put yourself into the picture at each of the eight stops on our fun-filled trail to fitness! Good health and lifetime leisure skills are yours if you follow this trail.

Complete an activity from a Contemporary Issues booklet or Issues for Girl Scouts booklet:

- ○ *Girls are Great*
- ○ *Tune In to Well-Being, Say No to Drugs: Substance Abuse* or
- ○ *Decisions for Your Life: Preventing Teenage Pregnancy*

OR

Participate in a council or neighborhood fitness event

Do the
- ○ **First Aid badge**
    or
- ○ **Safety Sense**

Do the
- ○ **Walking for Fitness**
    or
- ○ **Hiker badge**
    or
- ○ **Finding Your Way**

238

Complete
- ○ **Health and Fitness**
  or
- ○ **Exploring Healthy Eating**
  or
- ○ **Outdoor Cook**

Complete one of these:
- ○ **Doing Hobbies**
- ○ **Sports**
- ○ **Sports Sampler**

FINISH

HELP ORGANIZE A HEALTH FAIR, OLYMPIAD, FITNESS FAIR, OR ORIENTEERING MEET, OR HELP BUILD A PAR COURSE OR HIKING TRAIL.

FINISH

Complete an Outdoor Badge:
- ○ Horse Lover
- ○ Outdoor Creativity
- ○ Outdoor Fun in the City
- ○ Swimming
- ○ Water Fun

Sign of the Satellite

Participate in a service project that improves the earth for the future, such as recycling, scientific research (like monitoring acid rain or water pollution or participating in a bird count), pollution reduction, or energy conservation.

Complete
- ○ Celebrating People
  or
- ○ World Neighbors
  or
- ○ Geography Fun

Shadow someone who works in a government, science, or technological career that affects your future. Share your experience with others.

Do three activities from the Ecology or Eco-Action Badges

The Sign of the Satellite asks you to look at Planet Earth in a different way, using the World of Today and Tomorrow, the World of People, and the World of the Out-of-Doors as springboards. Color in the stars next to each of the seven activities as you complete them.

Interview someone in their 40's and someone in their 60's (or older). Ask each what inventions exist today that did not exist when each was 10 years old. How did the inventions change that person's life? What hopes and concerns did each have for the future when she was growing up? Make your own list of hopes and concerns for the future.

Complete the
O Ready for
Tomorrow Badge

Earn
O Sky Search
or
O Aerospace
or
O Weather Watch

Helps and Resources

HEALTH AND FITNESS

BECOMING A TEEN

ACTIVITIES 2 AND 6
The information you gather in Activity 2 can be used as a reference for Activity 6.

EXPLORING HEALTHY EATING

ACTIVITY 1
Some of the beginning cooking steps that you might want to teach a younger child could be reading the recipe, gathering the ingredients and necessary equipment, measuring dry and liquid ingredients, working safely in the kitchen, serving food attractively, and cleaning up.

FAMILY LIVING SKILLS

ACTIVITIES 7 AND 8
Your results from Activity 7 can be very helpful in completing Activity 8. The two activities can be planned together.

FIRST AID

To complete some of these activities, you will need to consult with or obtain resources from your local American Red Cross chapter, American Heart Association, hospitals, emergency medical services, colleges or universities, or other organizations that offer first aid training or provide first aid materials.

ACTIVITIES 2, 3, AND 6
Review the "First Aid Guide" in Chapter 3 of the *Junior Girl Scout Handbook* for instructions on how to do some of the first aid procedures in these activities.

First aid for stopped breathing and choking should not be performed on anyone without prior instruction from an adult certified in first aid. Keep in mind that the procedures are different for children and adults.

PET CARE

Another way to learn about how to care for a variety of pets would be to volunteer as a pet walker or sitter for a busy person or a vacationing family.

SAFETY SENSE

ACTIVITY 2
It may be very helpful if you publish the results of your accident survey and circulate it around your school or community. You can type or write out the results and have copies made for distribution.

ACTIVITY 3
Many organizations produce similar booklets or brochures and distribute them to businesses and nonprofit organizations that reach the public. Collect some brochures of interest to you from public libraries, doctors' offices, post offices, community centers, and other public buildings. Notice how they are written and illustrated.

These ideas will help you create your own booklet.

Safety Sense

The red arrows point to the safety hazards. How many did you find? The hazards include:

- plant vase on top of TV
- open drawer
- loose clothing piled on floor
- loose iron cord
- skateboard by doorway
- dangling lamp cord
- water glass by table edge
- scatter rug at top of stairs
- curtains blowing over stove top
- pot boiling over
- pot handle sticking out
- electric radio by sink
- knife out in open
- open paint cans
- water spilled on floor
- mop handle blocking doorway
- open scissors on table
- electrical cord across floor
- lamp that could be easily tipped over
- overloaded wall outlet
- electrical cords across floor
- fireplace without screen
- newspapers by fireplace
- plant on TV

SPORTS; SPORTS SAMPLER

For some of these activities you will need to get advice from a physical education teacher, coach, athlete, referee or other sports official, recreation leader, or fitness instructor. You might also work with a parks and recreation department, school, camp, church, or synagogue that offers a sports program. Libraries, local or school newspapers, and sports magazines can provide additional information on various sports activities and events.

WORLD CITIZENS

ACTIVE CITIZEN

Through Girl Scouting, each girl is encouraged to become a stronger member of her own religious group. Religious recognition programs are developed and administered by the religious groups themselves. If the recognition is a pin, a girl may wear it on her badge sash below the membership stars or on the right side of her uniform, level with her membership pin.

For girls of the Baha'i Faith: The Unity of Mankind program is earned by completing a six-, nine-, or 12-month project under the supervision of either the Baha'i representative appointed by the local Spiritual Assembly of the Baha'i in the community or a representative appointed by the Baha'i Committee on Scouting. For more information, contact: Baha'i Committee on Scouting, Baha'i National Center, Wilmette, Illinois 60091.

For girls of the Buddhist Faith: The Padma Award is designed to help a girl put into practice the ideals of the Buddhist faith and the Girl Scout Promise and Law. For more information, contact: National Buddhist Committee on Scouting, Buddhist Churches of America, 1710 Octavia Street, San Francisco, California 94109.

For Girls Who Are Christian Scientists: The God and Country program is designed to bring to Girl Scout activities a greater sense of serving mankind through living the teachings of Christian Science. For more information, contact: First Church of Christ, Scientist, Sunday School Activities, A142 Christian Science Center, Boston, Massachusetts 02115.

For Girls of the Eastern Orthodox Faith: The Chi-Rho program emphasizes learning about church, prayer, and worship and service to others. The Alpha Omega program emphasizes a girl's life and actions as an Orthodox Christian, the work and organization of her parish church, and service projects for the church. For more information, contact: Program of Religious Activities with Youth (PRAY), Box 6900, St. Louis, Missouri 63123.

For Girls of the Hindu Faith: The Dharma Award is a recognition that a girl receives after working on a program that helps a girl become more aware of God's presence in her daily life, especially within her home and community. For more information, contact: The North American Hindu Association, 46133 Amesbury Drive, Plymouth, Michigan 48170.

For Girls of the Jewish Faith: The Lehavah Award for Girl Scouts ages 6–9 emphasizes learning about oneself, one's family, and one's religion. The Menorah Award for Girl Scouts ages 11–17 is a program which gives more opportunities to learn about the Jewish religion and to participate in Jewish living. For more information, contact: the National Jewish Girl Scout Committee, Synagogue Council of America, 327 Lexington Avenue, New York, New York 10016.

For Girls of the Lutheran Faith: The God and Family program helps a girl find out more about herself and her relationships with her family, with God, and with the "family of God." Lutheran Living Faith, for girls ages 11–18, is designed to help girls become more active in their churches' programs and in community life. For more information, contact: Programs of Religious Activities with Youth, Box 6900, St. Louis, Missouri 63123.

For Girls of the Church of Jesus Christ of Latter-Day Saints: The Gospel in Action Award is for girls ages 10–11. For more information, contact: Salt Lake Distribution Center, The Church of Jesus Christ of Latter-day Saints, 1999 West 1700 South, Salt Lake City, Utah 84104.

For Girls of Protestant and Independent Christian Churches: The God and Country series has four units. God and Family, for ages 9–10 or grades 4–5, emphasizes understanding a girl's faith as it relates to her home and family and understanding the family's relationship to the church. God and Church, for ages 11–13 or grades 6–8, gives a girl the chance to participate in services and projects that will help her understand more clearly the mission of her church. For more information, contact: Programs of Religious Activities with Youth, Box 6900, St. Louis, Missouri 63123. The Episcopal Church has prepared a supplement to the God and Country series that is available from the same address.

For Girls of the Religious Society of Friends: The That of God Award is for girls in grades 2–5 to help explore their faith more deeply, particularly in relation to the Girl Scout Promise and Law. For more information, contact: The Friends Committee on Scouting, c/o Dennis Clarke, 85 Willowbrook Road, Cromwell, Connecticut 06416.

For Girls of the Reorganized Church of Jesus Christ of the Latter Day Saints: World Community has three age-level programs. Light of the World is for ages 8–10; Liahona is for ages 11–14; Exploring My Life and World is for ages 15–18. Girls complete a series of projects that provide growing experiences through all the important aspects of life. For more information, contact: The Youth Ministries Office, The Auditorium, P.O. Box 1059, Independence, Missouri 64051.

For Girls of the Roman Catholic Faith: I Live My Faith is a program for girls ages 9–11. With her parents, a girl will appreciate more deeply the place of God and religion in her life. For more information, contact: National Federation for Catholic Youth Ministry, 3700-A Oakview Terrace, N.E., Washington, D.C. 20017 or the local Roman Catholic Diocesan youth director.

For Girls of the Unitarian Universalist Faith: Religion in Life is a program of reading, thought, discussion, and action in Unitarian Universalist principles and action. For more information, contact: Unitarian Association, Distribution Center, 25 Beacon Street, Boston, Massachusetts 02108.

For Girls of the Unity Church: A spiritual growth program, God in Me, is for girls ages 6–11 to help deepen their faith and learn more about the Christ within. The Light of God program, for girls ages 11–13, is designed to give a practical method to achieve a basic spiritual understanding of the truths taught by Unity. For more information, contact: Association of Unity Churches, P.O. Box 610, Lee's Summit, Missouri 64063.

For Girls of the Islamic Faith: In the Name of Allah Award is for girls ages 9–11. With the help of counselors, the Junior Girl Scout will concentrate on the Islamic lunar calendar, Quranic verses, Islamic food laws, great women in Islam, and her own place in the Muslim community at large. For more information, contact: The Islamic Committee on Girl Scouting, 31 Marian Street, Stamford, Connecticut 06907.

For more information about religious recognitions in Girl Scouting, contact the local Girl Scout council or National/International Relations, Girl Scouts of the U.S.A., 420 Fifth Avenue, New York, New York 10018.

WOMEN'S STORIES

ACTIVITY 5
Here are some other famous women you can learn about for this activity:

Corazon Aquino on her first day as President of the Philippines, Junko Tabei reaching the top of Mount Everest, Sarah Winnemucca lecturing in Washington, D.C., about the mistreatment of her people, Rosalyn Yalow winning the Nobel Prize for medicine, Hannah Senesh parachuting into Yugoslavia during World War II, Amina, Nigerian queen, becoming the ruler of her country in 1576, Felisa Rincon de Guatier becoming the first female mayor of San Juan, Puerto Rico, Rachel Carson winning the Conservationist Award from the National Wildlife Federation, Fatima fleeing to Medina with her father, Mohammed, in 622, Anne Frank, in hiding, writing in her diary, Althea Gibson, winning at Wimbledon, Martha Graham receiving the Medal of Freedom in 1976, Queen Liliuokalani on her last day as Queen of the Hawaiian Islands, Annie Oakley winning the shooting match that started her career, Emily Dickinson choosing a topic for a poem.

• •

SCIENCE AND TECHNOLOGY

Sample troop budget

Troop # _____ Month _____

Income		*Expenses*	
Dues • • • • • • • • • $100		Equipment/supplies • • • $100	
Special project • • • 100		Troop trip • • • • • • • • • • • 50	
Total income • • • $200		Total expenses • • • • • • • $150	

BALANCE
Income $200 (minus) Expenses $150 (equals) Balance $50

Cash on hand as of _____ (last day of month)

MONEY SENSE

ACTIVITY 1
A sample troop budget is shown above.

READY FOR TOMORROW

ACTIVITY 2
Instructions for solar ovens are available from: Solar Box Cookers International, 1724 Eleventh Street, Sacramento, California 95814, or see diagram on the following pages.

Solar Box

Materials: Single plate of glass; corrugated cardboard for two large boxes with one lid and four "toppers"; aluminium foil; water-base glue; insulation (crumpled newspaper); thin, black metal tray; string and stick or wire.

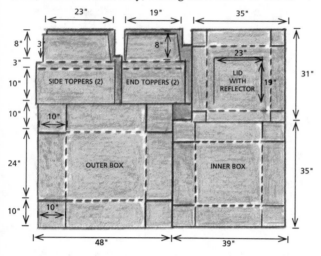

Instructions:

To make the box:

1. Glue aluminum foil to one side of *all* cardboard pieces except: Foil *both* sides of *inner* box and only the indicated parts of the four toppers.

2. Make boxes by folding up sides and gluing.

3. Fill bottom of outer box with crumpled newspaper to support inner box.

4. Add inner box and fill sides between boxes with more insulation.

5. Put toppers over top edges of boxes.

6. Put black tray in bottom of inner box. Tie or glue outer flaps.

To make the lid/reflector:

1. Fold lid piece over finished box.

2. Cut, fold, glue corners; cut three sides of reflector flap (a little smaller than the glass).

3. Spread strip of glue or caulk around edge of glass, set inside lid. Press flat until glue is dry.

4. Fold up flap for reflector. Attach stick or wire to hold up reflector.

Cooking Procedures:

1. Put foods into dark pots. Put lids on pots.

2. Put pots in cooker. Put lid on cooker.

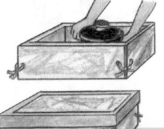

TYPE OF FOOD AND COOKING TIME ON A SUNNY DAY		
for 10 pounds (4 kilos) of food		
EASY TO COOK 1-2 hours	**MEDIUM** 3-4 hours	**HARD TO COOK** 5-8 hours
EGGS	POTATOES	MOST DRIED BEANS
RICE	PASTRY	LARGE ROASTS (all meats get more tender)
FRUIT	VEGETABLES (roots)	
VEGETABLES (above ground)	SOME BEANS, LENTILS	
	MOST MEATS	
FISH	BREAD	
CHICKEN		

TO PASTEURIZE WATER

Small jar-2 hours • Large jar-4 hours

COOKING TIME IS LONGER
- WITH LARGER AMOUNTS OF FOOD
- IF PARTLY CLOUDY
- WHEN THE SUN IS LOWER IN THE SKY

DARK, COVERED POT SUBSTITUTES: Blacken cookware with paint or soot/cooking oil. Shiny pots cook most poorly.

3. Set box in a sunny place so reflector will face toward the sun.
Then fasten prop stick so extra light shines on pots.

Enjoy a delicious meal!
5. TIME TO EAT! Be careful, the pots get very hot!

4. Leave 'til mealtime.... No need to stir food— it won't burn.

ACTIVITY 7

The Girl Scout Promise and Law are a credo that you have agreed to live by as a Girl Scout. To help learn more about writing a credo, refer to Chapter 3, "Developing Values to Last a Lifetime," in the Contemporary Issues booklet *Earth Matters: A Challenge for Environmental Action.*

SKY SEARCH

See *Outdoor Education in Girl Scouting,* especially the section on exploration tools in the chapter "Camping and Campcraft Skills" and the section on astronomy in the chapter "Outdoor Education Activities in the Five Worlds of Interest."

WATER WONDERS

ACTIVITY 6

For how-to's on purifying water, see *Outdoor Education in Girl Scouting,* the section on water supply in the chapter "Camping and Campcraft Skills."

ACTIVITY 9

Plankton net how-to's:

Purpose: To collect small aquatic organisms floating in the water of a stream, pond, or ocean.

Using the plankton net:

1. Tow behind a canoe or rowboat, or pull through the water while walking in a shallow area of a pond or body of salt water.
2. After several minutes, pull in the net and examine the contents of the bottle. Look at them closely with a hand lens.

The organisms in the plankton net represent the multitude of creatures that are basic to aquatic food chains. For example, microscopic algae are eaten by small animals, which are in turn eaten by small fish.

Plankton Net

Materials: Nylon stocking or pantyhose, wire, small plastic bottle, fishing swivel, fishing line and small lead weight, rubber band, needle and thread, tow rope.

Instructions:

1. Cut off a section of stocking about 12 inches long (remove the foot).
2. Cut a piece of wire and bend it to form a ring about 6 inches in diameter. Fit the wire ring into the larger end of the stocking and attach it with a needle and thread.
3. Cut three pieces of fishing line. Attach each to the ring at one end and to the fishing swivel at the other.
4. Insert a plastic bottle (such as a film canister) into the narrow end of the stocking and hold in place with the rubber band.
5. Attach a tow rope and small lead weight to the swivel.

ARTS AROUND THE WORLD

ART TO WEAR

These terms are used in this badge:

Appliqué Sewing a fabric decoration to a different type of fabric.
Batik A process for coloring fabrics using melted wax.
Brocade A rich cloth with a raised design.
Crewel Sewing a design or pattern using wool yarn.

Embroidery Sewing a design or pattern with colored thread using decorative stitches.
Finger weaving Using fingers as a loom to make small items like bracelets and belts.
Macramé Knotting thread, string, or rope to make a pattern.
Pile A cloth with a soft, velvet-like surface.

Silk screen Printing a design through a piece of silk or other fabric.

Stencil A cut-out pattern or design that is used to color fabric or paper.

Tabby A silk fabric with wavy markings.

Tapestry A heavy cloth woven with decorative designs and pictures.

Tatting A type of lace made using a shuttle.

Tie-dye Making a pattern or design on cloth by bunching the fabric, tying it, and dipping it into dye.

Twill A fabric woven in diagonal ribs.

Warp wrapping Taking warp threads and wrapping the weft threads over them.

CERAMICS AND CLAY

ACTIVITY 6

Graffito Decoration on clay made by scratching through the surface to show a different color underneath.

Slip decoration Painting decoration on clay using thinned clay.

COMMUNICATION ARTS

These terms are used in this badge:

Braille A printing system of raised letters used by the visually impaired.

Ham radio operators Licensed amateur radio operators.

Logo An identifying symbol.

Morse code A communication system in which dots and dashes are used.

Semaphore A signaling system in which arms, flags, or lights are used.

Sign language A means of communication through hand signals used by the hearing-impaired.

FOLK ARTS

These terms are used in this badge:

Ballad An ethnic or cultural poem or song that tells a story.

Quilling A way of making a design by curling strips of paper and gluing them to a background.

Origami The Japanese art of folding paper.

Piñata A decorative paper mâché or clay container filled with toys and candy. During some Mexican festivals, children are blindfolded and try to break the piñata, releasing the candy and toys.

Pysanky eggs A Ukrainian method of decorating eggs using wax and dye.

JEWELER

ACTIVITY 1

Paper beads Select a colorful page from a magazine, or use wrapping paper or aluminum foil. Draw zigzagged lines diagonally across the paper from top to bottom in 1" sections. Cut the sections out and curl them around a nail, knitting needle, or pencil (the good side of the paper should be on the outside). Glue the end to the bead and slip it off the nail. Cover the bead with glue. When dry, string on colored yarn.

Hardware jewelry Arrange the pieces of hardware on a piece of clear plastic wrap. Squeeze liquid solder on the pieces to join them in a design you like. Peel the clear plastic off and shine

the jewelry. Add a chain, earring backs, or a pin back.

ACTIVITY 5

Wash the seeds and let them dry on waxed paper. Arrange the seeds on a white background in the design you like best. String them with a heavy carpet thread. If the seeds are too hard to thread, soak them for several hours in warm water.

ACTIVITY 6

Ceramic clay is available at craft and art supply stores. You can also find clay in creek beds and river banks, but be sure you are digging up clay, not ordinary mud. You can make Baker's clay by mixing 1 cup of flour and 1 cup of salt with just enough water to make it feel like clay. You can color the dough with food coloring. Mold the clay into the shape of the jewelry. You can create designs and textures by pressing small objects into its damp surface and lifting them off to form a design. If you leave the object in the clay, make sure it won't melt, because your next step is to bake your object on a piece of wax paper in the oven at 200 degrees. You can paint the object with poster paints once it is dry.

ACTIVITY 7

Papier-mâché Make a thin flour and water mixture. Paste layers of newspaper over a form such as a cardboard box, bottle, or crumpled paper. Use colorful tissue paper for the last layer, or paint the object once it has dried.

Decoupage Cover a surface with paper cutouts. Then, coat with varnish for a permanent finish.

MUSICIAN

ACTIVITY 2

Minstrels were European traveling poets and singers during the Middle Ages. Troubadours were poet-musicians who lived in France and northern Italy during the eleventh to thirteenth centuries. Minnesingers were German minstrels during the twelfth to fourteenth centuries. Meistersingers were German workingmen who during the fourteenth to sixteenth centuries joined music and poetry clubs.

Pinhole Camera

Materials: Color or black and white 126 film cartridge, black adhesive tape, piece of black cardboard (1¼ inches x 5¾ inches), piece of black cardboard (1½ inches × 2¾ inches), piece of black paper (1 inch square), piece of aluminum foil (1 inch square), two rubber bands, needle.

Instructions:

1. Fold the cardboard into four equal sections.

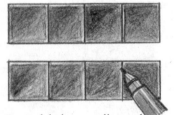

2. Fold the cardboard into a box and tape edges with black tape.

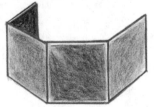

3. Make a small hole in the center of the piece of aluminum foil with the point of a needle.

4. Cut a 1 inch square in the center of the smaller piece of cardboard. Tape the foil over this opening.

5. Tape this piece of cardboard to the box you have made. Make sure no light gets into the box by covering all edges with black tape.

6. Attach the film cartridge to the box with two rubber bands. Place a small piece of black tape over the hole in the aluminum foil.

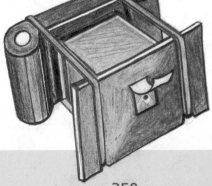

PHOTOGRAPHY

ACTIVITY 8

Using your camera:

Use a small coin to wind the film. Wind the film until the first number is showing. To take a picture, lift the black tape covering the pinhole. You must hold the camera perfectly still when you lift the tape or the picture will be blurry. Cover the pinhole and wind the film to take another picture.

You can also make a pinhole camera using other types of film. Write to: Eastman Kodak Co., Photographic Products Group, Rochester, NY 14650 for pamphlet, "How To Make and Use a Pinhole Camera."

POPULAR ARTS

ACTIVITY 5

You can look for examples in craft shops and gift stores, local museums, or in magazines, particularly *National Geographic* or *Smithsonian*. Craft cooperatives or books and magazines that celebrate different ethnic and cultural groups and their histories could also be good places to look.

ACTIVITY 8

Some folk instruments are the Irish tin whistle, the West African thumb piano, the Greek pan pipes, and an Indian sitar.

TEXTILES AND FIBERS

Batik Using wax on cloth to make a design.

Backstrap loom A portable loom that ties around the waist and is fastened to another object.

Flat frame loom A loom usually used for weaving tapestries.

Tapestry A flat kind of weave that incorporates a design.
Warp The basic threads strung on a loom.
Weft The crosswise threads used for weaving.
Finger weaving A weaving done using the fingers as the loom.
Appliqué Sewing one piece of fabric onto another to make a design.

TOYMAKER

ACTIVITY 4

Here are some examples of doll house furniture:

Tables can be made from a small purse mirror and two screws attached for legs, empty spools of thread or a small box lid covered with decorative adhesive paper with cork stoppers for legs. Upholstered furniture can be made from small emery boards or cardboard padded with scraps of foam rubber or cotton and covered with fabric. Large kitchen matchboxes can be used for beds when covered with fabric. Artificial greenery can be used for plants; braided rugs can be made from yarn scraps. Use the inside of a plastic bottle top or lid for a picture frame and attach an oval picture or aluminum foil on the inside for a mirror or picture. Birthday candles stuck in a button make a candelabrum, and small perfume bottles can be used for lamp bases. Many decorative items can be made from bottle tops or empty cosmetic containers. Make sure that all bottles, jars, and containers have been thoroughly washed and dried before you use them in your dollhouse.

EXPLORING THE OUT-OF-DOORS

HORSE LOVER

Remember: When horseback riding wear boots or shoes with at least one-inch heels, a hard hat with safety harness strapped under your chin, long pants, and other protective clothing.

HORSEBACK RIDER

Remember: When horseback riding wear boots or shoes with at least one-inch heels, a hard hat with safety harness strapped under your chin, long pants, and other protective clothing.

OUTDOOR CREATIVITY

ACTIVITY 4

To write a cinquain:

Line 1: Write one word that names an object, a feeling, or a theme.

Line 2: Put down two words that describe what you are thinking about.

Line 3: Write three words that tell what the subject is doing or how it is doing it (-ing or -ly words).

Line 4: Write a four- to five-word phrase (not a complete sentence) that describes the subject more, tells what or how it is doing, or makes a comparison.

Line 5: Write down a word that sums up the whole thought, how you feel, or relates back to your subject.

Example: grass
            green, soft
    growing, moving, sparkling
        swaying in the field
            spring

Japanese haiku is a poem that does not rhyme and is expressed in three lines with 17 syllables. The first line contains five syllables, the second line has seven syllables, and the third line has five syllables.

Example: Rain falls softly now
        a thousand tiny rivers
        as I look outward.

OUTDOOR FUN

Sun Tea Recipe.
Fill a clear gallon jar with cool water. Drop in 4 tea bags (try a mint or special herbal blend) and put on the lid. Let the jar sit in the sun all day or until the water turns a dark color. Refrigerate or pour over ice for a cool summer drink.

Sun Jam Recipe.
You will need:
    1½ pounds of ripe strawberries or blackberries
    1 cup sugar
    2 tsp. lemon juice
In the kitchen, wash the berries well. Cut hull in half and slightly mash. Put all the ingredients in a pan on the stove and boil for about 5 minutes without stirring. Remove from the burner and cool for 30 minutes. Pour the mixture into a baking pan

(9" × 9") and cover with plastic wrap. Place outside in the sunlight for 3–8 hours, until it is thick. Pour into a jar and place in the refrigerator, or use for a snack right away.

SMALL CRAFT

Remember: PFDs (personal flotation devices) should be worn while in any small water craft.

HELP (Heat Escape Lessening Position) is a position you can maintain in the water while wearing a PFD. In cool or cold water, this position helps you to maintain your body heat and reduce the chances of hypothermia. The most important thing is to keep your head out of the water. Then protect the sides of your chest with your arms, cross your ankles to keep your legs together, and if possible, raise your knees to protect your groin.

The Huddle position is done with several people in the water holding each other in a tight circle to preserve body heat and to keep up group spirit, too.

SWIMMING

Buddy system A safety practice in which girls are paired to keep watch over each other. In an activity (for example, swimming, hiking) the girls paired should be of equal ability.

Checkboard system A swimmer's safety check used by a waterfront supervisor to tell exactly how many persons are swimming at a given moment. Each swimmer has a numbered tag hung on a board. She reverses her tag on the board before going into the water, then turns it over again when she gets out.

TROOP CAMPER

"Walking softly" on the earth means that each of us must make a commitment to minimize our impact on the natural areas we use for outdoor activities. We should plan ahead and practice ways to leave no trace of our activities while camping, hiking, and so forth.

WATER FUN (see Small Craft)

Badge Index

· ·

Arts & media   *girls are great*

Across Generations   17
Active Citizen   52
Aerospace   95
Architechture   139
Art in the Home   143
Art in the Round   146
Art to Wear   148
Arts Around the World   134

Becoming a Teen   19
Books   150
Business-Wise   97

Car Care   99
Caring for Children   21
Celebrating People   54
Ceramics and Clay   153
Collecting Hobbies   23
Communication Arts   155
Computer Fun   101
Cookie Connection   228
Creative Solutions   57

Dabbler   14, 50, 92, 136, 190
Dance   158
Doing Hobbies   24
Do-It-Yourself   103
Drawing and Painting   160

Eco-Action   192
Ecology   195
Exploring Healthy Eating   25
Exploring the Out-of-Doors   188

Family Living Skills   27
Finding Your Way   197
First Aid   29
Folk Art   162
Foods, Fibers, and Farming   105
Frosty Fun   199

Geography Fun   60
Geology   107
Girl Scouting Around the World   62
Girl Scouting in the U.S.A.   64

Health and Fitness   12, 31
Healthy Relationships   33
Hiker   201
Horseback Rider   205
Horse Lover   203

Jeweler   165
Junior Aide patch   234
Junior Citizen   66

Local Lore   68

Making Decisions   35
"Making" Hobbies   37
Math Whiz   109
Money Sense   111
Ms. Fix-It   113
Musician   167
Music Lover   169
My Community   70
My Heritage   72
My Self-Esteem   38

Now and Then: Stories from Around the World   74

On My Way   77
Our Own Council's Badge   233
Our Own Troop's Badge   232
Outdoor Cook   207
Outdoor Creativity   209
Outdoor Fun   211
Outdoor Fun in the City   213

Pet Care   40
Photography   171

Plants and Animals   155
Popular Arts   173
Prints and Graphics   175
Puzzlers   117

Ready for Tomorrow   119

Saftey Sense   42
Science and Technology   90
Science in Action   122
Science in Everday Life   126
Science Sleuth   124
Sign of the Rainbow   237
Sign of the Satellite   240
Sign of the Sun   238
Sky Search   128
Small Craft   215
Sports   44
Sports Sampler   46
Swimming   218
talk
Textiles and Fibers   177
Theater   180
Toymaker   182
Traveler   79
Troop Camper   220

Video Production   184
Visual Arts   186

Walking for Fitness   222
Water Fun   224
Water Wonders   224
Weather Watch   132
Wildlife   226
Women's Stories   84
Women Today   82
World Citizens   48
World in My Community   86
World Neighbors   88

you & your community

The following badges are hidden in the Word Find on the inside front cover:

Safety Sense	Geography Fun	Money Sense	Jeweler	Theater
Health and Fitness	Women Today	Plants and Animals	Photography	Frosty Fun
Making Decisions	Dabbler	Puzzlers	Toymaker	Small Craft
My Self-Esteem	Active Citizen	Science in the Worlds	Architecture	Ecology
Sports	Local Lore	Sky Search	Art to Wear	Hiker
First Aid	My Heritage	Aerospace	Books	Horse Lover
Hobbies	On My Way	Computer Fun	Dance	Outdoor Cook
Pet Care	Traveler	Math Whiz	Folk Arts	Swimming
Sports Sampler	Car Care	Ms. Fix-It	Musician	Water Fun
Creative Solutions	Geology	Water Wonders	Music Lover	Wildlife

PROGRAM 9/90